Ilse Lenz, Helma Lutz, Mirjana Morokvasic,
Claudia Schöning-Kalender, Helen Schwenken
(eds.)

Crossing Borders and Shifting Boundaries

Vol. II:
Gender, Identities and Networks

Leske + Budrich, Opladen 2002

Die Schriftenreihe der Internationalen Frauenuniversität „Technik und Kultur" wird gefördert durch das Niedersächsische Vorab der VW-Stiftung

Coverbild: Gülsün Karamustafa „Mystic Transport"

Gedruckt auf säurefreiem und alterungsbeständigem Papier.

Die Deutsche Bibliothek – CIP-Einheitsaufnahme
Ein Titeldatensatz für die Publikation ist bei
Der Deutschen Bibliothek erhältlich

ISBN 3-8100-3494-0

Einband: design agenten, Hannover
Satz: Verlag Leske + Budrich, Opladen
Druck: DruckPartner Rübelmann, Hemsbach
Printed in Germany

Crossing Borders and Shifting Boundaries II

Schriftenreihe der Internationalen Frauenuniversität
»Technik und Kultur«

Band 11

Contents

Part III: Transnational Gender Democracy: Difference and Equality

Ilse Lenz, Helma Lutz, Mirjana Morokvasic, Claudia Schöning-Kalender, Helen Schwenken

Crossing Borders and Shifting Boundaries

1. Gender, Identities and Networks

New forms of migration and their gendered dynamism suggest fundamental changes around the turn of the millennium. New flexible forms of migration are increasing and transnationalism is becoming a marked trend. Female migration is no longer invisible but recognised as an important phenomenon in scholarly research and in policy making. The high percentages of women in labour, refugee, educational or marriage migration are believed to constitute a new trend. While this is a flawed view because women have always participated in migration movements, the focus on the gender dynamics of these developments is indeed new. Gender relations are now seen as fluid and changing: In the past, female migrants have been portrayed as symbols of national or traditional culture, expressed in clothes and body postures, or as representatives of different moral norms and life-styles, of chastity or communalism. However, in transnational communities young women and men are nowadays developing new flexible and syncretistic identities. Over the last years scholarly debates have redrawn the boundaries around the andocentric and national understanding of migration and have integrated gender as a core concept. Scholarly work shifted from describing women as passive objects or victims of migration structures to viewing them as social actors who conceive and follow strategies of their own in often difficult and complex situations. In short: Gender is interwoven with migration and gendered migration is on the move.

Contemporary feminist theory is marked by efforts to reflect on the links between gender, ethnicity and subjectivity in this new socio-political space. The metaphor of 'nomadic subjects' describes a way of thinking as well as living. Women are seen as moving between different worlds, languages, jobs and places without being bound to a fixed location (cf. Braidotti, 1994). This metaphor is attractive for feminist as well as for gender discourses. It promises a switching and exchanging of places marred by the experience of racism and sexism with new locations and a search for new options. To be on the move might be a strategy to avoid racism and sexism. Gender researchers have also wondered whether many people have turned into 'gender migrants'[1] in modern Western societies. They experiment or play with gender mixed identities, with queer or androgynous roles, with their individual gender designs and emancipation. It appears as if people can now choose their gender. However, these metaphors have their limits. „Having no passport or having many of them" (Braidotti, 1994, 33) are two totally different situations. Without a passport and other resources, one is not a voluntary nomad. Rather, celebrating mobility is only possible under certain circumstances. The apparent disappearance of borders and boundaries has its flip side: increasingly restrictive refugee and migration laws in many industrialised nations, the new 'Fortress Europe', the emergence of new forms of nationalism, the growth of racism, the repulsion of refugees as well as the denial of political and social rights for migrants. For many male and female migrants mobility is not a matter of choice, but the only way out of poverty, war, social pressure and other adverse conditions. In situations of sexual violence or rigid gender norms, e.g. considering childcare or public roles, the image of gender migrants is an illusion.

2. Conceptualising the Project Area 'Migration'

During the preparation for the *ifu* semester one of the German lecturers invited to take part in the project area migration sent an urgent mail, asking whether she would need to link her lecture on international feminist networking to the topic of migration. With her question the colleague unknowingly brought up the same difficulties the curriculum working group members[2] had been confronted with in their effort to name the project area adequately.

The process of conceptualising the *ifu* project area migration had started about two years before the actual *ifu* semester began, and the debates about the content are still reflected in the final title „Migration: People, Identities and Cultures in Process". The aim was to outline a project area which reflects the connection and interaction of different segments and processes in a globalising world: the gender dimension of regional and international migration movements and the reconfigurations of borders, meanings and identities which emerge in the conditionings of national borders and images, space as a realm and an „ob-

---

1   This is the argument of Hirschauer (1993, p. 351) from an ethnomethodological constructivist perspective.
2   The curriculum working group developed the curriculum of the first *ifu* semester on migration and invited colleagues from all over the world to present their research findings and describe their activism. Standing members were Mirjana Morokvasic (International Dean), Astrid Albrecht-Heide (Local Dean), Ilse Lenz, Helma Lutz, Maja Nadig, and Claudia Schöning-Kalender.

ject of continuous material and symbolic re-creation"[3], the phenomenon of shifting identities of those who move as well as of those who stay, and, last but not least, the identity discourses covering ethnicity, nationality as well as sexual preference and gender. Another important question was how the new migration is linked to the *persistence and actual upsurge* of racial images and racist aggressions on one side and to the border crossing transnational networking of feminist women's groups and organisations on the other. Actually the question of our colleague whether she should link her topic to migration once more pointed to our previous debates concerning the term migration – that the perception and understanding of migration might be too narrow to cover the wide concept and understanding we had in mind.

To address these concerns migration was linked to other issues such as globalisation, denationalisation and new national closures and racisms which are not necessarily caused by migration but in one way or another related to it. These linkages show that the definition and the coordinates of belonging and mobility, and the dynamics of inclusions and exclusions by gender, race and class are at stake and are being negotiated in migration processes.

The *ifu* project area proved to be a space of networking, relating and transnational cooperation. It has been called a temporary transnational home-space. 118 participants from Africa (11), Asia (31), Australia (6), Central Eastern Europe (6), Western Europe (16), Germany (29), Latin America (13), the Middle East (12) and North America (10) worked in this area. Lecturers came from 20 countries in Asia, Europe, the Middle East and North America. During the semester they developed projects ranging from the analysis of racism, the exploitation of female migrants, the criticising of the representation and politics of culture and difference at the world exhibition, the investigation of the home-pages of feminist and lesbian projects in Eastern Europe to developing mind maps of feminist networking from the experiences of feminist leaders present at the *ifu*. Lecturers often followed interdisciplinary approaches and used creative methods to link texts and analysis to art performances and images. Although there was criticism about the dense programme and the number of lectures and courses, as well as a vivid debate about eurocentric trends of the curriculum, in the end most students were satisfied with the theoretical and empirical content of the programme. Participants could also develop their own projects with the support of research assistants and some lecturers (see also Lutz & Morokvasic-Müller, 2002; Maiworm & Teichler, 2002; Metz-Göckel, 2002).

---

3   Cf. the project paper Tate and Varga.

3. The Gendered Spaces and Politics of Migration

In this volume we want to explore the tensions and interrelationship between new subjectivities and agency, shifting boundaries in gendered migration processes, and global and transnational structures both as restricting and enabling potentials. Whereas the first volume on migration and gender looked at the changing contexts of migration, we want to focus on migration, gender and agency from three perspectives in the second volume.

3.1 Nationalisms, Racisms, Ethnicisms

In the age of globalisation and massive migrant and refugee movements, nation states, which have functioned for a long time as political central units and as such regulated all levels of social life, are increasingly under pressure. The nation has been described as an 'imagined community' which includes people on the basis of certain common criteria, while excluding others. Nowadays the question about what the criteria for belonging are emerges as an issue of difference in power: between genders, social classes and ethnic groups (or "races"). Nationalisms, racisms and ethnicisms are not new phenomena, but have influenced the political discourses and activities in the past in a prominent way. Racist and nationalist violence as well as ethnic violence are now on the political agenda in many regions of the world and have gender-specific forms of expression.

Symbolic and material representations and discourses of the nation are still a crucial part of the collective identity construction of majority groups, but they are also found in the discourses of minority groups. Processes of 'othering', the defining and stigmatising of 'social Others' are essential for the stabilisation of national identities. In the same way, migrants, especially women, are excluded from social, economic and political citizenship. Nationality or ethnicity can be used as the basis for exclusion and boundary fortification.

These processes are aggravated by war and ethnicised violence and sexual violence against the 'ethnic Other' is legitimated by sexist and racist discourses. Feminist and peace movements have started to speak up against, analyse and understand the various sexual crimes against women, but also men, in ethnicised armed conflicts and by repressive regimes. In many countries, however, these issues are still considered a public taboo.

3.2. Space, Cultures and Identities in Process

Processes of inclusion and exclusion in the context of migration are often constructed in terms of culture, traditionally using a static concept of culture and cultural identity linked to a territory. A more process-oriented concept of culture and cultural identity focuses on power relations and on the interlocking systems of interpretable signs and actions that have to be decoded, systems which are shared by certain groups of people, and in which the concepts of the 'normal', the centre, and the 'Other' are constructed and implemented. Thus we have to analyse cultural identity not only in spaces that can be limited and classified, but also in transnational communities, informal economies and spaces in between. The core idea of this approach is no longer the sedentarity of people, concepts and relations, but rather mobility, change and interrelatedness. In the description and analysis of representations and discourses, and of the construction of collective and individual identities, *mobility* becomes a category that can help to transcend the dominant binaries. From the perspective of mobility, concepts of gender and ethnicity can be critically examined. In this approach the fragmentations, breaks and shifts of identities are considered not as deviations, but as the ordinary. The intention is to understand which self-spun, patchwork-like tissues of meaning and patterns of action are developed by people and groups in a world on the move. Identities in this perspective are seen not as primordial attributes, but as socially negotiated in processes of construction and self-constitution of subjects, communities and groups.

3.3. Transnational Gender Democracy: Difference and Equality

The third perspective addresses the agency and networking of migrants. Feminist and migrants' networks have been pioneers in globalisation from the grassroots. The UN-decade of Women created a global stage for the communication of feminists and activists from different cultures and provided a rapidly expanding opportunity structure. Discourses on women's and human rights, empowerment, paid and unpaid work and gender, development, peace and equality, and on sexual violence built bridges so that feminists developed discourses which aim for equality while respecting cultural difference. In developing this perspective, the contribution of black, migrant and lesbian women in the North as well as the feminisms in the South was crucial. The world action platform of the Fourth World Conference of Women in Peking 1995 can be read as a Charta of feminist programs and solutions to which the UN and the state governments have agreed. With their basic principles of empowerment and gender mainstreaming the platform provided an important impetus for the struggle of migrants as well. Mainstreaming migrant issues has been a demand in the feminist migrant networks in Europe.

Feminist transnational networks have increasingly confronted the counter-mobilisation of fundamentalist religious and ethnicised groups who try to roll back the empowerment and autonomy of women or minority groups. Secular women's and human rights approaches come under pressure in the Near East and in South Asia. In the US reproductive freedom or female autonomy is increasingly criticised by fundamentalist Christian groups. Whereas these groups try to instrumentalise and monopolise religion for their aims, the struggles for global gender democracy have to reflect on new ways to think about religious and secular values and visions. Secular and religious feminist networks are confronted with new issues.

Women's movements have developed concepts of gender democracy. In the context of migration they take up the issues of gender inequality, ethnic and cultural divisions, and look for new forms as well as normative foundations for equality and difference. *Social and political citizenship* work as inclusive factors for broad social participation in multicultural societies. But democracy must also emphasise *deliberative and procedural elements* in order to extend participation to marginalised groups. International networking of feminist movements (as well as antiracist groups or other NGOs) are working towards new global regulations in this sense.

The first section of this volume explores the re-drawing of gender boundaries by nationalisms, racisms, and ethnicisms and the diverse processes of inclusions/exclusions. Malathi de Alwis shows how gender is articulated in the making of culture and nationhood in Sri Lanka by focusing on the transformation of 'woman' into a pure and a-historical signifier of inferiority and 'tradition'. It is through this historical knowledge about the impact of the British colonial rule of control and repression that the notion of fixity of binary gender representation can be put into context. Similarly, in the second article Aneela Babar analyses the militarising discourse of contemporary Pakistani society through the creation of two binaries, the male warrior and the good woman. She shows how much the boundary making and mapping practices in this discourse rely on the construction of self vis-à-vis other nation states, in this case vis-à-vis India. Contrary to what is often thought, in the case of Europe the construction of belonging uses patterns and practises of inclusion and exclusion which are not so different from the ones identified in the Indian subcontinent, as Helma Lutz shows in the third article about racism, nationalism and ethnicism in Europe. She argues that borders and boundaries are currently in a process of fundamental re-definition; that their dissolution and reconstruction within European nation states have different effects on different parts of their populations: borders are increasingly permeable for 'indigenous' Europeans while they become increasingly inaccessible for those defined as outsiders, like the so called 'Third Nationals'. Ann Phoenix follows the same line of argument. In her case study of the British nation, Phoenix examines the continuities and discontinuities in the intersection of nationalism and racism. Using Michel Foucault's idea of examining the history of the present in order to understand how the world became normalised as 'regime of truth', she addresses the ways in which assumptions of who is to be included in the nation and who excluded have simultaneously remained the same and changed since the middle of the twentieth century. Continuities and discontinuities in the discursive practices of nation-making are at the heart of all four contributions for this part of the book.

The second section shows how culture becomes a crucial concept in the analysis of inclusions and exclusions in processes of power arrangements and shifts, in the meaning and importance of space, such as migration, economic globalisation, and construction or reassurance of collective identities.

In her approach to city and gender Ayşegül Baykan defines space as the realm that contextualises and grounds the ways of life, politics, power and ideology of different groups and subject positions. She introduces the vernacular as a general concept that refers to the totality of different agencies, their practices, meanings, and groups in resistance to appropriation of power by both the disciplinary regimes of knowledge and socio-economic and political interests; thus the vernacular is seen as the enunciative and performative presence of the subordinated. Elaborating on the process of space making in the city of Istanbul characterised by an ongoing rapid change through migration, new settlements, and economic globalisation, Baykan opposes forms of binaries and reifications which posit the enunciative presence of the subordinated at the edge or in opposition to the centre as the normative.

From the perspective of a political economist Saskia Sassen similarly argues that the dominant narrative about economic globalisation is that of eviction. According to her, the key concepts in the dominant discourse – globalisation, information economy, and telematics – all assume that place no longer matters, and suggest that the type of place represented by major cities may have become obsolete from an economic perspective. This eviction of a whole array of activities and types of workers from the narrative about the process of globalisation results in the exclusion of the variety of cultural contexts within which they exist, a cultural diversity that is as much a presence in processes of globalisation as is the new international corporate culture. The dominant account reconstitutes large portions of the city's economy in 'cultural' terms – the spaces of the amalgamated other, the 'Other' as culture. With her approach to spaces of intersection as 'analytic borderlands' Sassen reframes the terrain of the economy, incorporating the discontinuity between what is represented as economic and what is represented as cultural in the broad sense of the term – the centre as economy and the 'Other' as culture.

Neela Karnik discusses the excessive display of the tribal as the Other in tribal museums and in the politics of culture in India from the angle of cultural history and cultural representation. Whereas the very existence and the belief systems of the tribals have been threatened from colonial times to the present, it is tribal culture which is evoked most emphatically at national spectacles. Thus tribal art and culture are showcased as being distinct from a national culture (in terms of high culture as the normative centre) or are proffered as a national culture in an era of globalisation when boundaries of national art become porous and are blurred by a universal aesthetic. While tribal cultures are *visually* present as display and masked identity, they are absent from discursive space and function in contesting ways within and against dominant national orders, implicated either with narratives of 'cultural disappearance and salvage' or with the narratives of 'revival, remembrance and struggle'.

In the last contribution to this section Claudia Schöning-Kalender develops her argument about the ongoing visibility politics of the Turkish nation state through enforced changes in dress codes and norms. This political move of intertwining the construction of gender identity with the official self-concept of a 'modern', western nation state marks a multi-layered complex of gendered cultural representations that resists simple binaries in the interpretation. Although very different in the setting this article should be read with the contribution of Malathi de Alwis in mind who also explores the relationship of gender representation, culture and nationhood.

In the third section theoretical feminist approaches about globalisation, gender democracy and social movements are related to the experiences of diverse migrants' and women's movements around the world. In the first contribution for this section Ilse Lenz and Helen Schwenken analyse the interrelatedness of gender, migration and globalisation and argue that new inequalities as well as new options for women emerge. They trace these ambivalences on the basis of the experiences made at the UN World Conferences and the UN decades of women looking at the approaches to ratify global regulations to improve the situation of migrant workers. As the following contributions all deal with migrants and women organising in transnational contexts, Lenz and Schwenken use the concept of transnational social spaces and their crucial significance for the mobilisation of social movements: These spaces result from the activities of international migrants as they allow the negotiation and articulation of more egalitarian political norms and networking.

Marina Calloni elaborates on the importance of feminist and scholarly cross-border networking in order to support women and local women's movements in different parts of the world. Her examples of developments in Albania, the Russian Barent region, and China are based on her first-hand experiences in the *International Network for Research on Gender*. Theoretically she develops this practice-oriented approach by arguing that social justice only emerges from concrete daily life experience. Calloni also draws attention to the long-lasting debate about equality and difference, and relates it to the capability approach developed by Amartya Sen and Martha Nussbaum while framing it in a new perspective.

Amel Hamza's contribution provides further evidence of international co-operation for women in difficult political and societal situations. She describes the development of the international network *Women living under Muslim Laws* and how the social status of women is negotiated in different countries in which Muslim laws are valid. For a deeper understanding of their situation, Amel Hamza proposes to differentiate between Islam and Muslim thinking in important debates of feminist scholars in societies with Muslim laws.

Networking with female migrants in face of racism, sexual violence and legal problems is also discussed by Behshid Najafi and Jae-Soon Joo-Schauen. They present the work and political struggles of *agisra*, an information and counselling centre for female migrants and refugees in Cologne, Germany, which is also involved in national and international networking. They describe the situation of some of the refugee, migrant and undocumented women in Germany which is characterised by sexual and/or labour exploitation and limited rights due to restrictive foreigner laws. Joo-Schauen and Najafi also discuss their lobbying efforts to improve the situation of these migrants, especially those who are victims of trafficking in women. Although these women are victims, the authors argue against the easy equation of migrant women and victim and for acknowledging their subjectivity and courage.

Yayori Matsui gives an impressive and unsettling testimony of the international and Asian women's movements confronting gender violence and war. She describes the proceedings of the *Women's International War Crimes Tribunal* in Tokyo 2000 which dealt with the exploitation and violence by Japanese military towards Chinese, Korean, Indonesian, Filipina and Malaysian women as sexual slaves during World War Two. In view of the taboo around the issue in Japanese post-war society, women's networks in East Asia, including Japan, joined in creating a space for the testimony of the victims and showing the historic responsibility of the perpetrators – the military including soldiers at the front as well as the Japanese emperor. The tribunal has far-reaching historical significance and it opens a new future for international understanding and cooperation of Asian women's movements.

The contributions thus trace the tensions and contradictions of exclusions/inclusions in considering nationalisms, racisms, ethnicisms. They also look at the spaces and cultural representations created by migrant women. By linking this to feminist and migrant resistance, and networking and negotiating for global governance, we hope to do some justice to their various and courageous voices and practices.

Editorial work on the three parts of this volume has been carried out in the following way: Helma Lutz was mainly responsible for part I, Claudia Schöning-Kalender for part II and Ilse Lenz/Helen Schwenken for part III.

We want to express our gratitude to Ayla Neusel and Margot Poppenhusen for their generous, constant and patient support for the publication. We also want to thank Heike Alberts and Kyoko Shinozaki for their competent language editing. Thanks as well go to Kathrin Gawarecki and Dorothee Schwendowius for their support in proofreading. Special thanks are due to Lisa Mense and Charlotte Ullrich who kindly stepped in as support team in the last phase and have done proofreading, final corrections and editing. The work of the CAG migration at IFU *benefited* by the Marie Jahoda chair of International Gender Studies, Ruhr-University Bochum, and Mirjana Morokvasic takes this opportunity to acknowledge a generous support in her work from being Marie Jahoda Professor in the winter term 1999/2000. We want to thank the Ministry of Education and Science in North-Rhine-Westfalia, Germany, for supporting the chair and the University and all colleagues for their encouraging interest.

But most of all we want to thank all *ifu*-participants for their input, their ideas, their inspirations and their networking which provided the energy and impetus to follow the complex paths of this publication spanning across various spaces of feminist theories and practice.

Literature

Braidotti, R. (1994). *Nomadic Subjects*. New York: Columbia University Press.
Hirschauer, S. (1993). *Die soziale Konstruktion der Transsexualität*. Frankfurt/Main: Suhrkamp
Lutz, H. & Morokvasic-Müller, M. (2002) *Transnationalität im Kulturvergleich. Migration als Katalysator in der Genderforschung*. In: Neusel, A. & Poppenhusen, M. (eds). *Universität Neu Denken. Die Internationale Frauenuniversität Technik und Kultur*. Opladen: Leske + Budrich, pp. 111-124
Maiworm, F. & Teichler, U. (2002). *Die Internationale Frauenuniversität aus der Sicht der Teilnehmerinnen*. In: Metz-Göckel, S. (ed.) (2002). *Lehren und Lernen an der Internationalen Frauenuniversität. Ergebnisse der wissenschaftlichen Begleituntersuchung*. Opladen, Leske + Budrich, pp. 45-89.
Metz-Göckel, S. (2002). *Die Evaluation des ifu-Studienprogramms*. In: Metz-Göckel, S. (ed.). *Lehren und Lernen an der Internationalen Frauenuniversität. Ergebnisse der wissenschaftlichen Begleituntersuchung*. Opladen: Leske + Budrich, pp. 111-259.

Part I:
Nationalism, Racisms, Ethnicisms

Malathi de Alwis

'Housewives of the Public'
The Cultural Signification of the Sri Lankan Nation[1]

1. Positioning

„The anthropological concept of culture might have never been invented without a colonial theatre," notes Nick Dirks in *Colonialism and Culture*. Here he points to not just the production of 'culture' but also to the invention of the concept itself. „Culture was also produced out of the allied network of processes that spawned nations in the first place. Claims about nationality necessitated notions of culture that marked groups off from one another in essential ways, uniting language, race, geography, and history in a single concept" (1992, p. 3). The violence that has ensued from such formulations of culture continues to be a part of our everyday realities today.

In this paper, I would like to focus on how gender articulates with the making of culture and nationhood in Sri Lanka; how woman is transformed into a pure and ahistorical signifier of interiority and tradition. In this project of narrativization, I follow in the footsteps of that remarkable feminist historian Joan Scott who insisted that the point of new historical investigation „is to disrupt the notion of fixity, to discover the nature of the debate or repression that leads to the appearance of timeless permanence in binary gender representation" (1989, p. 94).

Thanks to the pioneering work of social historians and feminists, it is an accepted fact among social scientists today that a sexual division of labour i.e., linking women with domesticity and the 'private' – epitomised in the notion of 'motherhood' – was a corollary of industrial capitalism, and was systematically propagated by the emerging middle classes in 19th century Euro-America (for example, Ehrenreich & English, 1979; Ryan, 1975; Davidoff & Hall, 1987).

1   This paper was presented at the Nanyang Technological Institute, Singapore, several years ago. I am particularly grateful for the comments I received at that time from Janadas Devan and Wei Wang-Ling, and to Pradeep Jeganathan for his critical engagement with it from its inception. An earlier version of this paper was published in Coomaraswamy, R. & Wickremasighe, N. (co-eds.) (1994). Introduction to Social Theory. Colombo: ICES.

Yet, in South Asia, as has been pointed out for Africa as well, 'the home' has long been „a crucial, and hitherto neglected focus of European efforts to colonise" (Comaroff & Comaroff, 1992). As the work of anthropologists such as Jean Comaroff (1985) and Ann Stoler (1989), and historians such as Partha Chatterjee (1989), Nancy Hunt (1988, 1990), and Lata Mani (1986, 1987), has demonstrated, the colonisers' involvement in these projects of domestication also provided them with an important avenue to radically transform the relations of power between genders and classes within these colonial societies.

However, Comaroff and Comaroff also rightly underscore the danger of assuming that a „full-grown, stable model of 'home life' was exported from Europe to the colonies" or that the „concept of the 'domestic domain' can be freed from its particular historical context and used as universal" (1992, p. 4). In seeking to understand the domestication of Sinhala women within its particular historical and cultural context, I have been especially enabled by the historical schema that has been posited by Partha Chatterjee (1989). Chatterjee traces the discourse of Indian nationalism during the colonial period along the gendered axes of the spiritual and material. This discourse was later condensed into the more ideologically powerful dichotomy of the feminised interior (*ghar* or home) and the masculinised exterior (*bahir* or world). Chatterjee points out that in the unequal relations between the coloniser and the colonised, „it was in the material sphere that the claims of Western civilisation were the most powerful. Science, technology, rational forms of economic organisation (...) had given the European countries the strength to subjugate the non-European people" (1989, p. 239). Therefore, the Indian nationalists realised that in order to overthrow colonial domination, they would have to learn those „superior techniques of organising material life and incorporate them within their own cultures" (ibid.).

However, this could not mean an imitation of the 'West' in every aspect of life, as this would erase the very distinction between the East and the West namely that of the spiritual and the material. The Indian nationalists had eagerly embraced the Orientalist myth that the East was superior to the West in the spiritual domain[2]. Therefore, great effort was taken to protect this distinctive spiritual essence of Indian culture which the nationalists believed could be contained and nurtured within the home by the women while men waged the battle for independence on the treacherous terrain of the profane, materialist outer world.

Thus, Indian women, and I would like to emphasise, especially middle class Indian women, were not seen merely as the representatives of tradition, spirituality, and the essence of Indian culture, but they were also considered the protectors and disseminators of it (ibid., pp. 238-240), or to use R. Radhakrishnan's

---

2   For a brilliant exposition on the tensions between Nationalism and Orientalism see
      Chatterjee, 1986 especially pages 38-39.

evocative paraphrasal, „woman becomes the mute but necessary allegorical ground for the transactions of nationalist history" (1992, p. 84). I would like to posit a similar formulation of Sinhala Buddhist nationalism within Sri Lanka in which debates between the missionaries/British colonialists and the Sinhala nationalists over women's roles in society and the family were not really about changing the status of women, but rather about re-casting a specific kind of middle class Sinhala womanhood that was appropriate for, and emblematic of, an emerging nation state.

However, an important divergence between the Indian nationalist movement and its Sri Lankan equivalent must be stressed here. In Sri Lanka, unlike Chatterjee has argued for India, the very status of the nationalist movement did not hinge upon the resolution of the 'woman's question' which included such controversial and volatile issues such as $sati^3$, child marriages, $purdah^4$ and the ban on widow remarriages. As Kamala Visweswaran has pointed out, the 'woman's question' in India was the „usual shorthand to signify a range of issues concerning women which [were] also read as references to the nation. For example, British appeal to the degraded status of Indian women was one of the primary ways of legitimising continued colonial presence" (1990, p. 65). In Sri Lanka, much of the nationalist debates revolved around the issues of female education.

Sri Lanka has a long history of colonisation. Resistance to imperialism during the Portuguese and Dutch occupations was continuous, from small-scale revolts to major uprisings. However, it was only during the British occupation that an organised nationalist movement began to take shape. This emerging nationalism of the late 19th century was primarily religiously motivated in outlook and content through a re-assertion of Buddhist values and reactions against Christian missionary enterprise. Though the population of Ceylon was multi-ethnic and multi-religious „the nationalism that developed became identified with the Sinhala Buddhist majority, with the result that, at certain times, nationalism and chauvinism became synonymous" (Jayawardena, 1986, p. 122).

The political overtones of Sinhala Buddhist nationalism became especially pronounced in the early period of the 20th century with the growth of its ancillary movement, the temperance agitation. Temperance agitators „indulged in criticism of the government by associating it with the evils of intemperance; and diatribes against foreign vices and Christian values were cleverly scaled down into more restrained and subtle criticisms of a 'Christian' government" (de

---

3   "Sati is the traditional Hindu practice of a widow immolating herself on her husband's funeral pyre," (www.kamat.com/kalranga/hindu/sati.htm.)

4   Purdah is the translation of screen or veil. "Purdah is the practice that includes the seclusion of women from public observation by wearing concealing clothing from head to toe and by use of high walls, curtains, and screens erected within the home. Purdah is practiced by Muslims and by various Hindus, especially in India," (www.kings.edu/womenshistory/purdah.html.)

Silva, 1981, p. 350). The temperance movement also provided the training ground for the first generation of Ceylonese[5] political leaders and was a useful bridge between the 'constitutionalists' who stood for a limited program of political action within the framework of the classical Liberal political system and the Sinhala Buddhist 'nationalists' who were committed to the regeneration of a 'traditional' religion and the cultural and linguistic elements associated with it (de Silva, 1986, p. 20).

Alongside their concern with the widespread incidence of intemperance in Ceylon, the Sinhala Buddhist nationalists, like their Indian counterparts, were also extremely concerned with the dominance of the missionaries in the field of education. By the end of the nineteenth century, a whole new class of anglophone, Christianised elites had been spawned in these missionary schools. Particularly deplored were the effects of missionary education on the Sinhalese girls. In the 1890s, Anagarika Dharmapala, one of the pioneers of Buddhist education and Sinhala Buddhist nationalism, noted with much foreboding that „girls [were] being educated under western principles by Christian educationalists" and therefore it was „impossible to expect that a race of true Buddhists could be produced in Ceylon" (Guruge, 1965, p. 798).

2. Missionary Education: A Study in Domestication

During the early period of British domination, the colonial administration, which was concentrating its efforts on economic and military matters, took little interest in the question of education (Jayawardena, 1986, p. 118). It was only with the arrival of Governor Sir Robert Brownrigg in 1812 that many Christian missions received encouragement to pursue proselytising and educational activities on the island. The eight year administration of Brownrigg saw the coming of the Baptist Missionary Society in 1812, the Wesleyan Methodist Missionary Society in 1814, the American Missionary Society in 1816, and the Church Missionary Society in 1818 (Gratien, 1926, p. 1).

The Ceylonese women, viewed through the lenses of an ideal Victorian womanhood, were seen as epitomes of bigotry, ignorance, and degradation[6]. They soon became the target of both American and British missionaries, who were convinced that „no real growth in civilisation or Christianity could be

---

. 5   Though I have used the more nationalist title of 'Sri Lanka' in much of this paper, I will resort to the colonial title of 'Ceylon' whenever I refer to the time periods in which it was used – the nineteenth and mid-twentieth centuries.

6   The attributes of 'True Womanhood' by which a woman judged herself and was judged by her husband, neighbours, and society at large, could be divided into four cardinal virtues – piety, purity, submissiveness and domesticity (Welter, 1966).

made in Ceylon unless its women were educated" (Harrison, 1925, p. 4). The 1848 Church Missionary Society Report noted, „it has been calculated from experience and observation...that the training of one female is, on the whole, equivalent in value to that of five boys" (quoted in Wilson, 1976, p. 59).

Many of the girls from low income families were enticed to the mission schools with gifts of cloth and other 'prizes', and in the north of the island even by offers to provide their dowry at the end of their schooling period (Winslow, 1835, p. 135; Tennant 1850, p. 160). They were taught in the vernaculars, either Tamil or Sinhalese (Jayawardena, 1986, p. 118), and their 'education' was limited to the '3 Rs' and needlework[7], which were intended to provide them with "minimum skills for their role as housewives in their low status social environment" (Jayaweera, 1990, p. 326). On the other hand, many upper class girls – daughters of rich merchants or conservative land-owning families, who would not come to the mission schools – were visited daily by Bible Women (Rev. Jones, 1912) or had governesses (sometimes foreign) to teach them English, arithmetic, needlework, music and drawing in their own homes (Jayawardena, 1986). By the 1850s, these women had adopted Victorian dresses and fashions, and in the 1860s, wedding gowns were imported from London for the brides of this class (ibid). The girls who attended the government-run Female Superior Schools in the urban centres (established between 1842 and 1869 due to popular demand by the anglophone Ceylonese) were restricted to a narrow urban elite (Jayaweera, 1990). In 1868, 87% of these girls were reported to be Europeans and Eurasians or Burghers (ibid.). The colonial governor's wife and the wives of other colonial administrators gave their patronage to these elite schools as a part of their philanthropic and social 'reformist' activities (Hardy, 1864, p. 47; Selkirk, 1850, p. 154).

The British missionaries and administrators, who were often the products of elite British educational institutions which „reflected the ethos of the British ruling class with its authoritarianism and social exclusiveness" (Heussler, 1963, p. 48), continued the transmission of these values and biases through their educational policies in the colonies. Thus, social differentiation was accentuated in Ceylon through the establishment of urban-based fee-levying English high schools catering to a small urban elite, and free, ill-equipped elementary schools teaching in the vernaculars for the majority of the population (Jayaweera, 1990, p. 324). Missionaries from other European countries and North America, who

---

7   Deborah Gaitskell has an interesting 'reading' of the stress on needlework in colonial societies. She points out that sewing did not have narrow domestic connotations as it could lead to employment in the dressmaking industry. However, it was also presented as an indispensable accomplishment for Christian womanhood, which leads her to suggest that it might be partly a survival of the centrality of Western clothing as a sign of conversion (1983).

also played an important role in the field of education in Sri Lanka, tended to share similar racial and social biases (ibid).

Along with their social values and biases, the missionaries and administrators also brought along with them Victorian notions of 'separate spheres'. This model of a binary opposition between the sexes, which was socially realised in separate but supposedly equal 'spheres', underwrote „an entire system of institutional practices and conventions" that ranged from a sexual division of labour to a sexual division of economic and political rights (Poovey, 1988, pp. 8-9). This gender dichotomy was also apparent in the colonial power structure and in the missionary organisations (Jayaweera, 1990).

The missionary's wife, who epitomised Victorian domesticity and motherhood, was seen as being the most important vehicle of civilisation to those of her 'degraded sex', and wherever possible, the missionaries attempted to establish female branches of schools or separate female schools at their 'stations' under the direction of their wives (ibid., p. 325). Missionary wives were also joined by unmarried women missionary educationists, who had made religion and education their avocation in life, and subsequently by nuns from Roman Catholic organisations, who established convent schools in the second half of the 19th century. According to Swarna Jayaweera, the most important role of these European women educators was perceived as being to assist in the 'transformation' of „indigenous society on the metropolitan model as a facet of cultural colonisation" (ibid)[8].

Since the major medium of instruction in the city mission schools was English, many middle class households in Colombo and other major towns spoke English at home and used Sinhala or Tamil only as the 'language of command' (Cohn, 1985) even at Independence in 1948[9]. Gombrich and Obeyesekere note that in this respect Sri Lanka was more like a French colony in Africa than a part of South Asia because „in India hardly any Hindu or Muslim household adopted English as their mother tongue" (1988, p. 209). However, the influence of Christianity was rarely more than „skin-deep (...) the majority of schoolchildren (...) attended Christian scripture lessons at school and were examined in

---

8   However, Kumari Jayawardena disputes the notion that women missionaries and educators were merely crass imperialists. She points out that many of these women were influenced by the movements for democratic rights and women's rights and were themselves examples of the developments in these movements as independent single women travelling abroad, heading schools and often combating 'the authoritarian attitudes and male chauvinism of the church hierarchies" (1994, p. 8). Fired with an enthusiasm to „rescue" their „degraded sisters," these 'new women' of their time saw „Christianity itself, as a liberating factor for women in both the West and East" (ibid., cf. Forbes, 1986; Rendall, 1985).

9   Interestingly, under the 1911 Census Reports categorisation of persons who were literate in English and not in their own language women constituted 37.4% of this group (Denham, 1912).

their knowledge of the Bible, but returned home to Buddhist households" (ibid.). Thus, Gombrich and Obeyesekere suggest that „the Sinhala anglophone class must have come to regard Christianity as the civic religion of the day, Christianity for public life, Buddhism for private" (ibid.), or as one Ceylonese gentleman described himself, „a Christian of the Buddhist faith!" (quoted in Eckard, 1844, p. 45).

It was specifically because of this reason that it was deemed necessary to increase the number of girls' boarding schools. In this way, the missionaries were not only able to monitor the girl's academic/public life but also dissuade her from resorting to „old customs and manners" of „idolatry" in her private life (Tennant, 1850, p. 147; Wilson, 1976, p. 61). As the Director of Public Instruction noted: „ (...) if the Government wished to pay for permanent and indelible rather than transitory results, the money paid for one girl educated in a Mission boarding school or a Convent was worth ten times the sum for a girl taught in a day school" (quoted in Bruce, 1910, p. 32). Unlike the day mission schools, which often charged a nominal fee once they had become sufficiently established, the girls' boarding schools consistently attempted to provide free education with the help of generous benefactors from churches abroad. As a result, a novel feature arose, where each girl in the boarding schools was named after her benefactress abroad. Thus, Annamah could become Mary Walton overnight (Tennant, 1850; Ruberu, 1962; Wilson, 1976).

The major foci of the girls' schools were the study of Christian scriptures and prayers and Victorian forms of social 'disciplining' such as orderliness, thrift, cleanliness and accounting that were encompassed under the title of 'Domestic Science'[10]:

> Training in home life is well provided for by the domestic science course, and will become still more practical when Senior girls can live in the model cottage[11] and finance and plan their own domestic life. The destiny of most Uduvil girls is to become wives and mothers, and though there is much that mothers and wives can learn only by experience, yet school days should lay the foundations for that orderliness and care, that wise thrift, that ready courtesy, that loving and unselfish spirit which comprise the ideal of a true home"(Harrison, 1925, pp. 155-156).

---

10 Under the 1914 Revised Code of the Education Department, a girls' school could only qualify as a secondary school if it provided practical instruction in Domestic Science preceded by a course in Elementary Experimental Science (Seneviratne, 1975).

11 The Domestic Science Cottage, which could house five girls at a time, was donated to the Uduvil Girl's School by Mrs Franklin Warner of Oberlin, Ohio in 1925. The use of 'practice cottages' and model homes as 'laboratory settings' was very popular in America at this time as well, and they were especially used as vehicles to transmit „middle-class 'home values' to ethnic minority groups and the working class generally" (Ehrenreich & English, 1979, p. 176).

Many of the girls in these boarding schools were not merely groomed to be good housewives, but rather good Christian housewives. They were „gently encouraged" to marry young Christian men who had, in turn, been groomed in the boys' boarding schools and were now pastors and teachers (ibid., p. 67; Winslow, 1835, p. 273)[12]. These Christian wives and mothers were expected to be the epitomes of „domestic virtue" in the midst of „abounding vice." One such example „in a dark heathen neighbourhood [was] like a star on the thick brow of night" (Winslow, 1835, p. 273).

When the Cambridge examinations were introduced to Sri Lanka at the beginning of the 20th century, the value of giving the same examination-oriented education to girls as to boys was the subject of much spirited debate in Ceylon. The strongest demand for a similar education for boys and girls came from European women educators, who were mainly concerned with the social role 'their girls' would have to play as wives and mothers in elite families that operated within the framework of patriarchal social relations (Jayaweera, 1990, p. 329). Nevertheless, there were also heads of schools who suggested 'diluted' curricula for girls. As one headmistress pointed out, „as long as they know how to keep the house accounts and check bills, I think it is sufficient" (quoted in ibid.). The latter argument was also taken up by some Ceylonese women (Denham, 1912; Jayawardena, 1986), and demonstrates to what extent the Ceylonese bourgeoisie had naturalised this position and women had become equated with domesticity and the 'home'.

3. Sinhala Buddhist Counter-Discourse: Disciplining in the Name of the Nation

Simultaneous with the debates on the feasibility of a parallel education for boys and girls was a rising dissatisfaction among the Ceylonese bourgeoisie over the „thoughtless imitation of unsuitable European habits and customs" (Jayaweera, 1990, p. 327), and a 'Christianising' education (Jayawardena, 1986, p. 124). The strongest calls for resistance to these influences came from two different segments of Ceylonese society.

One group was made up of the products of the urban English schools who had been able to further their education in Europe, had often married European women, were at the forefront of the anti-colonial movement, and now wanted to

---

12 Jayawardena also points to the fact that most fee-levying secondary English schools for the daughters of the bourgeoisie were often 'paired-off' with boys' schools of similar calibre. What is most interesting, however, is that this 'pairing-off' had to be denominationally correct, e.g. the 'sister school' of Kingswood College (Anglican) was the Girls' High School (Anglican) (1986, p. 119).

resuscitate 'national culture' and their countrymen and women to be on par with the Western world. The other group was made up of the products of government-run vernacular schools, where the medium of instruction was either Tamil or Sinhalese. These schools' curricula were much more limited in scope as their basic aim only was to create a mass of white collar workers who could fill the lower ranks of the colonial bureaucracies. Since social mobility and economic advancement were still dependent on the acquisition of an English education, this emerging bourgeoisie was treated as the 'poor relations' of the former group, but they were, nevertheless, a very articulate body of 'organic intellectuals'.

Both the anglicised elite and the Sinhala-speaking bourgeoisie agreed with each other on the issues of anti-colonialism and the imminent necessity for a good Buddhist education for their children[13]. However, while the anglicised elites viewed Buddhist women's education as an essential part of a national and political awakening and a means of emancipating women, the better represented Sinhala-speaking bourgeoisie believed that a Buddhist education should be primarily geared to producing good Buddhist wives, but with the modicum of modern knowledge necessary for the times (Jayawardena, 1986). One of the dominant leaders among the latter conservative group was Anagarika Dharmapala, the son of a Sinhala furniture merchant and a devout Buddhist housewife.

Dharmapala's attitudes towards the status of Ceylonese women was an ambivalent one. Though he had been influenced by several independent foreign women such as Helena Blavatsky and Annie Besant, he „particularly deplored the effects of missionary activity on Buddhist girls who had adopted not only Western ideologies but also European dress" (ibid., p. 126). In the same way that he wanted to purify Buddhism, he wanted to purify the Europeanised men and women of Sri Lanka. In many of his speeches and articles, he constantly ridiculed the Victorian hats and crinolines that were worn by the women of the bourgeoisie and advocated the Indian *saree* as a suitable garment for Sinhala women as it covered their „black legs, navel and midriff" (Guruge, 1963)[14]. Dharmapala's own mother was the first to wear this new form of attire in Dec. 1884 on a pilgrimage to Bodh Gaya in India, and it soon became the standard 'national' dress for women in the low country (Obeyesekere, 1979)[15].

---

13 Similarly, there was a parallel movement amongst the Tamil Hindu revivalists.
14 The saree has an interesting genealogy within India as well. For a fascinating discussion of how the Brahmika saree (a form of wearing the saree in combination with the 'western' influences of blouse, petticoat and shoes) became an accepted standard for middle class women in India (see Borthwick, 1984; Chatterjee, 1989).
15 Similarly, he advocated the cloth and banana for men but this form of attire was not adapted so quickly or so widespread as was the saree (Guruge, 1965).

Dharmapala's attempt to re-cast the Sinhala woman was dependent on the positing of a set of identities on the one hand, and the simultaneous operation of a set of exclusions. He was an unabashed advocate of Sinhala Buddhist domination of the island and believed that the loss of masculinity and cultural regression of the Sinhalese people was due to the erosion of their original Aryan qualities (cf. Chakravarti, 1989). Therefore, he was extremely assiduous in holding up the Aryan woman as the Sinhala woman's role model.[16]

> The Aryan husband trains his wife to take care of his parents, and attend on holy men, on his friends and relations. The glory of woman is in her chastity, in the performance of household duties and obedience to her husband (Guruge, 1965, p. 345).

Along with the Aryan woman, the contemporary role models posed were of the Japanese woman and, secondly, the Burmese woman (note that Japan and Burma are both Buddhist countries), who were supposed to be renowned for their grace, obedience and cleanliness; they bathed daily and constantly washed their garments (ibid., p. 85).[17]

The Sinhala Buddhist woman was also constituted in opposition to women of other religions and ethnicities. According to Dharmapala, womankind was degraded forever in the Bible through the original sin of Eve, the Koran equated woman to a field that was owned by her husband, and various Hindu texts referred to women in a derogatory fashion. Thus, only Buddhism provided freedom and respect to women (ibid.). The *saree* was chosen for Sinhala Buddhist women, because Dharmapala felt it was essential for the woman's body to be a marker of her ethnicity, modesty and uniqueness – the Tamil women wore *pottus*, the Muslim women covered their heads, but the Sinhala women wore immodest dresses and ridiculous hats and could not be told apart from the Europeanised riff raff. Dharmapala also attempted to constitute Sinhala Buddhist women in opposition to the 'completely' Europeanised upper class women who continued to wear European dresses, drink alcohol, smoke and not pay sufficient attention to their homes, as well as the lower class women and the peasantry who were seen as being coarse, immoral, unclean and frequently beaten by their husbands (Guruge, 1963).

---

16 Dharmapala's propaganda bore a remarkable similarity to that of the champion of Aryan/Hindu resurgence in India, Dayananda Sarasvati. Both men not only had a specific vision of a golden past that their cultures (meaning Aryan) had experienced at one time, but their goals were to actually rejuvenate this past. Therefore, they both wrote detailed treatises that laid out how this golden age could be regained through the highly disciplined everyday practices of people (see below).

17 Similarly, Dharmapala challenged the Sinhala Buddhist male with this contemporary role model: „Let us take the Japanese as our example, let us be enterprising, let us cultivate manliness, and make every effort to develop our brains and our body" (Guruge, 1965, pp. 511-512).

In his extremely influential pamphlet, the Gihi Vinaya, *The Daily Code for the Laity*, which was published in 1898, Dharmapala clearly spells out how women's sexuality and their everyday lives should be constructively regulated through practices of sanitation and religiosity, so that they could be suitable role models for their children (cf. ibid.). The making of this new bourgeois woman required that she would either be pried loose from her Christian and Western-ised upbringing or have the „peasant" in her (with whom were associated such „bad" and „slovenly" habits as indiscriminate betel chewing, afternoon siestas and a preoccupation with hair lice) reformed (ibid., pp. 31-46). This religious and moral re-juvenation of women was regarded as being synonymous with the re-juvenation of Ceylonese (which for Dharmapala meant Sinhala Buddhist) so-ciety. It was part of a Foucauldian moral order, „a silent edifice in which family and home served as internalised mechanisms of self-discipline and social con-trol" (Comaroff & Comaroff, 1992, p. 4).

Dharmapala's rigid notions of morality and his ethic of disciplined work spurred on by rationalised and purified Buddhist beliefs (cf. Gombrich & Obeyesekere, 1988, pp. 212-215), had a special appeal for the emerging Sinhala bourgeoisie, who were swiftly pushing out the feudal brown raj in the 20th century arena of increasing capitalisation and industrialisation. A large portion of the wealth that was accrued by this entrepreneurial class was freely donated to fund a plethora of Buddhist schools that were being started by the Theo-sophical and Mahabodhi Societies under the aegis of Anagarika Dharmapala and his followers. Among the donors were several wealthy Sinhalese women (Jayawardena, 1986; Jayawardena, 1992).

4. The Homogenisation of a 'Domestic Identity'

One of the 'legacies' of the colonial system that remained in Sri Lanka after it gained Independence from Britain in 1948 was the system of education. Though more Buddhist and nationalist in content, many of the ideologies behind the structural elements of the old system, e.g. the importance of Domestic Science courses for girls, remained. However, it was in the practices of disseminating such ideologies of domesticity that the post-colonial state in Sri Lanka drasti-cally differed from its former colonisers.

Foremost among the state strategies of dissemination was (1) the stan-dardisation of the major medium of instruction in schools through the decla-ration of Sinhala as the official state language in 1956, (2) the nationalisation of almost all schools in the island in the early 1960s and the provision of free education in all these schools and the national universities, and (3) the dis-banding of the Cambridge Examinations and the introduction of a Sri Lankan version of the British Ordinary Level and Advanced Level national examinations.

When Sinhala was declared the national language of Sri Lanka and almost all the schools on the island were nationalised, the system of education, which hitherto had been divided along the colonialised lines of privately-funded, exclusive English-medium schools (Christian and Buddhist), and poorly-equipped government-run vernacular schools, was largely 'democratised'.[18] It drastically changed the political dominance of the anglicised Sinhala elite and the hegemony of the few exclusive English-medium schools. With the introduction of the national examinations, the passing of which were crucial to the procurement of any job with adequate pay, even the few Christian and Catholic private schools that had managed to stave off the government take-overs and continued as fee-levying institutions had to prepare their students for these exams and follow the syllabi put out by the state. As Laclau and Mouffe have aptly noted, every hegemonic formation is „constructed through regularity in dispersion" (1985, p. 142).

The ramifications within female education were equally telling. For the first time girls from a variety of class backgrounds met in the same schools, conversed in the same language and learnt from the same books. All girls taking the Ordinary Level Examination were required to sit for papers in Home Science and Health Science and use standardised government textbooks. This ethic of service and 'motherhood' that was propagated through the national curriculum was reconciled with the increasing capitalisation of the Sri Lankan economy by relegating the majority of women to a continuation of their domestic chores in the 'public' domain – teaching, doctoring and nursing the sick, providing secretarial services, cleaning and serving in tourist hotels, making garments in export-oriented factories, using their 'vocational' skills at home rather than being agricultural producers, and migrating abroad (mainly to Singapore and the Middle East) as housemaids and nannies (Jayawardena & Jayaweera, 1986).

Another manifestation of the propagation of this ethic of service was the consistent promotion of 'social service' as an appropriate vocation for upper and middle class women. Their participation in the 'public' domain in this context was coded as being a continuation of their 'housewifely duties' in the 'private'. In the same vein that the missionary mothers had counselled their Christian flock of women to pursue the noble task of social service, Anagarika Dharmapala, too, had exhorted women of the new bourgeoisie to donate the six yards of cloth that were needed to sew a *saree* to lower class women, and firmly noted

---

18 However, this greatly hindered the opportunities of minority groups like the Tamils, Muslims and Burghers whose first language was not Sinhala. Unfortunately, this aspect of state policy is beyond the scope of this paper and cannot be adequately discussed here.

that their responsibility as Sinhala Buddhist women was to work towards the 'upliftment' of their less fortunate Sinhala Buddhist sisters (Guruge, 1965). Therefore, being philanthropic was closely associated with religious virtue and the power of pious and moral women to demonstrate by example (cf. Hall, 1979).

This extension of 'housewifely duties' for both the converted Christian woman and the 'new' Buddhist woman mainly centred around the 'upliftment' of the lower class women of the slums (Jayawardena, 1986). Most often, the philanthropists did not view these women „from a social height which precluded any specific sense of female solidarity", but rather saw them as „potential agents of domesticity, the means by which working class men might be brought home off the streets" (Summers, 1979, p. 59). It was in the slum then, to paraphrase Stallybrass and White, that the bourgeois spectator surveyed and classified her own antithesis (1986).

As Partha Chatterjee has pointed out, „The new patriarchy advocated by nationalism conferred upon women the honour of a new social responsibility, and by associating the task of female emancipation with the historical goal of sovereign nationhood, bound them to a new, and yet entirely legitimate subordination" (1989, p. 249). Ironically, the words of Sirimavo Bandaranaike, the world's first woman Prime Minister, amply affirm this:

> I feel most strongly the home is a woman's foremost place of work and influence and looking after her children and husband duties of highest importance for her to perform. But women also have their vital role in civic life, they owe a duty to their country, a duty which cannot, must not be shirked, and some at least of their time should be devoted to social welfare work (quoted in Seneviratne, 1975, p. 151).

It was also Sirimavo Bandaranaike's training in social work that was held up by some as an example of her readiness to enter the political arena as the Prime Minister (ibid., p. 156). However, the majority of people's reaction to the news of her being sworn in as Prime Minister was best captured by Sir Paul Deraniyagala: „What does she know of politics? In Solla's time Sirima presided over nothing fiercer than the kitchen fire" (quoted in Gooneratne, 1986, p. 160).[19]

More contemporaneously, Madam Hema Premadasa, the wife of President Ranasinghe Premadasa, has also used her social service activities to establish her political clout and to further the cause of the Sri Lankan state. Consider this example, on July 12th 1990, during a lull in fighting between the Sri Lankan army and the Tamil militants, Madam Premadasa flew to the battlefront in the north to spend a few hours with the soldiers. Accompanied by all the high-ranking members of the Air Force Seva Vanitha Unit, she went armed with

---

19 Mrs Bandaranaike's reply to this constant taunt through the years was: „A woman's place is everywhere and anywhere duty requires her to be and *also* in her kitchen" (quoted in Seneviratne, 1975, p. 204, emphasis in original).

„delicious lunch packets" and other gifts for the soldiers. While the troops feasted on the special lunch that had been brought for them, the First Lady and her entourage of elite women insisted that they should be served the usual camp diet. During her flight back to Colombo that same day, Madam Premadasa proudly exclaimed: „Next time we won't take cooked food (...) we will go there and do the cooking for these men ourselves" (Daily News, 13 July 1991).

However, it is also important to recognise that in their continuation of 'housewifely duties' in the 'public', these women also had an opportunity to escape a life that was bounded by the physical confines of home. This new 'freedom' was optimally mobilised by Madam Hema Premadasa, who carved a separate identity for herself through her Presidentship of the Seva Vanitha Movement.

Partha Chatterjee has also argued that the 'new patriarchy' of post-Independence nationalism subtly „inverted the ideological form of the relation of power between the sexes" through the adulation of woman as goddess and mother (1989, p. 248). Though the symbol of goddess did not feature in Sinhala Buddhist nationalism, the mother definitely stood as a sign for the Sri Lankan nation and the land through her spiritual qualities of self-sacrifice, benevolence, devotion and religiosity. This specific spirituality facilitated women to go out into the 'world' under conditions that would not threaten their femininity: „In fact, the image of woman as (...) mother served to erase her sexuality in the world outside the home" (ibid.). Here, the image of mother could encompass all nurturing, empathic and morally directive public services and roles such as social worker, teacher, nurse, etc.

However, as Kamala Visweswaran points out, this formulation only shifts the site of discourse from 'wives' to 'mothers'. „From the standpoint of feminist analysis, one subject position is exchanged for another, and a new strategy for containing women is set into play" (1990, p. 66). Yet, from a nationalist standpoint, she notes that „such a shift is both oppositional and hegemonic" (ibid.). It is oppositional, because by stressing the de-sexualised, spiritual 'mother' it resists the British sexualising of all Indian women as potential 'wives', and hegemonic, „because the other side of the British equation of the sexual Indian woman was the asexual, spiritual Victorian woman" (ibid.). Her argument is further complicated through her final suggestion that „nationalist discourse itself must incorporate the very terms it opposes, for in order to be a mother, one must first be a wife" (ibid.).

Chatterjee also suggests that by de-sexualising and 'normalising' their mothers, sisters and wives, the nationalists displaced all their notions of promiscuous sexuality on the lower classes and the 'Europeanised others' (1989). However, I find this easy split between the 'moral mother' and the 'whore' rather problematic. How do we account for violence against women within the home? I would like to suggest that even though middle class women were valorised as mothers, a simultaneous subterranean discourse of sexuality existed that always undercut it.

This simultaneous mothering and sexualising was best illustrated in 1960, when Sirimavo Bandaranaike was first sworn in as Prime Minister. Though she attempted to win the sympathy of the people through her widowhood and as a mother of three fatherless children, a counter-discourse of rumours and cartoons in newspapers portrayed her as having conceived her children out of wedlock and as sleeping with a leader of a Left party with which she was hoping to align her party (cf. Dissanayaka, 1975). The international press did not seem to do any better. Yasmin Gooneratne describes how the newspapers in Lausanne carried pictures of Mrs Bandaranaike, „her face pale, her eyes rimmed with dark shadows campaigning from public platforms in Ceylon (...). They used the terms *volupteuse* and *seducteuse* to describe [this] placid lady" (1986, p. 160). Sir Paul Deraniyagala seems to have sensed the possibilities of such 'tarnishing' that would have to be faced by a woman in the public eye: „She'll end by *spoiling* her personal reputation and *ruining* the family name" (quoted in ibid., emphasis mine).

However, Mrs Bandaranaike also often manipulated her domestic identities to her advantage in the 'public' sphere. Her major platform was that she was merely carrying out the political pledges her husband had made to his beloved voters like any dutiful wife. At the Non-Aligned Conference in Belgrade in 1961, she „electrified her audience" by speaking to them „not only as the Head of a Government, but even more as a woman and mother" (quoted in Kanakaratne, 1972, p. 17), when she proclaimed: „I do not believe for one moment that there is a single mother in the world who can bear to contemplate the possibility of children being exposed to atomic radiation and lingering death" (quoted in Seneviratne, 1975, pp. 184-185).

But this identity could also be used against her. For example, when Sirimavo was unable to keep to her 1970 election pledge that she would increase the free rice subsidy to two *serus* (measures), the opposition party circulated a pamphlet in which a mother sings a lullaby about her inability to provide food for her son (Sirimavo Nohot Avicara Samaya, n.d., p. 2). In a similar vein, when Sirimavo's government brutally put down a popular youth uprising in 1971, the opposition came out with various *kavi kola* (poetry broadsheets) that referred to the mother who shot her own children (ibid., p. 6). The fact that all three of her children, as well as her brothers and their wives and many other close as well as distant relatives, were given posts in her 1970 government led to many snide comments that even in politics Sirimavo's family came first! However, Neville Kanakaratne, the Sri Lankan Ambassador to the USA in 1972, gave these insinuations a slightly different valence, when he noted: „Friend and political foe alike agree that the woman, the wife, and the mother are all still in her and have not been allowed to take second place to her position as her people's elected leader" (1972, p. 17).

5. Conclusion

In conclusion, I want to re-invoke Gayatri Chakravorty Spivak's warning and focus our attention once again on how the materiality of women's bodies continues to be erased in the formulation of Sinhala motherhood within the postcolonial context of today, where the sovereignty of the Sri Lankan nation state continues to be challenged by the Tamil militants in the north and east of the island (Spivak, 1988). As Cynthia Enloe has pointed out, it is in such periods of national crisis that ideas of feminised sacrifice and masculinised valour become even more exaggerated (1989, p. 197).

This is best illustrated by two vivid images that I have seen in Sri Lanka: (1) A poster which was put out by the Ministry for Women's Affairs at the height of the government's offensive against the Tamil militants in 1986-87. It depicted a woman, bearing the obvious cultural markers of a Sinhalese, breast feeding her baby while dreaming of a man dressed in army fatigues. The Sinhala caption below read: „Give your life blood in breastmilk to nourish our future soldiers." (2) A colour photograph published on the front page of the Sunday Times at the start of the third major government offensive against the Tamil militants in July 1990. The photograph was titled „Defender of the Faith." It depicted a youthful soldier with his machine gun beside him and a necklace of ammunition draped around his neck, with the caption: „A lone soldier stands guard at a Buddhist temple on the Vavuniya border" (Sunday Times, 1 July 1991).

With regard to the first image cited above, the anti-State, Sinhala-chauvinist militants in the South, the Janatha Vimukthi Peramuna (JVP), adopted a similar tactic a few years later by circulating pamphlets banning Sinhalese women from using contraceptives. They noted that it was unpatriotic to use contraceptives, because it would reduce the possibility of potential fighters for their cause. A newsletter put out by the female wing of the JVP at the height of their offensive against the government in 1989 contained a special column titled „The Notes of a Courageous Mother". This mother documents how she is constantly left alone at home while her sons and daughters participate in anti-State activities. During one of these 'forays', her younger son is caught by the police. For the first time in her life she has to visit the police station to plead for her son's release. While the mother is there she becomes the horrified observer of police brutalities and suddenly realises that all these suffering youths, who are ready to sacrifice their lives for a cause that she does not quite grasp, are really all her children and that their pain becomes her pain, too (Sebaliya, June 1988, p. 3). This 'courageous' mother is not only being upheld as a role model for all Sinhalese mothers, but she also symbolises the patient and suffering 'Motherland' who will be eternally grateful and appreciative of the militants' efforts.

In a situation of patriarchal militancy and violence, Sri Lankan women are not only expected to sacrifice their bodies and the products of their bodies – their children – but they are also made into metaphors of the dishonoured nation patiently waiting to be avenged by the courageous and virile 'sons of the soil'. Throughout Sri Lankan history, the masses have been exhorted to defend the 'Motherland' and their 'Mother tongue' from foreign invaders/rulers or their own countrymen like the Tamil Eelamists demanding a separate Tamil state. Buddhist monks, who supported the JVP youth uprising in 1971, articulated their concern through the slogan: „The Motherland or Death!" (Jiggins, 1979, p. 147), while student activists in the universities protesting the occupation of the Indian Peace Keeping Forces (IPKF) in 1987-89 rallied under the slogan: „First Our Motherland, then Our Degrees".

Graffiti written on the walls (attributed to members of the JVP) during the signing of the Peace Accord between the President of Sri Lanka, J.R. Jayawardene, and the Prime Minister of India, Rajiv Gandhi, in the summer of 1987, was especially remarkable for its sexual explicitness. For example, an image that was constantly evoked through graffiti in various parts of the south was: „J.R. is in the kitchen while Rajiv is buggering J.R's mother in the arse." The mother here, once again, is the nation state of Sri Lanka. Her sodomisation is doubly heinous, because (a) on a rather literal level, as the mother of such an old man as J.R. Jayawardene (who is in his 70s) it would be extremely disrespectful to even consider her as a sexual being and here she is being violated by someone who is young enough to be her grandson and (b) her son, who is expected to protect her at all times, is within hearing distance of her denigration and still does nothing. The un-manning of J.R. Jayawardene and his simultaneous domestication and feminisation is achieved with one word – J.R. is in the „kitchen". The key discursive tropes used here are of 'outraged modesty' and 'wounded masculinity' for as Kamala Visweswaran reminds us, „a woman's modesty is emblematic of the masculinity of her community. [She] becomes the symbol of violence as the shame and subjection of her community is represented in her" (1990).

The irony behind both the state and anti-state discourses is that the metaphor of the 'mother' as passive, vulnerable and violated remains as the stable terrain upon which these debates are waged. As Kamala Visweswaran too has argued, „it is precisely the enshrining of women in nationalist ideology as 'mother' which establishes the sovereign male subject of nationalism" (1990).

References

Borthwick, M. (1984). *The Changing Role of Women in Bengal 1849-1905.* Princeton: Princeton University Press.

Bruce, C. (1910). *The Broadstone of Empire.* London: Macmillan and Co. Ltd.

Chakravarti, U. (1989). Whatever Happened to the Vedic Dasi? Orientalism, Nationalism and a Script for the Past. In Sangari, K. & Vaid, S. (eds.), *Recasting Women: Essays in Colonial History.* New Delhi: Kali for Women, pp. 27-87.

Chatterjee, P. (1986): *Nationalist Thought and the Colonial World: A Derivative Discourse?* New Delhi: Oxford University Press.

Chatterjee, P. (1989). The Nationalist Resolution of the Women's Question. In Sangari, K. & Vaid, S. (eds.), *Recasting Women: Essays in Colonial History.* New Delhi: Kali for Women, pp. 233-253.

Cohn, B. (1985). The Command of Language and the Language of Command. In Ranajit, G. (ed.), *Subaltern Studies*, vol. IV. New Delhi: Oxford University Press, pp. 276-329.

Comaroff, J. (1985). *Body of Power, Spirit of Resistance.* Chicago: University of Chicago Press.

Comaroff, J. & Comaroff, J. (1992). *Of Revelation and Revolution.* Chicago: University of Chicago Press.

Comaroff, J. & Comaroff, J. (1992). Home-made Hegemony: The Civilizing Mission and the Making of Domesticity in South Africa. In Tranberg Hansen, K. (ed.), *African Encounters with Domesticity.* New Brunswick: Rutgers University Press, pp. 37-75.

Davidoff, L. & Hall, C. (1987). *Family Fortunes.* Chicago: University of Chicago Press.

de Silva, K.M. (1981). *A History of Sri Lanka.* New Delhi: Oxford University Press.

de Silva, K.M., (1986). *Religion, Nationalism and the State in Modern Sri Lanka.* Tampa: Dept. of Religious Studies, University of South Florida.

Denham, D.B. (1912). *Ceylon at the Census of 1911.* Colombo: Government Press.

Dirks, N. B. (1992). Introduction. In Dirks, N. B., *Colonialism and Culture.* Ann Arbor: University of Michigan Press, pp. 1-25.

Dissanayaka, T.D.S.A (1975). *Dudley Senanayake of Sri Lanka.* Colombo: Swastika Press.

Eckard, J.R. (1844). *Ten Years in Ceylon.* Philadelphia: Perkins and Purves.

Ehrenreich, B. & English, D. (1979). Microbes and the Manufacture of Housework. In *For Her Own Good: 150 Years of the Experts Advice to Women.* New York: Anchor/Doubleday, pp. 141-182.

Enloe, C. (1989). *Bananas, Beaches and Bases: Making Feminist Sense of International Politics.* Berkeley: University of California Press.

Forbes, G. (1986). In Search of the 'Pure Heathen': Missionary Women in 19th Century India. *Economic and Political Weekly*, 21(17), pp. Ws2-Ws8.

Gaitskell, D. (1983). Housewives, Maids or Mothers: Some Contradictions of Domesticity for Christian Women in Johannesburg, 1903-39. *Journal of African History*, 24, pp. 241-256.

Gombrich, R. & Obeyesekere, G. (1988). *Buddhism Transformed: Religious Change in Sri Lanka.* Princeton: Princeton University Press.

Gooneratne, Y. (1986). *Relative Merits: A Personal Memoir of the Bandaranaike Family of Sri Lanka.* New York: St Martin's Press.

Gratien, L. J. (1926). *The Founding of the Mission Schools.* Colombo: Ceylon Historical Association.

Guruge, A. (ed.) (1963). *Dharmapala Lipi.* Colombo: Government Press.

Guruge, A. (1965). *Return to Righteousness: A Collection of Speeches, Essays and Letters of the Anagarika Dharmapala.* Colombo: Government Press.

Hall, C. (1979). The Early Formation of Victorian Domestic Ideology. In Burman, S. (ed.), *Fit Work for Women*. New York: St Martin's Press, pp. 15-33.

Hardy, R.S. (1864). *Jubilee Memorials of the Wesleyan Mission*. London: Wesleyan Methodist Missionary Society.

Harrison, M.H. (1925). *Uduvil, 1824-1924: Being the History of One of the Oldest Girls Schools in Asia*. Tellippalai: American Ceylon Mission Press.

Heussler, R. (1963). *Yesterday's Rulers: The Making of the British Colonial Service*. Oxford: Oxford University Press.

Hunt, N. R. (1988). Le Bebe en Brousse: European Women, African Birth Spacing and Colonial Intervention in Breast Feeding in the Belgian Congo. *International Journal of African Historical Studies*, 21, pp. 401-432.

Hunt, N. R. (1990). Domesticity and Colonialism in Belgian Africa. *Signs*, 15(31), pp. 447-475.

Jayawardena, K. (1986). *Feminism and Nationalism in the Third World*. London: Zed Press.

Jayawardena, K. (1992). White Women, Arrak Fortunes and Buddhist Girls' Education. *Pravada*, I(10), pp. 13-16.

Jayawardena, K. (1994). *The White Women's Other Burden*. London: Zed Press.

Jayawardena, K. & Jayaweera, S. (1986). *A Profile on Sri Lanka: The Integration of Women in Development Planning*. Colombo: Women's Education Centre.

Jayaweera, S. (1990). European Women Educators Under the British Colonial Administration in Sri Lanka. *Women's Studies International Forum*, 13(4), pp. 323-331.

Jiggins, Janice (1979). *Caste and the Family in the Politics of the Sinhalese, 1947-1776*. Cambridge: Cambridge University Press.

Kanakaratne, N. (1972). The World's First Woman Prime Minister. *Ceylon Today* 21(1-2), pp. 15-17.

Laclau, E. & Mouffe, C. (1985). *Hegemony and Socialist Strategy: Towards a Radical Democratic Politics*. London: Verso.

Mani, L. (1986). Production of an Official Discourse on Sati in Early Nineteenth Century Bengal. *Economic and Political Weekly/Review of Women's Studies*, 21(17), pp. 32-40.

Mani, L. (1987). Contentious Traditions: The Debate on Sati in Colonial India. *Cultural Critique*, 7, pp. 119-56.

Obeyesekere, G. (1979). The Vicissitudes of the Sinhala-Buddhist Identity Through Time and Change. In Roberts, M. (ed.), *Collective Identities, Nationalisms and Protest in Modern Sri Lanka*. Colombo: Marga Institute, pp. 279-313.

Poovey, M. (1988). *Uneven Developments: The Ideological Work of Gender in Mid-Victorian England*. Chicago: University of Chicago Press.

Radhakrishnan, R. (1992). Nationalism, Gender and the Narrative of Identity. In Parker, A. et al. (eds.), *Nationalisms and Sexualities*. New York & London: Routledge, pp. 77-95.

Rendall, J. (1985). *The Origins of Modern Feminism: Women in Britain, France and the United States 1780-1860*. London: Macmillan.

Rev. Jones, J.P. (ed.) (1912). *The Year Book of Missions in India, Burma and Ceylon*. New Delhi: Christian Literature Society for India.

Ruberu, R. (1962). *Education in Colonial Ceylon*. Kandy: The Kandy Printers Ltd.

Ryan, M. P. (1975). *Womanhood in America: From Colonial Times to the Present*. New York: New Viewpoints.

Scott, J. (1989). Gender: A Useful Category of Historical Analysis. In Weed, E. (ed.), *Coming to Terms: Feminism, Theory, Politics*. New York & London: Routledge, pp. 81-100.

Selkirk, J.(1850). *Recollections of Ceylon*. London: Hathard & Sons.

Seneviratne, M. (1975). *Sirimavo Bandaranaike*. Colombo: Hansa Publishers.

Sirimavo Nohot Avicara Samaya. *n.d. Illustrated political pamphlet*.

Spivak, G. C. (1988). A Literary Representation of the Subaltern: A Woman's Text from the Third World. In Spivak, G. C. (ed.), *In Other Worlds: Essays in Cultural Politics*. New York & London: Routledge, pp. 241-268.

Stallybrass, P. & White, A. (1986). *The Politics and Poetics of Transgression*. Ithaca: Cornell University Press.

Stoler, A. L. (1989). Making Empire Respectable: The Politics of Race and Sexual Morality in 20th Century Colonial Cultures. *American Ethnologist*, 16(4), pp. 634-660.

Summers, A. (1979). A Home from Home: Women's Philanthropic Work in the Nineteenth Century. In Burman, S. (ed.), *Fit Work for Women*. New York: St Martin's Press, pp. 33-64.

Tennant, Sir Emerson (1850). *Christianity in Ceylon*. London: Murray.

Visweswaran, K. (1990). *Family Subjects: An Ethnography of the Women's Question in Indian Nationalism*. PhD Thesis. Stanford University.

Welter, B. (1966). The Cult of True Womanhood. *American Quarterly*, no. 18, pp. 151-174.

Wilson, D. K. (1976). *The Christian Church in Sri Lanka*. Colombo: Government Press.

Winslow, H. W. (1835). *A Memoir*. New York: Leavitt, Lord & Co.

Aneela Babar

The Militarizing of Civil Society: Creation of the *Mujahid* (Warrior) and the 'Good Woman' in Pakistani Society

1. Introduction

War rhetoric often revolves around the preservation of the patriarchal state and encourages what policy makers assume to be the natural characteristics of the male citizens. These natural and essential characteristics are constructed in the state discourse in hyper masculine terms of bravery, aggression, conquest, fearlessness and dominance. Imbibing these characteristics is deemed necessary to protect the honor of the motherland, and the mothers and daughters of the nation. The soldier/son's role is to protect and defend the nation/mother/land by sacrificing his life (which is a debt received from the mother/land) whenever the nation/mother/land is besieged by enemies and dangerous 'others' (Khattak, 1994). The role of women in national security has been ambiguous: Defined as those whom the state and its men are protecting, women have had little control over the condition of their protection (Tickner, 1992). With the overriding presumption that only men participate in combat, the rule of men is justified, as only they will have the requisite courage and honor.

2. Setting the Parameters

The following paper is based on my fieldwork in Pakistan and India from March to May 1999 when 'jingoistic' nationalism stepped up the pressure for the social acceptance of the nuclear tests conducted in May 1998. Academic syllabi, newspaper and journal articles for this specific time period, and images in the electronic media (especially programs co-produced by the Inter-services Public Relations in Pakistan), war songs, books, videos and other publicity materials were reviewed and analyzed. After this in-depth study, forty-five people, including representatives of the military, religio-political leaders, feminists, students, academics, policy makers and media persons in both countries were interviewed. Discussions encompassed the above literature, the statements they themselves had made in press releases earlier, and other topics relevant to the theme of gender identity formation in Pakistan and India. However, due to space constraints and to maintain thematic continuity, I will now concentrate on militarism in Pakistan and the feminist critique that accompanies it.

May 28, 1998, the day Pakistan conducted nuclear tests, is now named *'Yaum-I-Takbeer'* (literally Day of God's Greatness). The state of Pakistan calls for celebrating the anniversary of the tests in a 'befitting manner' and people are called upon to renew their pledge to the nation-state. Every year, including 1998 when the tests were conducted, there are national rallies and parades, thanksgiving prayers and countrywide festivities. As ever, citizens like myself feel left behind standing on the periphery/margins in the midst of these 'nationality tests'. On occasions like this when the spirit of nationalism increases and is verbalized, identities are more vigorously demarcated. The boundary-making and mapping practice is a gendered construct (when it intensifies/underlines the creation of the 'other') leaving some of the populace feeling like 'others' in one's own nation. This leaves some of us coping with the very boundaries of our identities and the duties assigned to us by their very definition.

At the time, conducting the nuclear tests translated not only into security considerations, but also into obeying a divine command. At the same time, it was equated with an exhibition of manhood and a policy of restraint was deemed effeminate. This was reflected in the popularity of nationalist songs in Pakistan with lyrics like *„war is not a game effeminates play."* Feminists in Pakistan criticized the state discourse as they felt that the policy makers in the defense and political echelons used highly psychosexual metaphors. Feminists in India were equally vehement in their criticism of the rhetoric. They believed that the 'other' was portrayed as 'rapacious' and threatening the helpless mother/ nation, so the Indian Hindu had to become aggressive and show his strength by taking revenge. There was an establishment of consolidating one's honor based on the dishonor of the other nation. But policy makers in both Pakistan and India took a different stance and spoke in terms of having proved their manhood, of exhibiting virility and strength, of having the courage and ability to fight. Further the symbol of femininity is used with negative connotations. It is not only the biological entity 'woman' that suffers but the symbol of the feminine is used to rob any oppositional movement (to the prevailing dominant thought of the nation state) of legitimacy. For instance, peace is taken as a sign of submissiveness if it is not on one's own terms. Aggressive peace is more acceptable than passive (read feminine) peace. To be passively peaceful means to be spineless, translating into a sign of weakness, which would encourage the enemy to trample all over one. That is why the Pakistani and Indian public continues to be more comfortable with the nuclear deterrent rather than a policy of restraint and dialogue.

3. Engendering the Nation State

To critique the chauvinistic nationalism at play today in Pakistan and India, one has to understand the historical process of nation making in the two countries. Pakistan has been a rhetorical construction imagined, carved and created out of the binary discourse of the two-nation theory. The polar opposition created by positing Hindus as the other of Muslims enabled the construction of the Indian Muslim nation as a separate ideological entity different from the Hindus in every respect. The Hindu revivalists at the same time argued that the great Hindu Aryan tradition had been weakened by the ravages of Mughal (read Muslim rule) (Saigol, 1995). This kind of cultural xenophobia persists even today in the discourses of right-wing political and religious groups like the Jamaat-I-Islami[1] in Pakistan, and Hindu revivalist and militant groups like the Bajrang Dal and Vishwa Hindu Parishad (VHP) in India, which professes that they want to cleanse/purify society from the layers of contamination resulting from co-existence with the other. Saigol points toward the gendered construction of the two-nation theory by showing how the state of Pakistan continues to contrast the Islamic principles of justice, fairness, tolerance, brotherhood, and equality with (presumed) Hindu intolerance, injustice, infighting and inequality (Saigol, 1995, p. 229). A hero/villain theme underlined by masculine/feminine consciousness runs throughout Pakistani state discourse in that the attributes usually reserved for describing women are used for Hindus and masculine attributes are reserved for Muslims.

In an interview with Dr. Rubina Saigol, the author of a study on educational discourse in Pakistan, the educationist stated that on examining the social studies textbooks from grade three to eight, she found page after page filled with the two-nation theory, which can be basically analyzed as Pakistani nationalism. On the articulation of the two-nation theory in educational discourse, she observes:

> It is replete with gendered constructs.. the Hindus and enemy as weak, vegetable eating, feminized [...] as those who cannot fight, those who attacked us very sneakily in the middle of the night [...] that's interesting, how when they are constructed as weak enemies, they are feminized. We (*Pakistan*) can beat them easily (*and one of us is*) equal to ten of them..but they are highly masculinized when we talk of their cruelty [...] so sometimes they are hyper-feminized and at other times we hyper-masculinize them. Muslims and Hindus are complete opposites of each other, there is absolutely nothing overlapping in them, they are weak, we are strong, they are cruel, we are kind. This was to me in terms of binary oppositions, a very gendered look.[2]

Speaking with resource persons in India, I found out that a similar process was being executed there. Azra Razzak, who has researched educational textbooks

---

1   The literal translation is 'congregation of Islam'.
2   Personal interview, Lahore, Pakistan, March 1999.

and the emergence of Muslim identity in India, states that looking at history textbooks children learn through the portrayal of Muslim rulers that Muslims are associated with plunder, loot, intolerance, and religious bigotry (Razzak, 1998, p. 235). She concludes that most children would grow up with 'negative images' of the other; in this case, of the Muslim child in school, or Muslims in general. She also comments on a complete absence of stories in textbooks representing the partition from the Muslim angle. In her opinion, most students will probably look at issues from a majority point of view (textbooks may be the only reading material they go through), which identifies the minority as being the problem. Thus Muslims, for her, have to live in India with the stigma of being fanatics, sadists, and intolerant (Razzak, 1998, pp. 230-235).

The creation of Pakistan witnessed immense bloodshed, violence and rioting and an unprecedented displacement of human population, the memories of which continue in the state of animosity prevalent in the two countries today. The 'embodiment of violence' in Pakistan and India can be gauged by surveying the violence committed against women of both Hindu and Muslim during the historical process of partition of the sub-continent. Nationalism is based on purity, so sexual violence was the 'ultimate weapon'. In most cases, women were violated in religious spaces, which was seen as a double of desecration of the 'sacred space and the seed' (of future generations). As defense of women has long been a cultural hallmark of masculine pride, these violent acts were interpreted by the men of the 'vanquished' community as evidence of their impotence (Brownmiller, 1990) leading to further incidents of sexual assaults on women of the 'other' community. Very large numbers of women were forced into death to avoid sexual violence against them, to preserve chastity and protect individual, family and community 'honor'. In interviews with a cross-section of religious elite in Pakistan and India regarding their views on these 'honor killings', on both sides of the border the religious elite gave religious sanction to these heinous acts.

As the Deputy-Director of Jamat-I-Islami put it:

> If the only other choice is that they will get in the enemies' hands then it is the dictate of our ghairat (honor) that we kill these women. There were two risks, so rather than risk their dignity and honor, it was justified to take the other risk and kill them. *(I repeated my question if it was not an extreme measure to kill the women or coerce them into taking their lives).* No, it was not extreme, as they would have died anyway. Once the enemy had used them he might have killed them, so it was all right if you killed them before.[3]

These perceptions have seeped down into all sections of society. I received similar justifications when I posed this question to the political and military elite. The act was equated with 'euthanasia', 'mercy killing' and the only recourse for the 'defeated women' to escape indignity and humiliation.

---

3   Personal interview with Maulana S, Lahore, Pakistan, March 1999.

4. Militarizing of Civil Society

How we visualize our world and our relation to it is not dependent on our individual creative initiatives. Rather, our concepts are influenced by technologies
and the institutions – the media, the corporations, the academy – , which codify
information. If one looks at the articulation of cultural/national identity as it is
expressed in visual form in Pakistan, one can note that from public spaces to
public monuments, from the iconography of a Muslim national identity to the
self-image of the people internalized by them, cultural spaces, cultural signs,
cultural iconography, all reflect the national ideology of a predominantly Muslim, masculine identity/consciousness (Lalarukh, 1997). One would note that in
Pakistan's official ideology the hero is almost always a military hero, and even
if he is not from the military, the metaphors used to describe him will be always
militaristic (as in calling Jinnah, the founder of Pakistan, a soldier of Islam).
Such heroes are created by war and warlike societies, and moments of crisis reinforce the dominance of masculine conceptions of virtue and worth.

Pakistan and India's permanent state of hostilities produce a psychological
mind-set for the production of images to justify the militaristic agenda of the
two governments (Pakistan and India). The people are fed with images of militaristic heroism, brutality, and relentless pursuit of aggrandizement. On the
other hand, images that grow out of peace, tolerance and universal goodwill, are
systematically denigrated. In fact, any attempt at developing an alternative voice
to this national project has been quelled quite harshly by the political administration of the two states, as independent reports on the human rights situation in
the two states show.

Pakistan's educational policy states that in order to demonstrate a desire to
preserve the ideology, integrity and security of Pakistan, the Pakistani school
child would be expected to make speeches on jihad (holy war) and martyrdom
in class. The child is also expected to proclaim her/his readiness to fight against
India. In the actual construction of the 'feminine' and the 'masculine', the curriculum uses Islamic personalities and individuals (Saigol, 1995). Similarly, the
world-view of the Pakistani military affected the choices exercised by Pakistani
college students. As a student in a Federal Government college administered by
the Pakistan Army, I had to sign a pledge that make-up/cosmetics are contra-
band, the chadar (shawl) is an integral part of my uniform;DDK

and 'I will resist (sic) from political conversation'. The extent of militariza-
tion can be judged by the educational discourse. For example, Saigol points out
the following extract from the Class VI civics textbook:

> Every Pakistani has to be a soldier. He has to be ready to render physical and financial
> help. If someone cannot join the army, he can be otherwise helpful to the defenders of the
> country. If he is unable to carry a gun, he can at least become a member of Hilal-e-ahmar

(Red Cross) (Social studies Textbook for Class VI, 1975, p. 86 as quoted by Saigol, 1995, p. 300).

In Pakistan and India I interviewed small groups of schoolgirls and boys aged 14-16 years with similar socio-economic backgrounds to find out the gendered images and the attitudes towards violence that had been disseminated to these children. Students from both countries could not recollect any reference to famous women in their history textbooks and concluded that women lacked the initiative to participate in the history-making processes. For instance, the heroes in the Pakistan Studies textbooks were all recipients of Nishan-e-Haider (the highest Pakistani military honor). When inquired regarding their perceptions of personal security in light of the images they received from school texts, families and media, the male students unanimously believed that a gun would be the best guarantor of security for them. Their female colleagues, by contrast, consider their character, and whether they took the veil or not, more important. The schoolgirls in their replies commented that the boys were 'already secure' whereas they, the girls, had to depend on their families for security.

Asked to justify their support for the nuclear tests, it was interesting to see how the young women internalized the conflict situation for themselves. In the interim period between the conduct of nuclear tests by India and Pakistan, one Pakistani schoolgirl confessed: „I was scared that we would have a Taleban-like situation here if there were a crisis. We are a weak country, and when Muslims are in trouble then they fall back on Islam, and it gets more repressive for women."[4] On the contrary, the schoolboys said, „India doesn't have the guts to attack us now [...] We were the first Islamic state to become (nuclear) power. Good for Islam, not getting repressed".[5]

5. The Religio-Military Nexus in Pakistan

The military in the case of Pakistan has exercised a decisive influence on Pakistan's state policy, either by directly taking over the structures of government or indirectly by controlling and/or manipulating the civil ruling elite (Hussain, 1996). The Muslim religious groups in Pakistan have played their role in justifying militarism in Pakistan. In my interviews with them in Mansoura (the city that the Jamaat-I-Islami have set up for themselves)[6], a former head of the Jamat-I-Islami who also served in the 1980s in the hand-picked legislative assem-

---

4   Personal interview with R, Karachi, Pakistan, April 1999.
5   Personal interview with O, Karachi, Pakistan, April 1999.
6   A literal inside/outside divide for the Jamaat-I-Islami. Inside are the devout Muslims living their lives according to the true faith. While outside are those who are not one of them and have not found 'the truth'.

bly set up by the then military regime of General Zia, was very clear in his support:

> The real task is to conduct jihad, to propagate the word of Islam everywhere [...] God has instructed us to spread His law all over the word. Therefore if we have to use power or force to convince the people it is justified. We have been instructed to put our lives in the path of God, as it is the cause of truth.[7]

This, of course is a very monotheist definition of what jihad signifies. In less extremist countries, jihad means fighting all evils, including the sins outlined in Islam and not just physical violence against infidels. In recent years, extremist forms of Islam have tended to emphasize the physical side of jihad and ignore the rest. The Deputy-Director of Jamaat-I-Islami accepted this broader view, while stressing his own interpretation:

> Jihad is a very broad term to strive to spread the Creator's will and law. The best way to prove our devotion to Him is qatal fi sabeel Allah (kill in the way of God). Those who do not have a complete picture of religion cannot participate in jihad. The various forms of worship like prayer and charity prepare us for the supreme form of worship, which is jihad.[8]

Opting for the military is then not just a career choice. In Pakistan, the military officer is not just a professional. Placed on a pedestal, he is glorified as a hero. The public feels he is performing his religious duty. As the religious elite described it,

> the Pakistani military is competing against a country of non-believers [...] so the soldier is a martyr and conqueror in the religious sense. As we are taking his time and effort so we have to pay him for this service as well. Defending the country is a jihad, it is said that to keep a vigil on the borders is better than one who prays all night.[9]

Religious groups in the period preceding Pakistan's nuclear tests constantly urged the then Pakistan Prime Minister Nawaz Sharif to be a 'real man' and conduct the nuclear tests, as it was a matter of national pride and masculine honor. The 'divine sanction' to the tests in Pakistan could be gauged by the photographs of Thanksgiving prayers being offered (on the Friday immediately following the nuclear tests) in the mosques on the successful conduct of the nuclear tests. These photographs were carried on the front pages of all the national dailies, and the video footage was a part of the news bulletins on national television. The religious elite in their interviews justified the nuclear tests as fulfilling God's command.

> They are justified in Islam as God has instructed us to be as well prepared as we can as far as power is concerned. This power includes nuclear power. So by attaining nuclear

---

7   Personal interview with Chaudhry T, Lahore, Pakistan, March 1999.
8   Personal interview with Maulana S, Lahore, Pakistan, March 1999.
9   Personal interview with Maulana S, Lahore, Pakistan, March 1999.

power we have fulfilled God's command. He has instructed us to be strong so that the enemy of God is afraid of that power.[10]

Subsequently, there were reports in the national media that the religious groups in Pakistan have come to a national consensus regarding the Comprehensive Test Ban Treaty (CTBT) as being against the dictates of Holy Quran: A column in the Urdu Press declared that signing the CTBT would violate verse 60 of Surah-e-Anfal of the Holy Quran which enjoins the Muslims to keep their war-horses ready for the enemy (Nuggets-selections, 1999).

In Pakistan, the martial law regimes have made use of Islam to legitimize their rule, and it can be signified by the inclusion of terms like 'making Pakistan a fortress of Islam', the soldier as the mard-I-momin (Muslim superman) and so on in state discourse. Military dictators like General Zia-ul-Haq in the 1980s also implemented a series of 'reforms' designed to bring laws in conformity with tenets of Islam. More recently, the Chief Executive of Pakistan General Pervez Musharraf, who is referred to as a 'secular Muslim', had to backtrack on certain reforms proposed in the notorious blasphemy laws, in face of domestic pressure by the religious lobby. As recently as February 2002 he had to invoke a verse from the Holy Quran to claim divine authority for his rule and counter criticism of crackdowns on militant Muslim groups.[11]

The military elite's constant reference to Quranic verses and sayings of the Holy Prophet to justify militarism in Pakistan society was reflected in their 'divine justification' of the nuclear tests as well. „There are limits to the number, to the period of time we fast, the pilgrimage. But religious war is one Divine Command that has no such constraints. It is a continuous process of human endeavor to prepare ourselves".[12]

Keeping in mind the religio-military nexus in Pakistan, cultural values have placed a premium on military service, and as Stephen Cohen, in his profile of the Pakistan Army, describes it: „A Pakistani who cannot share equally in the obligations and rewards associated with such a central institution as the military is not truly a citizen in the full sense of the word" (Cohen, 1990, p. 50). For a society, which grows up with the images of the valiant warrior hero fighting in the path of his religious beliefs, one would want to know how women in such

---

10   Personal interview with Maulana S, Lahore, Pakistan, March 1999.

11   „I tell these people, who have become the custodians of Islam or who think that they understand Islam better, that it is Almighty God who gives honor or authority to anybody [...] This is our faith that God Almighty gives honor to whoever He wants and snatches honor from whoever He wants. If this is our faith then God Almighty has brought me to this position...this position, this authority has been bestowed by God and as long as I hold this authority, and whatever work I am doing with full responsibility, all Pakistanis should have confidence in that because this is our faith" (Power bestowed by God, 2002, p. 1).

12   Personal interview with Gen MAB, Rawalpindi, Pakistan, March 1999.

societies could achieve glory. In such a scenario, one would assume that Pakistani women would face a grave crisis of citizenship, as they are not participating in active combat. This is important, because there have often been arguments, both by feminists and by those who opposed them, that the entry of women in the military is the precondition for women's achievement of full citizenship rights. One does not expect that peacetime fatwas (religious edicts) restricting women's mobility and defining their position in society would be challenged. However, would there be scope to maneuver some space for women or would any 'window of opportunity' be open to women in times of crisis?

A look at the religious discourses in Pakistan will show that they maintain and continually reconstruct the public/private, modernity/tradition and East/West divide when they talk of the role women can play at the time of war. Khawar Mumtaz of Shirkat Gah (a research institute working on women living under Islamic laws) narrated how after the creation of Pakistan there were efforts to start the National Voluntary Guards where 'women guards' would be given some military training in return for a monthly stipend. There was a lot of hue and cry, as the religious leaders could not tolerate women marching like soldiers. There were religious edicts against women 'parading with their heads uncovered and bosoms exposed'. They protested that these women would be staring into men's eyes and would have no shame and dignity. During the same time, some women's social service groups started as well. They did not fare badly, as women were viewed doing what was 'their kind of work'. These women did community work in a voluntary capacity without any salary. In contrast, the 'women guards' were getting remuneration for their services, which would give them some degree of economic freedom. This did not go down well with the public. After the 1971 war between Pakistan and India, the religious elite defined the role of women in national reconstruction as follows:

> Now that the war is over, the duties of women are not so much in the battlefields as these are in the hospitals, help-centers, camps for the bomb-stricken etc. What most demands their particular attention is the care and rehabilitation of the family members left by our soldiers, many of who are now in East Pakistan. It is the education of their sons, marriage of their daughters and general care of their wives and mothers and sisters. Nature has given special gifts to women for the service of nursing. According to the dictates of Islam, even giving encouragement or inspiration, giving comforting and grief-effacing talk, smiling and making others smile, has been listed as holy war [...] so apt for women. (Maulana Asadul Qadri, 1972, p. 4).

So, the religious elite appeal to biological determinism to allot the role for women in society. Women are also instructed to be responsible for their men performing their religious duties. One has to note the life goals the Maulana (member of the Islamic clergy) has allotted to daughters and sons – marriage for the girls and education/career for the boys. This theme is repeated in advertisements in Pakistani media, particularly for purchasing insurance policies, where parents are instructed to safeguard the future of the children. The son is shown in a graduation gown clutching an academic degree in his hands, while the daughter is decked up as a bride. Likewise, other members of the Pakistani clergy were quick to emphasize:

> It goes to women's courage that they manage the house when the men are away. And as they cannot leave the housework they cannot participate in combat. But they will receive the same level of divine reward for their work. God has not created men and women equal to each other. For women is the task of reproduction, of taking care of the education of the young, to take up the responsibilities of the house. God has Himself made such divisions among men and women.[13]

By making a gender division of tasks and roles, divinely ordained, any attempt to challenge these limits becomes very difficult and tantamount to questioning the will of God. Within parameters that make sacred the sexual dichotomy by positioning a divinely ordained, bipolar universe, any violation of the different roles and functions assigned to the female and male acquires a cosmological significance (Bouhdiba, 1985).

Similar to the religious elite, the military elite in Pakistan in their interviews vehemently believed in biological determinism ('a dominance of men ordained by nature') as a basis of the naturalization of the gender division of labor in the military and civil world. The Pakistani military elite at no time believed that a policy of keeping women in non-combat positions is discriminatory. They felt that they were doing so to save 'our women' the 'indignity' that women in the West were facing (as in sexual harassment from the superiors). This conveniently absolves them of any responsibility as 'the source of temptation' is removed. As one of the interviewees described it:

> If our women have been kept in non-combat positions like doctors and nurses in the Pakistan Army, one way of looking at it is discrimination, but the other way to look at it is protecting the honor of our women. That she should not be forced in a situation where embarrassment becomes a way and she cannot even openly say what has happened to her, and yet damage may be done [...] it is not discrimination, I will call it discretion.[14]

In his response he conveniently juxtaposes 'the licentious West' with the protective environment for women in the East to put forward his point. He mentions the embarrassment a Pakistani woman would face in coming out with accusations of sexual harassment (compared to her Western sister who was forthright in her accusations). So it is to protect her from humiliation that the benevolent Pakistani military steps in to keep her in 'safe positions'. Notice also how he shifts to the patriarchal discourse of not allowing 'his women' to go through such discomfort. The military elite in its discourse kept on referring to here (virtuous values, control of female sexuality in the two countries) and the

---

13   Personal interview with Chaudhry T, Lahore, Pakistan, March 1999.
14   Personal interview with SMR, Rawalpindi, Pakistan, March 1999.

over there (loose sexual morals of the West). Their own nation is seen to triumph over the more liberated West as they kept their women in segregation, while the West is portrayed as repenting over its mistakes. However, this self-righteousness on the part of the military leads to its feeling that it knows best how social relations should be organized. One can analyze how the Pakistani military, for instance, continues to control women's mobility. This has ranged from the repressive laws passed by the martial law regimes to the 'instructions' given from time to time by the military elite. For example, in the 1980s, the Director of Education for Federal Government Colleges got instructions from the General Headquarters (of the Pakistan Army) to make the chadar (shawl/shroud) a part of the uniform for the girl students, and, as mentioned earlier, all college students were required to sign a pledge if they wanted admission to a Federal Government college.

There have also been reports, which were confirmed during my interviews, that when the Pakistan military was posted as a peacekeeping force, they (the Pakistan peace troops) refused to allow Bosnian women to work at the Pakistan stations 'unless they were properly covered.' The 'women-as-temptress' theme reappears again, for in order to protect the valiant soldier from distraction and 'raving madness', it is simpler to give ultimatums to the women. The military fears women who are trying to modernize as they feel such efforts would reduce the boundary between 'us' and the 'other'. Feminists who have analyzed the articulation of gender in state discourse conclude:

> The purdah (veiling of women) chadar wali aurat (a woman who covers herself) is a very strong boundary between the Western woman and ours. That she (the Western woman) has stepped outside the home, her legs are showing, she is exposed to the colonizing male, and this is our (moral) victory, that even if they (the West) have colonized us, we protected our women from the penetrating, intrusive gaze of the colonial. So the fear of the military that if our women were modernized, and if there is emancipation, freedom for women, modernity, women speaking of women rights, then somehow there would be no difference between the Western woman or women of other nations and ours. Where will the difference lie? (It will lie in what) our women can do or cannot do.[15][16]

---

15   One's moral superiority lay in the fact that the colonizer's 'impure and tainted' ideology could not reach the home where women protected and preserved cultural traditions to protect the beleaguered self. The whole process symbolizes protection of Islamic identity, communal dignity and social and cultural continuity and draws the boundaries between 'Muslim culture' and non-Muslim other.

16   Personal interview, Lahore, Pakistan, March 1999.

6. Reading the Tests: The Mis/Representation of Women in Social Text

As it was in the case of the military elite, the journalists working for the print media in Pakistan have the same agenda of using the conduct of gender relations as boundaries demarcating 'us' against 'them'. The 'other' (in this case India) is portrayed as lax in sexual morals and their women as unprincipled and without honor in most articles in the vernacular press. There is a standard fare that keeps on appearing in the national press of the Indian intelligence agencies sending groups of 'pretty girls' to 'entrap and corrupt' prominent Pakistani men to the Indian cause. Through their women the Indians are shown as manipulative and conspiring to allure good Muslim men.

If one takes up the war songs popular in Pakistan, the female voice is always shown as inciting the man to save her, her honor, her dignity. Or she appears in the form of the 'good women' who have sacrificed their men for the war effort. Verbal behavior is part of socialization, one learns one's role in life, including one's place in the power structure, from the way one speaks and is spoken to. This can be tested by comparing the phrases/ metaphors used to describe the men and the women in the nationalist songs. For the men the metaphors are:

Mard-I-mujahid: warrior hero, Shujaat: bravery, jawan Mardi: gallantry, jiyala: headstrong, daleyr: courageous, sarfaroshi: willing to sacrifice his life in a just cause, madar-e-watan kay aabroo kay muhafiz: the guardian of the motherland's chastity, sheyr-e-bahadur: lion-hearted.

For women were the terms: shama-aman: lamps of peace, tan-I-pak: pure bodies, deys ki izzat: the nation's honour, aabroo (chastity), paykar-I-haya: embodiment of modesty, vareejaana: unrestrained emotions of love.

These metaphors have been used by the various educational, political and religious elites in society to establish ideological control over women. By glorifying them for their ability to sacrifice, and conceptualizing them as 'mothers of nations', women are reduced to reproductive roles in society and marginalized from the educational and professional sector. There is a very false sense of what constitutes honor, power and national pride. The Pakistani state, for example, had orchestrated public displays at the time of the nuclear tests, in one instance in terms of veiled women from right-wing political parties taking out processions 'thanking the government for protecting them and exhibiting their ghairat (male honor and pride)' (Jang, 29 May, 1998, p. 2).[17] The language employed was again very patriarchal, of women's honor being defended by the strong arm

---

17   Jang is a daily newspaper in Urdu. Page two of this daily contains nothing but untitled photographs and no further text. The examples given are taken from this particular page.

of the army. These images were contrasted by photographs of men in public rallies firing in the air with ammunition displayed prominently in national newspapers for a week following the tests conducted by Pakistan with the caption:
„(Prime Minister) Nawaz Sharif has proved with the blasts that Pakistan is a
land of ghazis (conquerors), ghairatmand (honorable), juntas (courageous men),
and jan-nisar (men willing to sacrifice their lives)" (Jang, 30 May, 1998, p. 2).

7. He Said/She Said: The Feminists on the Texts of War

Feminist activist organizations like the Women's Action Forum (WAF) were
formed in direct response to General Zia's Islamization measures in the 1980s.[18]
The most profound changes undertaken in the course of Islamization were directed at women. Along with Hadood Ordinance (which commands public flog-
ging and/or death for crimes like adultery, theft, rape and the consumption of alcohol) came a series of rulings which implied control over women's bodies,
space and ability to maneuver: their dress, behavior, their public appearance,
their participation in the sphere of politics and paid work; principally a relentless message that women were not equal to men.

The religious right wing also took a long-term view of imparting their ideology among a wider section of women. As a measure to actively mobilize
women belonging to an emerging middle class, there was a mushrooming of religious seminaries in major cities and towns of Pakistan. These institutions im-
parted a selective reading of Islamic texts and discourses and prepared them for
jobs in segregated settings as teachers of Arabic and religious studies in state-
run schools. Mumtaz notes:

> The stated reason for establishing one such institution, Madrassah Faisal-al-Banat in
> Lahore, in 1979, was to rectify the neglect of women's spiritual education – considered
> essential to counter, in the words of the brochure of the madrassah,[19] Westernization that
> has affected women, who under the pretext of emancipation and liberation are in reality
> spreading obscenity and immorality (Mumtaz, 1994, p. 231).

These images of the 'immoral' and the 'moral/good' woman remain in public
perception. One can take up the case of Ms Benazir Bhutto, and her dramatic
entry into motherhood. As a single woman the critics would always situate her

---

18 Before this, the major organization of women was the All Pakistan Women's Association formed in the late 1940s. This group had a history of lobbying and co-operating with
   the state throughout changes in the government, with the understanding that the state
   would not assert its authority by forcing women to conform to Islamic codes of behavior,
   and the women would not challenge the state and its 'Islamic credentials' (Gardezi,
   1997, p. 101).
19 Religious seminary.

in the land of Western wickedness. Although she had initially tried to locate herself at the other end of female archetypes, that of the Amazon or hero, and later as the daughter of a Great Man, her father Zulfiqar Bhutto, it was as a mother that she finally found political success. This was because in a nation afraid of female sexuality, of sexuality as such, an Amazon could never last (Inayatullah, 1996).

The Women's Action Forum operated in such a climate as an umbrella organization of women's groups within urban areas that united to fight Islamic laws and subsequently became involved in other issues relating to women's oppression. In 1982 the Sindhiani Tehreek (Sindhi women's movement) was formed in the province of Sindh and operates as the largest women's organization in the country, by addressing issues of gender, class and national oppression (Said Khan, 1988, p. 15). These groups have been successful since then to build alliances with other civil liberties groups to build up an effective counter-hegemony.

In Pakistan they had been protesting for disarmament in South Asia since the beginning. They pressed upon the political elite of Pakistan to follow a policy of restraint and to resist from conducting nuclear tests. A leaflet issued in the public interest by the Women's Action Forum stating their position on nuclearization read:

> What will the nuclear program provide? Safety from police brutality? End of corruption? End to violence? Money for development? Freedom from fear of death, radiation and disease?
>
> Our Needs: Education, Food, Clean Air and Water, Not bombs.
> Our Desire: Healthy Babies, Your Plans: diseased births for untold generations.
> Our Priority: well being for all, not only the powerful and the elite.
> Use resources to benefit majority, not to boost egos.
> Live in Peace, not fear.
> We nurture life, not destroy it.
> We want radiation free air for our children; our children have a right to live too.
> Nuclearization – a mindless ego boost.

In their interviews they brought up the monolithic interpretation of courage on the part of the Pakistani public, in terms of the power to defeat, to attack, to take over, to demolish the consolidation of one's honor based on the dishonor of the other country. One could see the disappearance of courage in terms of the ability to sacrifice or to remain silent in one's lexicon. However, the significance of these terms is not restricted to the level of discourse alone. They reflect all the ways it resembles the rest of society in which behaving in a particular manner carries power and privilege. Women being the victims of violence for so long particularly abhor the state sanctioning a policy of aggression.

Along with this is the phenomenon of the masculinization of the mind. Given the structure of power and the patterns of male-oriented socialization, empowerment, and liberation for women is equated with 'being like men' and professionalism means taking the 'hard' masculinist option. Women, to survive in male dominated professions, have to emulate masculine behavior or risk getting sidelined. Chenoy and Vinayak state that when women support war, conflicts or the military, they do so because of patriarchal socialization (Chenoy & Vinayak, 2002).

8. Demilitarizing the Texts

The making of the national idea in Pakistan and India has so far involved the propagation of myths – myths of a glorious past, of an 'imagined community', of demon enemies, of what the 'valiant heroes' and 'good women' of the state can do or not do. Discourses in the two states continue to valorize a belligerent rather than a more rational and pacifist attitude towards each other. The myths are present within the educational discourse where knowledge is constructed to suit the powers that be. They continue with the media where there are strict images and roles for the men and women of the state. The religious elite who one would have expected to employ a language of ethics has actively incited the public by inflammatory speeches. One should also keep in mind that there is no separation of the church and the state in Pakistan and India, in fact one would find members of the religious elite and militant religious groups as members of parliament. Therefore they can easily quell civil movements by proclaiming eternal damnation for anyone challenging the status quo.

Gendered images dominate the language of Pakistani foreign policy discourse. In the Pakistani context, India is projected as the villain, sometimes acquiring the visage of a big threatening force many times Pakistan's size and sometimes a dangerous scheming woman trying to manipulate international opinion against Pakistan (Khattak, 1997, p. 43). A future project could be the exploration whether security discourses in the post-September 11th world can be critiqued as highly gendered if one witnesses the strong binary divisions in policy discourse.[20]

---

20 i) President Bush's ultimatum: You are either with us or with the terrorists; ii) US Secretary of State Colin Powell said in an interview with the New York Times that he delivered a virtual ultimatum to General Musharraf: „Mr. President, you have a choice to make" (Amir, 2001, p. 7); iii) in the global media: from September-November 2001, the information spots for BBC Asia Today (which are aired daily at regular intervals) featured footage of street demonstrations in Pakistan with the voice-over 'Pakistan at the Cross-roads: medieval Islam or secular democracy'. In both instances these are images that are constantly repeated.

Historically policy-making institutions have valorized militarism and masculine conceptions of virtue and worth. Could the solution lie in having a greater percentage of women in the policy-making institutions? But as critics have already noted, the aggressive and insecure nationalism that defines the security perceptions of Pakistan and India towards each other decisively restricts the scope for feminizing such perspectives in a more positive direction. To put it another way, having more women with the same kind of masculinist minds in the senior policy-making apparatuses of the two countries is likely to make only a limited difference, especially if there is a special obligation on women to show they can be equally aggressive in their defense of national interest. However, my caution regarding women pursuing hawkish policies should not be taken as an excuse to not to include women in policymaking. The goal then should be to include more women and men who are sensitive to these gendered definitions of power.

What an alternative discourse demands for rectification is a radical restructuring of thought and analysis which valorizes and enhances what are conventionally known as masculine values: violence, eagerness to retaliate, or a tendency towards brutality. There is a need to follow what Gerda Lerner describes as stepping outside of patriarchal thought. To learn to be skeptical towards every known system of thought; being critical of all assumptions, ordering values, and definitions. As long as both women and men regard the subordination of half the human race to the other as 'natural', it is impossible to envision a society in which differences do not connote either dominance or subordination (Lerner, 1986, p. 84).

An option can come out by demilitarizing the social texts of the two countries. There is an urgent need to allow an alternative feminist/civil society voice to develop. There are feminist organizations and civil movements at work in the two countries today that employ this alternative discourse. In such a scenario it is essential to document the experiences and instances of resistance, solidarity and agency disseminated through alternative voices, activist movements and channels in the transnational and regional media, those that have remained skeptical of hegemonic discourse. And those that have provided a platform in communication technology for dialogue and debate with others outside one's community. For one has to realize that though globalization literally refers to an increase in inter-connectedness, we must recognize that in the case of Pakistan there is a history of 'deglobalization' as well (for example the banning of Indian cable channels and South Asian satellite news channels at times of conflict for 'spreading propaganda and disinformation', or controlling the physical movement of actors involved in civil movements). There is a need to permit these movements to flourish and to learn from them as well. At the moment, the rest of the world sees these two countries as regions where civil liberties are overridden in the name of religion and male power, where peace never stood a chance to suit the militaristic agenda, where a majority of people lives in abysmal conditions which suits political agendas. This image can be repaired if the civil society builders are willing to learn from the alternative discourses based on freedom, dignity, and human/women's rights.

References:

Amir, A. (2001, November 30). Pragmatism of the supine. *Dawn*, p.7.

Bouhdiba, A. (1985). *Sexuality in Islam*. London: Routledge, Kegan and Paul.

Brownmiller, S. (1990). *Against Our Will: Men, Women and Rape*. New York: Bantam Books.

Chenoy, A. & Vinayak, A. (2002). Promoting Peace Security and Conflict Resolution: The Impact of Gender Balance in India and Pakistan. In Skjelsboek, I. & Smith, D. (eds.), *Gender, Peace and Conflict*. London: Sage Publications, in print.

Cohen, S. (1990). *The Pakistan Army*. New Delhi: Himalayan Books.

Gardezi, F. (1997). Nationalism and State Formation: Women's Struggles and Islamization in Pakistan. In Hussain, N., Mumtaz, S. & Saigol, R. (eds.), *Engendering the Nation State*, vol. 1. Lahore: Simorgh Publications, pp. 79-110.

Hussain, N. (1996).Women in Pakistani Context: An Overview. In Malik, M. & Hussein, N. (eds.), *Reinventing Women*. Lahore: Simorgh Publications, pp. 11-21.

Inayatullah, S. (1996). Mullahs, Sex and Bureaucrats: Pakistan's Confrontations with the Modern World. In Bahri, D. & Vasudeva, M. (eds.), *Between the Lines: South Asians and Post Coloniality*. Philadelphia: Temple University Press, pp. 121-136.

Khattak, S. (1994). A Reinterpretation of the State and State Discourse in Pakistan (1977-88). In Said Khan, N., Saigol, R. & Zia, A. S. (eds.), *Locating the Self: Perspectives on Women and Multiple Identitie*s. Lahore: ASR Publications, pp. 22-40.

Khattak, S. (1997). Gendered and Violent: Inscribing the Military on the Nation-State. In Hussain, N., Mumtaz, S. & Saigol, R. (eds.), *Engendering the Nation State*, vol. 2. Lahore: Simorgh Publications, pp. 38-52.

Lalarukh (1997). Image Nation: a Visual Text. In Hussain, N., Mumtaz, S. & Saigol, R. (eds.), *Engendering the Nation State*, vol. 2. Lahore: Simorgh Publications, pp. 75-101.

Lerner, G. (1986). *The Creation of Patriarchy*. Oxford: Oxford University Press.

Maulana Asadul Qadri (1972, January 1). The role of women in national reconstruction. *Dawn*, p.4.

Mumtaz, K. (1994). Identity Politics and Women: 'Fundamentalism' and Women in Pakistan. In Moghadam, V. (ed.), *Identity Politics and Women: Cultural Reassertions and Feminisms in International Perspective*. Boulder: Westview Press, pp. 228-242.

Nuggets-selections from the Urdu press (1999, July 9-15). *Friday Times*, p. 8.

Power bestowed by God, says Musharraf (2002, February 6). *Dawn*, p. 1.

Razzak, A. (1998). *Education and the Emergence of Muslim Identity in India*. Ph.D. thesis, Delhi: University of Delhi, Department of Education.

Said Khan, N. (1988). *Women in Pakistan: A New Era*. Lahore: ASR Publications.

Saigol, R. (1995). *Knowledge and Identity: Articulation of Gender in Educational Discourse in Pakistan*. Lahore: ASR Publications.

Tickner, J. A. (1992). *Gender in International Relations: Feminist Perspectives on Achieving Global Security*. New York: Columbia University Press.

Helma Lutz

The Long Shadows of the Past. The New Europe at a Crossroad

1. Intro: Just a Normal Week ?!

The world is turning at an increased speed, and as images follow images, we all follow their flow. A critical look at the media representation of the murderous attacks of September 11th, 2001, shows how a certain interpretation of images can create 'communities'. By repeating the same pictures over and over, and, by emphasising that this attack is not comparable to any other incident in history, the media contributed to the scandalisation of the event in such a way that it is now considered a turning point in American and world history. Other events pale to insignificance besides it. But what happens to the violent incidences which do not become corner stones of collective memory, but, instead, are quickly forgotten? I start my article by examining two incidents from the year 2000 on the basis of which I want to develop my argument.

In the night of June 11th, 2000 three male Germans, aged between 16 and 25, hung around a park in Dessau (Germany), drinking beer and listening to right wing rock-music. When 39 year old Alberto Adriano walked by, he was beaten into a coma and died from his injuries the next morning. The young men were white while their victim was black.

This was not the only violent racist attack that week. The statistics indicate 4972 registered racist incidents in the year 2000 in Germany[1] (see Bundeskriminalamt, 2001). Only when people died from the attacks or were severely injured, newspapers took notice. Racist violence has become a part of everyday life in Germany.

Seven days later, on June 19th, British customs officers opened the doors of a Dutch truck in Dover and found two survivors along with fifty-eight casualties. The men and women from China, declared as a load of tomatoes, had died from suffocation. European political leaders, at that very moment debating about Europe's future in Portugal, reacted to the event by blaming each other

---

1   The Federal Criminal Police Office distinguishes between anti-semitic criminal offences
     and those against foreigners (fremdenfeindliche Straf- und Gewalttaten); I have added up
     these two categories as 'racist incidences'.

for failing to adequately protect their countries' borders, thereby providing loopholes for illegal immigrants. They promised to intensify border controls, to invest in X-ray-scanners and other equipment, and to track down the illegal border-crossers more effectively.

Numerous parties were immediately declared responsible and guilty for this incident: a) the Chinese Mafia (the 'snake heads'), who smuggles people for 3-30,000 Euro per person from the province of Fujian to a West European country, b) the Chinese restaurant owners in London, who are dependent on cheap labour and therefore collaborate with the snake heads, c) the Russian police which tolerates an estimated 200,000 Chinese trespassers on their way to Western Europe, d) the agency which ran the truck, including the lorry driver and e) finally, the victims themselves, who were considered criminal offenders because they entered the European Union border without papers and appropriate visa.

The refugees did not appear in the newspapers by name. Neither their biography nor their motives to embark on this risky journey were investigated. Since they had no right to come to Europe there was no memorial service by European state leaders and no public outcry except by the people who found their horror scenarios of a Europe flooded by illegal immigrants confirmed. In China, too, the victims did not receive much attention.

Just a normal week? Business as usual? Other subjects have captured the attention of the media since then, and Europe has other problems to worry about. In this article I want to examine the links between these two incidents. I intend to show what these incidents tell us about migration, nationalism, racism, ethnicism and gender. In particular I want to develop a theoretical framework in which the intersections between them are emphasised. I will start by analysing the socio-political landscapes of the 'New Europe', its changing geographies and populations which are connected to new ways of belonging, its new identities, and, in particular, its new forms of social exclusion. I will then turn to examining how European feminism has dealt with these questions. Finally I develop a theoretical framework that allows to examine the intersection of a large number of lines of social difference, aiming for a better understanding of how nationalism, racism, ethnicism and gender shape our everyday lives.

2. The New Europe of Post 1989

The breakdown of the Soviet Union, the fall of the Berlin Wall, the reunification of Germany, the end of the Cold War, the war in former Yugoslavia, and last but not least the Nato War on Yugoslavia/Serbia show that the political and social map of Europe has changed significantly since 1989. Another important change with far-reaching consequences was the abolition of borders between the member states of the European Union, started by seven Schengen[2] countries in March 1995, and the decision to enlarge this community towards the East and the South East. We are now speaking of a 'New Europe' (see Koser & Lutz, 1998; Anthias & Lazaridis, 2000; Brah, 1993, 1996; Bade, 2000). This New Europe, with the introduction of the Euro also united by a common currency, seems to be heading for a new political entity.

Meanwhile, the socio-political transformations have brought into sharper focus questions surrounding the definition of Europe and its boundaries (Balibar, 1990; Brah, 1996). Before 1989, Europe was often understood to comprise the member states of the European Economic Community (the predecessor of the EU) and the other parliamentary democracies of *Western* Europe. Since then, a search for commonalties uniting the European states has been going on, which often focused on the elusive concept of 'European civilisation' or a so called common Judeo-Christian culture. In fact, since the de-colonisation process after World Wars I and II, the redefinition of what Europe is has been an ongoing project. The 'Old Europe' was characterised by a discourse about its superiority and domination over the South and was constructed through the process of colonisation, namely the settlement of Europeans in other parts of the globe, the formation of empires, and the struggles against indigenous populations (Balibar, 1990). In contrast, the 'New Europe' seems to be a rather defensive discourse of striving to construct a 'pure Europe' as a symbolic continent, cleansed of foreign and 'uncivilised' elements. In the search for intrinsic features of 'Europe', discourses of culture, politics and space have become closely intermeshed with discourses on nationalism, racism and 'home' versus 'foreigners' and 'otherness', a point I will elaborate on later in this paper (Lutz, Phoenix & Yuval-Davis, 1995; Brah, 1996; Räthzel, 1995; Yuval-Davis, 1997).

Migration movements have been and still are at the heart of the cultural and political developments in Europe. Since 1989 an estimated four million migrants have come to Europe; another estimated five million refugees have fled or been expelled from the territory of the former Yugoslavia (see Koser & Lutz, 1998, p. 1). Migration remains a complex issue in Europe because it can be examined at two different scales: the nation state and the European Union. These two perspectives are often divergent because of different constitutional traditions, the political composition of national governments and the weakness of the European Parliament as a legislative assembly. In fact, the political institution

---

2   The Schengen Treaty was first signed in 1985 by France, Germany and the Benelux countries. It aims to implement common visa policies throughout the Schengen territory and control entry and movement of non-EU citizens including asylum seekers through a common electronic database system. The 1985 agreement has been specified by the 1990 Implementing Agreement. In addition to the five original states, the treaty has been signed by Spain, Italy, Greece, Austria, Denmark, Finland, Iceland, Norway, Portugal and Sweden.

which decides European policies and formulates treaties is not the European Parliament but the Council of Ministers, composed of the heads of the member states. Due to the constitution of European citizenship, migration is thus considered in an ambivalent way.

The definition of European citizenship, formulated in Article 7 of the Maastricht Treaty (1992), had internal as well as external consequences. The right of all Europeans to partake in local elections of the country of their residence has not only permitted a stronger cohesion between European citizens, but has also accentuated their difference from so called 'others', that is non-Europeans. This right is especially important for those Europeans residing in a European Union member state outside their own. Thus, a Dutch citizen living in Germany for a limited time can exercise his/her local political rights, while a German-born Turkish citizen is prevented from it. The same mechanism is in operation with regard to the elections for the European Parliament, because all those who are not in possession of the membership status of a nation state are ineligible.

An ambivalent dialectic related to the constitution of a common 'European identity' and the exclusion of 'others' can also be observed in the present new border policies. Treaties on boundaries indicate that new cultural and political dynamics are at stake. A look at the Schengen treaty elucidates how, on the one hand, it permits the opening up of borders between the EU member states on the basis of the liberal principle of the free movement of people and goods. On the other hand, it creates new borders inside the states and between human beings with regard to foreigners. Now boundaries are no longer equivalent to state borders, but are constructed inside states, as well as around the European Union (see Calloni & Lutz, 2000). Thus, the border police today is not only operating along the borders, but is entitled to search and arrest every suspicious person in public places like undergrounds, airports and harbours which are earmarked as border spaces or dangerous places. All European citizens can potentially be dangerous border crossers, but in reality only those who are 'suspicious looking', since September 11th mostly Middle Eastern people, are exposed to this procedure. The former *inside* becomes the new *outside*. Many European 'mainports' (main airports) now have extra-territorial zones where refugees are kept and from where they can be deported. Since they do not enter the country, they do not have the right to ask for political asylum.

Not only Europe has changed significantly over the last decade, but the rest of the world is marked by profound changes as well. Apart from the Soviet Union, South and Central Africa, South and Central America, China and other Asian countries, have experienced political upheavals, wars and genocide. Some states disappeared, and some have lost large parts of their population while new ones have emerged. All this is contributing to the world's new cartographic and mental maps. The 'New Europe' drives these changes as much as it is affected by them.

However, the more things change, the more they stay the same, a proverb says. Historical analysis shows that the application of the term 'new' to a social phenomenon is arbitrary and therefore debatable – transitions are incomplete and boundaries can be blurred. Describing a phenomenon as 'new' corresponds with the modern desire to order and arrange the history of societies according to certain characteristics, of which the expression of time in sequential structure is a major principle. It is an example of an a posteriori description which is often challenged at a later date on the basis of different ordering principles.

In order to understand what is new, we first have to investigate the old. A closer look at the two incidents I described at the beginning makes clear that they cannot be analysed without the knowledge of the past. This past goes back more than two hundred years, to European colonialism, to the socio-biological construction of races, and to the implementation of racism as a major ideology and organising principle for European nation states. All three aspects are closely interconnected.

The fact that Alberto Adriano was killed has nothing to do with his reasons to leave Mozambique and come to Germany[3], but with the racist world view of those who killed him. These young people simply had a boring night, and the bashing of blacks or 'others' has become a widespread way of passing the time among young males, particularly in East Germany. Their view that Blacks just do not belong here is shared by large parts of the population. The youngsters can therefore legitimate their actions as being an execution of the people's will. Indeed, they have the moral support of many fellow countrymen. They are proud of producing 'tick-free' zones, as they call it, regions purified from 'vermin'. In mainstream social sciences these deeds of racist violence are explained by the rapid social changes in Germany after its reunification. It is assumed that these youngsters are members of fringe groups, the losers of modernity, who could not cope with the changes of the political system and act out their frustration by clinging to xenophobic ideology and using violence (Heitmeyer et al, 1992; Ausländerbeauftragte, 2000). This is a comfortable explanation because it reduces racism to its violent expressions and ignores its ideological and discursive aspects as well as its social contexts. It also situates its existence within marginal youth groups (such as skin heads) and outside of dominant society (see Leiprecht et al, 1997; Leiprecht, 2001). Finally it ignores the gender aspect: the fact that the male young perpetrators perform masculinity in a way which differs from its 'normal' expression only by the degree of violence. In Germany, the debate on xenophobia (which was triggered by the bomb attack on a group of Jewish immigrants from the former Soviet Union in July 2000) has failed to address racism as a problem at the centre of society – in-

---

3   Some newspapers have portrayed Adriano as refugee; however, Adriano had come to the former GDR as contract worker and had lived in Germany for 20 years. He was married to a German woman and had three children.

cluding the production of racist images on various levels – and racist violence as a gendered phenomenon. A look at the list of 93 reported victims killed by right wing youngsters (see Frankfurter Rundschau & Tagesspiegel, 14 September, 2000) in the ten years since the German reunification (1990) shows that the majority of the victims are male; this is also true for their perpetrators. There are only two incidents reported in which (young) women actively took part. However, this does not mean that women are not racist. Recent research in Germany has shown that young women express racist opinions and racist aggression verbally rather than in a physical way, although they often support their male peers emotionally in activism and in physical attacks (Holzkamp & Rommelspacher, 1991; Horn-Metzger & Riegel, 1995). In other words, racism is a gendered phenomenon with specific male and female forms of expression. It needs to be examined as a major structural problem of society, requiring a public debate and a variety of different counter-measures.

The reasons why to this day a wider discussion on racism – instead of xenophobia – is avoided in Germany are manifold (see Lutz, 2001): First, there is a particular way of dealing with the legacy of German fascism, in which the term racism is reserved for the murderous crimes of German fascism, the Holocaust, and consequently non-existent after 1945. Second, a dominant belief that there is no reason to deal with the colonial past and its expression in post-colonial societies since Germany had few colonies in the past. German colonialism compared to National Socialism appears as an evil of minor relevance, writes Birgit Rommelspacher (1999, p. 22). As a consequence, racism is characterised by its most extreme expressions and not in the subtle forms of discrimination and exclusion, short of murder and extermination. In this context it is interesting to note that when Roman Herzog, the former President of Germany, visited Namibia, a former German colony in South Africa, in 1998, he refused to apologise for the twenty years of German colonial rule in the country and for what is now called the first *ethnic cleansing* of the 20th century on the African continent. In 1904 at least 60,000 Herero and 10,000 Nama people were killed by German soldiers, members of the so called *Schutztruppe* (colonial army) which carried out a command of extermination. The killing of Hereros and Namas was followed by the settlement of German farmers in Namibia who came to own a large percentage of the fertile land. In connection with developments in the neighbouring countries like Zimbabwe, these farmers are currently experiencing difficulties due to property claims by the former landowners. This issue has become a political instrument for the power play of the post-colonial African elite who uses it for its very own purposes. A closer look at this issue shows that the ideological basis of colonialism does not end simply because of the retreat of the coloniser from the colonised territory, but that colonialism has repercussions and consequences for the societies for many generations. This goes so far that white British and German farmers who decide to leave Namibia, Zimbabwe or

South Africa due to farm ownership disputes, can claim British and German citizenship on the basis of their ethnic origin – whereas this is denied to any offspring of a mixed marriage between black and white. Thus, whiteness can be a resource and a long-lasting asset.

As in the German case, a look at two centuries of European nation states' histories reveals the close connection of Europe's history to literally every part of the world. Be it as explorers, invaders, colonisers, missionaries, teachers, doctors, travellers or civil servants in duty of the motherlands, as revolutionaries or intellectuals, Europeans have left a mark on the non-European territories as much as these territories have inscribed themselves into Europe (see also Knowles, 2000; Pattynama, 2000). The legacy of this past becomes visible in the analysis of current socio-political phenomena. Few European countries did not have a share in the conquest and exploitation of 'others', be it within their own territories, within Europe, or outside. Europe as a whole has to deal with its long shadows of the past. A look at the German case is again illuminating for understanding why this is such a troublesome task.

The German reluctance to deal with its colonial past does not stand by itself, but is part of Germany's difficulties to deal with any of its pasts: The philosopher Jürgen Habermas has used the Freudian term '*Deckerinnerungen*' (cover memories) (Freud, 1899/1960) to characterise the German way of coming to terms with its past ('*Vergangenheitsbewältigung*') (Habermas, 1994, see also Rosenthal, 1998). Habermas points to the fact that the collective memories of fascism have been covered up by those of expulsion and flight of millions of Germans after World War II, and by the Stalinist and socialist state oppression of East Germans thereafter. In other words, the collective memory of being perpetrator is superseded by that of being victim. I would add that tracing back a century's memories, layer after layer of cover memories can be detected in which perpetration, co-perpetration, or at least indifference to atrocities are covered up by *sufferance and victimisation*. It is this particular social construct which lies at the heart of racist and nationalist legitimisation: producing an image of oneself as victim of oppression by others, having suffered for such long a time, asking for revenge and claiming a territory of one's own – this is the rhetoric used by nationalists in Serbia, Croatia, Albania, Ireland etc. as well as by racists in France, Britain, Belgium, Germany etc. The idea of an ethnically cleansed community, therefore, is not new – it is an intrinsic feature of a particular form of 19th century nationalism.

If, as it seems, the discourse of victimisation is powerful and productive, it is not easy to deconstruct the victim-perpetrator binary and analyse the space in between.[4] What is needed instead is a layered contextual analysis of positional-

---

4   This is supposedly one of the reasons why anti-racist and anti-nationalist interventions are relatively ineffective.

ity, meaning that people can be perpetrators in one situation and victims in another, or both at the same time.

In the next part I will look at how gender studies in Europe have dealt with the phenomena described.

3. European Feminism and the New Europe

Firstly, it needs to be said that there is and was no unified 'European' debate on these issues. Rather there was a very diverse discussion in different countries. Drawing on American feminism's focus on the race-class-gender-debate (see Lutz, 2001), women and gender studies in England pioneered the analysis of 'race-relations' in a post-colonial society. In this context it is now generally agreed that the concept of race is a social construct which makes use of a historically variable nexus of social meanings. Avtar Brah has given a very elaborate definition of the phenomena in question:

> Any number of characteristics – colour, physiognomy, race, culture, gene pools –
> may be summoned as signifiers of 'race'. Certain forms of racism will highlight
> biological characteristics as indicators of supposed 'racial' difference. Other forms
> may single out cultural difference as the basis of presumed impervious racial
> boundaries between groups. Cultural racism may even deny any notion of biological
> superiority or inferiority, but what characterises it specifically as racism is the subtext of
> innate difference that implicitly or explicitly serves to denote a group as a 'race'. In other
> words, racism constructs 'racial' difference. (Brah, 1993, p. 11).

For historical reasons, the term racism is not used in many Western societies as it is in the British and North American context even though the phenomena described are comparable. In some European countries the social construction of minority groupings takes the form of racialisation, in others it is rather ethnicisation or culturalisation. „If a phenomenon is to be identified as racism, the collective signified within it must be represented as being inherently different," writes Avtar Brah (idem, p. 11). Thus, racism can be produced by similar mechanisms, using race or ethnicity as a means of exclusion. I agree with Ann Phoenix (1998, p. 10) who argues that „the terminology of 'race' and 'ethnicity' are in constant flux, largely because no entirely satisfactory terms have been found." This is obviously due to differences in social order systems and historical developments. Whereas 'race' as an official category used by the state to differentiate between its citizens, as for example in the US, reproduces the discourse about races and engenders racialisation, in the German or Dutch context the term race is totally avoided by policy makers and state institutions. Instead, the terms ethnicity and culture are used for the same purposes. This, however, is not an indicator for the absence of racism from state policies. On the contrary, as many authors (see Wekker, 1995; Essed, 1990, 1995; Lutz, 1991) have emphasised, institutionalised racism is present in the Dutch and German foreigner law as much as 'race talk' is part of everyday encounters and media discourses. Race and ethnicity overlap and can „become particularly confusing since ethnic groups also have racialised positions." (Phoenix, 1998, p. 11)

While the Dutch debate on nationalism, ethnicism and racism follows the English-American one, the feminist discussion in Germany can be described as a special case (see Lutz, 2001). As Birgit Rommelspacher (1999) shows, the term racism in Germany is inseparable from the atrocities of fascism and the Shoa in which millions of people were killed, with Jews and gypsies being the main targets of the extermination machinery. Thus, racism is always identified with its most extreme form of expression. Because of this, since 1945 the term xenophobia or 'animosity against foreigners' is preferred when speaking about contemporary phenomena. As a result, the whole discourse is one of *discontinuity*, excluding different forms and expressions of racism from the perception. As already mentioned, German colonialism almost disappeared from the analysis, hiding behind National Socialism (Rommelspacher, 1999, p. 22). Rommelspacher rightly stresses this fact as a reason why German feminists have detached their debates from those in Britain or the Netherlands where the emphasis is more on *continuity* of racist ideology and the features of racism in everyday life. In addition, the lack of citizenship rights for immigrant women contributed to their weak presence in the German feminist discourse (see Lutz, 1997). The German reunification in 1990 is another reason for the distinctly German discourse because it interrupted a debate about racism and nationalism among feminists that had only started in the 1990s, initiated by authors, who, by drawing on the British literature, emphasised similarities in the social positioning of migrants in Germany and post-colonial immigrants in the Netherlands and Britain (see Kalpaka & Räthzel, 1986; Lutz, 1991; Gümen, 1996; Lutz & Huth-Hildebrandt, 1998).

Because of all these reasons one can say also that German feminism contributed to the debate in a unique way. The accusation that German *women* helped Hitler to power (see Koonz, 1986) triggered a long-lasting debate over the involvement of women in fascism on different levels. While there was a strong feminist desire to deny this fact by clinging to the notion of woman as the (morally) superior gender, it is now widely agreed that German women profited from the empowerment strategies (The mother of the fatherland) of the Nazis and that they have at least acted as co-perpetrators or accomplices (Thürmer-Rohr, 1989). This debate has also become the starting point for identifying the special female character of right wing extremism by providing important tools for the analysis of the current situation. However, the research dealing with National Socialism is still not connected to the research about current expressions of racism and ethnicism in relation to post-1945 immigration. Whereas researchers as myself focus on the 'othering' of the Muslim woman and Anti-Islamism as a meaningful aspect of identity-building in the context of the European unification (Lutz, 1991, 1997; Inowlocki & Lutz, 2000), others write about the continuing existence of Anti-Semitism (Rosenthal, 1998). Unfortunately with few exceptions (Rommelspacher, 1995) the analysis of common features in facism and post-war society racism is neglected and a dialogue between researchers is missing. The tension between East and West German women with regard to the different pasts and the common future is making this task even more difficult.

Whereas the focus on women's involvement in National Socialism is quite strong in the German feminist debate, this very aspect is completely missing in many other European countries. National Socialism and Anti-Semitism are constructed as a specific German characteristic which must not to be dealt with in the formerly occupied countries. In my view, however, the theoretical concept of 'Mittäterschaft' (collaboration) might prove a very powerful tool for understanding contemporary phenomena of racism and nationalism in Europe. This would imply a research agenda which is not reduced to analysing the outcome of processes of social exclusion but includes the production of 'othering' and its actors in the analysis.

4. From Race-Class-Gender to Intersectionality

The race-class-gender-debate in Europe (see the pioneering work of Anthias & Yuval-Davis, 1992) has been very important for understanding identity construction in contemporary Europe.

> Recent conceptualisations of identities emphasise the way in which individuals occupy multiple positions and therefore have a range of fragmented identities, which become salient in different contexts and conceptualise identities as always in the process of being formed, rather than achieved and fixed (Phoenix, 1998, p. 9).

This position is very much in accordance with post-modern concepts of mobility ('the nomad'), fluidity, masquerade, hybridity (the cyborg) and syncretism (diaspora space) (see also the second part of this volume).

When scholars like Stuart Hall, Homi Bhabha, Gayatri Spivak, Trinh T. Minh-ha, Rosi Braidotti, Donna Haraway, Avtar Brah and many others started this debate, it was mostly welcomed as liberating and breaking new theoretical grounds. Stuart Hall's famous 1987 speech on migrant identities is often quoted in this context. Hall talked about the way in which his identity changed over time in different contexts – he would never have considered himself black while living in the Caribbean as a child and a young man, whereas this identity was forced onto him when he came to Britain as a student. Later, he adopted it or identified with it as a political identity, whereas he lately identifies himself as a post-colonial or diaspora migrant. And he adds:

> Thinking about my own sense of identity, I realise that it has always depended on the fact of being a migrant, on the difference from the rest of you.. Now that, in the postmodern age, you all feel so dispersed, I become centred. What I've thought of as dispersed and fragmented comes [...] to be the representation of postmodern experience! Welcome to migranthood! (Hall, 1987, p. 63).

By evoking the notion of difference, Hall not only problematises the use of this term as detached from power relations, but he also mimics the desire of post-modernists to create equality through evoking multiple differences: all different, all equal, all equally different. Ann Phoenix (1998) has taken this argument further by asking ironically: Are we all marginal now? She answers: „[...] our identities can all be said to be marginal now, in at least some ways, but we are not equally marginalized. Recognition of the complexity of positioning is crucial if Otherness is not to be re-inscribed in work which seeks to disrupt Othering." (idem., p. 30).

To me this is a very important statement, and I would like to elaborate on the passionate debate about difference as a scientific concept. Within feminism it has been immensely helpful to recognise differences between women in order to understand social positionings, representations and articulations. I want to argue that as analytical tool difference can be a very useful concept. However, as Phoenix reminds us, by conceptualising identities as fragmented and marginalised, we must not forget that people are not equally victimised, and that old racist and sexist notions of difference and otherness are still invoked and in operation. In short, power relations have not vanished by the pure act of rhetorical ignorance. Phoenix sees the task of critical feminist researchers in the recognition of everyday articulations of difference and power relations, while reconstructing gendered, racialised and ethnicised identities.

I would suggest that this concept has to be elaborated to incorporate lines or axes of difference. These 'lines of difference' always co-exist and intersect with each other. Starting from Patricia Hill-Collins'(1990) 'interlocking systems' this idea is based on what Valerie Smith (1998) and Kimberlé Crenshaw (1994) have later called intersectionality. As Crenshaw says, only a fool can live on an intersection – but, in fact, all of us do so. Intersectionality is a concept for understanding the context of social positionings as well as identities emerging from it, in which in addition to gender, class or race, other lines of difference are in operation. No matter whether they are visible or invisible, these are the lines along which social inequality, exclusion, marginalisation and discrimination are articulated.

14 lines of difference

Categories	Basic Dualisms
Gender	male – female, masculine – feminine
Sexuality	Heterosexual – homosexual
„Race"/Skin-colour	white – black
Ethnicity	dominant groups – ethnic minorities
	non-ethnic – ethnic
Nation/State	members – non-members
Class	high – low
Culture	„civilised" – „uncivilised"
Ability	able-bodied – handicapped
Age	adults – children, old – young
Sedentariness/Origin	sedentary – nomadic,
	settled/established – immigrated
Wealth	wealthy – poor
North – South	the West – the Rest
Religion	religious – secular
Stage of social	modern – traditional
Development	(progressive – backward
	developed – undeveloped)

See Lutz & Wenning, 2001, p. 20.

The problem with these binaries is that they are by no means complete; others have to be added or re-defined. Also, by presenting them as binaries they are at the same time constructed as such, and it becomes a challenge to consider the spaces in between. Yet, if it is agreed that complex realities call for the differentiation of analytical tools, then this list could be a starting point. In addition, considering these lines of difference in such a way that they can illuminate social positions means to analyse how they work as 'patterns of normalisation' – how they privilege one side over another by and through disadvantaging, discriminating and harming others.

It is also important to stress that to work with these lines of difference does not mean that one has to consider all of them at the same time. Rather, it is desirable to ask what Mari Matsuda (1991) has called the 'other question': In many cases the category which is most crucial in a particular situation seems obvious, but what if we look at race or ethnicity while gender is the focus, or at class when nation is the main category of analysis? This 'other question' may help us to detect layers of underlying meaning.

5. Conclusion: The Long Shadows of the Past

I finally want to demonstrate the relevance of this theoretical exercise by coming back to the two incidents I described at the beginning of my article. In an effort to understand the murder of Alberto Adriano we have to take into account that more than one line of difference helps to explain the event: Race is the most obvious one, and was used by the murderers to legitimise their deed. They saw it as an act of purification and of safeguarding their people and its territory. Their symbolic territory, in this case the park, had to be defended against a *male* intruder. They presented themselves as an endangered species, the potential victims of invasion. Here, the gender aspect becomes crucial, as Adriano would have been treated differently had he been a woman (Similar cases show that physical violence is used first and foremost against men while women are more likely to be sexually harassed). Of equal relevance to race and gender seems to be the North-South-divide, a mentality of 'Europism' or 'welfare chauvinism' (see Leiprecht, 1991; Habermas, 1992) according to which non-West Europeans are 'Schmarotzer', or people living off others, who except for legally recruited workers have no right to enter the territory of the EU. A closer analysis of the police interviews and trial transcripts (which I cannot elaborate further in this article) also illuminates how the youngsters were influenced by society with regard to their attitude towards immigrants from another continent, where East Germans were not allowed to travel under the Socialist regime. This deprivation might have created feelings of hatred. Avtar Brah (1993) suggests that racialised differentiation is not only the result of a bi-polar matrix of negativity versus positivity, superiority versus inferiority, exclusion versus inclusion, but that it is also about a deep ambivalence between envy and desire, admiration and repulsion. The desire for the racialised 'other' is as much codified in Orientalism as it is in erotic Exoticism. Asking the 'other question' in this context may shift the attention to the categories of class, age or religion. It is likely that a more in-depth analysis would result in the uncovering of even more overlap and entanglement between categories.

The second incident can be analysed along similar lines. The question who belongs to Europe and whether the New Europe will take the form of a (federal) nation state or will develop as an economic – but not a political – unit, is subject of many current debates. Notwithstanding all disagreements, a common border control policy has been implemented since the beginning of the 1990s. In order to compensate for the abolition of borders within the European Union, the external borders are more strictly guarded. Thousands of additional officers were hired, and millions of Euros invested in improved equipment like infrared cameras and x-ray scanners.[5] One could remind the European leaders that the x-

---

5   According to the Times, June 25th 2000, Britain is going to invest 1.5 Mill. £ in Dover alone on this equipment.

ray scanners had originally been used at the East German border to detect refugees hidden away in car trunks who fled the socialist countries of Eastern Europe. In those times, smugglers were not considered criminals by Western Europeans, but providers of freedom. This is also true for the smugglers who helped Jews to leave Nazi Germany. Although I do not want to deny the fact that smuggling is a criminal business, it has to be said that many refugees would not have reached a safe country without their help. Like their predecessors during the Cold War and the Nazi period, these smugglers are making a lot of money with this activity, but it is important to note the changes in their portrayal in different historical contexts.

The new European politics of exclusion are responsible for this new attitude: welfare chauvinism legitimises the measures to keep undesired migrants out. A Dutch NGO (UNITED) counted 3026 people who lost their lives between 1993 and June 2002 when trying to enter the EU illegally. They either died crossing the Mediterranean or the land borders. The new policies, which also include stricter rules concerning asylum, are legitimated by the idea that Europe is flooded by immigrants if it does not take counter-measures. What does not surface in this rhetoric is the fact that without the cheap labour of undocumented workers in the service sector the European economy would completely collapse (see Lutz, 2002 a, b; Bade, 2000; Rat für Migration, 2001). A Dutch newspaper (de Volkskrant, 21 September 2000) reported that as a result of the stricter enforcement of British border controls after the Dover death tragedy in June 2000, thousands of Chinese trespassers stranded in Rotterdam. In other words, if one European country 'solves' illegal immigration by closing its borders, another one has to deal with the immigrants.

Categories like nationality, level of development, and the North-South divide are obviously important factors for the analysis of racist events. Posing the 'other question' in this case might bring us to class and gender issues, too. It may lead us to the legacy of colonial ties between Britain and China, and new, post-modern and globalised ways of exploitation and exchange.

It was my aim to show in this article how racism, nationalism, ethnicism and gender are entangled, interwoven and contradictory at the same time. Any attempt to understand the current situation requires a look back into history.

In the view of the feminist philosopher Rosi Braidotti (1999, p. 53) European, in contrast to American Feminism, has to be praised for its broad view on issues of multicultural and gender identity, because „... given the legacy of colonialism, it is much easier for Europeans to address social questions related to far-away places, than to stare at the problems of our own backyard." In this article I have tried to point to what is missing in this view. The long shadows of the past consist of colonialism *and* fascism, including a history of perpetration, victimisation *and* resistance. I agree with Braidotti that we need situated perspectives on the politics of location. This requires an effort to reappraise our pasts and uncover layer after layer of cover-memories, taking into account the 14 lines of difference.

By way of inference I propose that 'staring at our own backyard' is not such a bad thing, if we muster the courage to face the ghosts in the garden and to finally address them and learn from them.

References

Anthias, F. & Yuval-Davis, N. (1992). *Racialized Boundaries: Race, Nation, Gender, Colour and Class and the Anti-Racist Struggle.* London: Routledge.

Anthias, F. & Lazaridis, G. (eds.) (2000). *Gender and Migration in Southern Europe: Women on the Move.* Oxford & New York: Berg.

Ausländerbeauftragte, Die (ed.) (2000): *Bericht der Beauftragten der Bundesregierung für Ausländerfragen über die Lage der Ausländer in der Bundesrepublik Deutschland.* Bonn & Berlin.

Bade, K. (2000). *Europa in Bewegung.* München: Beck.

Balibar, E. (1990). *The Nation Form – History and Ideology.* Review, Vol. XIII (3), pp. 329-361.

Braidotti, R. (1999). *Gender, Identity, Multiculturalism and the Question of the European Union.* In Lutz, H., Amos, K. & Rodriguez, E.G. (eds.), *Ethnicity, Difference and Gender Relations.* Frankfurt a.M.: Zentrum für Frauenstudien und die Erforschung der Geschlechterverhältnisse, Uni Frankfurt, pp. 51-56.

Brah, A. (1993). *Re-framing Europe: En-gendered Racisms, Ethnicities and Nationalisms in Contemporary Western Europe.* Feminist Review, 45 (Autumn), pp. 9-28.

Brah, A. (1996). *Cartographies of Diaspora: Contesting Identities.* London & New York: Routledge.

Bundeskriminalamt (Hg.) (2001). *Jahreslagebericht 2000: Daten zu rechtsextremistischen, fremdenfeindlichen und antisemitischen Straf- und Gewalttaten.* Wiesbaden.

Calloni, M. & Lutz, H. (2000). *Gender, Migration and Social Inequalities: The Dilemmas of European Citizenship.* In Duncan, S. & Pfau-Effinger, B. (eds.), *Gender, Economy and Culture in the European Union.* London & New York: Routledge, pp. 143-170.

Crenshaw, K. (1994). *Mapping the Margins: Intersectionality, Identity Politics, and Violence Against Women of Color.* In Fineman, M. & Mykitiuk. R. (eds.), *The Public Nature of Private Violence.* New York: Routledge, pp. 93-118.

Essed, P. (1990). *Everyday Racism: Reports from Women of Two Cultures.* Alameda, CA: Hunter House.

Essed, P. (1995). *Gender, Migration and Cross-Ethnic Coalition building.* In Lutz et al. (eds.), *Crossfires: Nationalism, Racism and Gender in Europe.* London: Pluto Press, pp. 48-64.

Freud, S. (1960). *Über Deckerinnerungen.* Gesammelte Werke, vol. 1. Frankfurt a.M.: Fischer, p. 465. (Original work published 1899).

Gümen, S. (1996). *Die sozialpolitische Konstruktion 'kultureller' Differenzen in der bundesdeutschen Frauen- und Migrationsforschung.* beiträge zur feministischen theorie und praxis, 42, pp. 77-89.

Habermas, J. (1992). *Faktizität und Geltung.* Frankfurt a.M.: Suhrkamp.

Habermas, J. (1994). *Die Last der doppelten Vergangenheit.* Die Zeit, 13 May, no. 54.

Hall, S. (1987). *Minimal Selves.* In Hall, S., *The Real Me – Postmodernism and the Question of Identity.* London: ICA Paper.

Heitmeyer, W. et al. (1992). *Die Bielefelder Rechtsextremismus-Studie: Erste Langzeituntersuchung zur politischen Sozialisation männlicher Jugendlicher.* Weinheim & München: Juventa.

Hill-Collins, P. (1990). *Black Feminist Thought: Knowledge, Consciousness and the Politics of Empowerment.* Boston: Unwin Hyman.

Holzkamp, C. & Rommelspacher, B. (1991). *Frauen und Rechtsextremismus.* Päd.Extra/ Demokratische Erziehung, 1, pp. 33-39.

Horn-Metzger, T. & Riegel, C. (1995). *Geschlecht und politische Orientierungen: Zur Notwendigkeit einer geschlechtsspezifischen Herangehensweise.* In Held, Josef et al. (eds.), *Gespaltene Jugend.* Düsseldorf: Hans-Böckler-Stiftung, pp. 207-236.

Inowlocki, L. & Lutz, H. (2000). *Hard Labour: The Biographical Work of a Turkish Migrant Woman in Germany.* The European Journal of Women's Studies, 7(3), pp. 301-320.

Kalpaka, A. & Räthzel, N. (1986). *Wirkungsweisen von Rassismus und Ethnozentrismus.* In Kalpaka & Räthzel (eds.), *Die Schwierigkeit, nicht rassistisch zu sein.* Berlin: Express Edition, pp. 32-91.

Koonz, C. (1986). *Mothers in the Fatherland.* New York: St. Martin's Press.

Knowles, C. (2000). *Home and Away: Maps of Territorial and Personal Expansion 1860-97.* The European Journal of Women's Studies, 7(3), pp. 263-280.

Koser, K. & Lutz, H (1998). *The New Migration in Europe: Contexts, Constructions and Realities.* In Koser & Lutz (eds.), *The New Migration in Europe: Social Constructions and Social Realities.* London: MacMillan, pp. 1-17 .

Leiprecht, R. (1991). *Rassismus und Ethnozentrismus bei Jugendlichen.* DISS-Texte, 19, Duisburg: Duisburger Institut für Sprach- und Sozialforschung.

Leiprecht, R. (2001). *Alltagsrassismus: Diskurse, Repräsentationen und subjektive Umgangsweisen. Eine Untersuchung bei Jugendlichen in Deutschland und den Niederlanden. Münster,* New York, München & Berlin: Waxmann.

Leiprecht, R. et al. (1997). *Racism in the New Germany: Examining the Causes, Looking for Answers.* In Hazekamp, Jan L. & Poppel, K. (eds.), *Racism in Europe: A challenge for youth policy and youth work.* London: ICL Press, pp. 91-122.

Lutz, H. (1991). *Welten Verbinden: Türkische Sozialarbeiterinnen in den Niederlanden und Deutschland.* Frankfurt a.M.: IKO.

Lutz, H. (1997). *The limits of European-ness: Immigrant Women in Fortress Europe.* Feminist Review, 57, pp. 93-111.

Lutz, H. (2001). *Differenz als Rechenaufgabe: über die Relevanz der Kategorien Race, Class und Gender.* In Lutz, H. & Wenning, N. (eds.), *Unterschiedlich Verschieden: Differenz in der Erziehungswissenschaft.* Opladen: Leske + Budrich, pp. 215-230.

Lutz, H. (2002a). *In fremden Diensten: Die neue Dienstmädchenfrage als Herausforderung für die Migrations- und Genderforschung.* In Gottschall, K. & Pfau-Effinger, B. (eds.), *Zukunft der Arbeit und Geschlecht.* Opladen: Leske + Budrich (in press).

Lutz, H. (2002b). *At your service, Madam! The Globalisation of Domestic Service.* feminist review (in press).

Lutz, H. & Huth-Hildebrandt, C. (1998). *Geschlecht im Migrationsdiskurs.* Das Argument, 224(40), pp. 159-173.

Lutz, H., Phoenix, A. & Yuval-Davis, N. (1995). *Nationalism, Racism and Gender – European Crossfires.* In Lutz, Phoenix &Yuval-Davis (eds*.), Crossfires: Nationalism, Racism and Gender in Europe.* London: Pluto Press, pp. 1-25.

Lutz, H. & Wenning, N. (2001). *Differenzen über Differenz – Einführung in die Debatten.* In Lutz & Wenning (eds.), *Unterschiedlich Verschieden: Differenz in der Erziehungswissenschaft.* Opladen: Leske + Budrich, pp. 11-24.

Matsuda, M. (1991). *Beside my Sister, facing the Enemy: Legal Theory out of Coalition.* Stanford Law Review, 43, July, p. 1189.

Pattynama, P. (2000). *Assimilation and Masquerade: Self-Constructions of Indo-Dutch Women.* The European Journal of Women's Studies, 7(3), pp. 281-300.

Phoenix, A. (1998). *Reconstructing gendered and ethnicised identities: Are we all marginal now? Inaugural speech for the chair Feminisme, Humanisme en Emancipatievraagstukken.* Utrecht: Universiteit van de Humanistiek.

Rat für Migration (ed.) (2001). *Integration und Illegalität in Deutschland.* Osnabrück: IMIS.

Räthzel, N. (1995). *Nationalism and Gender in Western Europe: The German Case.* In Lutz et al. (eds.), *Crossfires: Nationalism, Racism and Gender in Europe.* London: Pluto, pp. 161-185.

Rommelspacher, B. (1995). *Schuldlos-Schuldig? Wie sich junge Frauen mit Antisemitismus auseinandersetzen.* Hamburg: Konkret-Literatur.

Rommelspacher, B. (1999). *Ethnizität und Geschlecht: Die feministische Debatte in Deutschland.* In Lutz, H., Amos, K. & Rodriguez, E.G. (eds.), *Ethnicity, Difference and Gender Relations.* Frankfurt a.M.: Zentrum für Frauenstudien und die Erforschung der Geschlechterverhältnisse, Universität Frankfurt, pp. 19-32.

Rosenthal, G. (ed.) (1998). *The Holocaust in Three Generations.* London & Washington: Cassell.

Smith, V. (1998). *Not just Race, not just Gender: Black Feminist Readings.* London: Routledge.

Thürmer-Rohr, C. (1989). *Vagabundinnen: Feministische Essays.* Berlin: Orlanda.

Wekker, G. (1995). *'After the last sky, where do the birds fly?' What can European Women learn from the Anti-Racist Struggles in the United States?* In Lutz et al. (eds.), *Crossfires: Nationalism, Racism and Gender in Europe.* London: Pluto, pp. 65-87.

Yuval-Davis, N. (1997). *Gender and Nation.* London: SAGE.

Ann Phoenix

A Monocultural Nation in a Multi-Cultural Society?

British Continuities and Discontinuities in the Racialised and Gendered Nation

1. Introduction

Following the attacks on the World Trade Centre and the Pentagon in the USA on September 11th, 2001 and the subsequent 'War on Terrorism' by the USA and its allies (including Britain), issues of nationalism and racism have again received attention around the world. In both Britain and the USA, those constructed as 'Arab' and/or Muslim have increasingly been subjected to attack. However, apparently 'new' forms of exclusion from the nation and racism are often longstanding because the past leaves us with legacies that continue to operate (see, for example, Lutz et al., 1995). An understanding of nationalisms, racisms, and ethnicisms therefore requires a complementary understanding of the ways in which they are socially and historically produced (Lutz, 2002). It is partly because there are continuities that 'post-colonial' periods cannot be viewed as disconnected from colonialism. As Michel Foucault suggested, we need to examine 'the history of the present' and the conditions of possibility that allow particular ways of viewing the world (discourses) to become normalised as 'regimes of truth'.

This chapter examines continuities as well as discontinuities in the intersection of nationalisms and racisms in the British context. It particularly addresses the ways in which assumptions of who is to be included and who excluded from the nation have both remained the same, and changed since the middle of the twentieth century, when Britain was bowing to nationalist pressures in its 'colonies' and beginning to decolonise. In the British case, 300 years of slavery and status as the world's largest modern coloniser provide the backdrop to twentieth and twenty-first century racisms and nationalisms. They also partly account for British reluctance to cede sovereign power to the European Union and to give up the pound in favour of the Euro (although this is perhaps inevitable). The chapter focuses on changes since the Second World War since, for Britain, the post-war period was a busy one in the (re-)construction of the British nation. For example, 1948 brought together:

- the introduction of the Welfare State
- the independence of India and the partition of India and Pakistan,
- the creation of Israel, and
- the arrival of the Empire Windrush, the troopship which brought migrants from the Caribbeans to Britain, which is often seen as *the* symbolic moment for the start of 'mass' Caribbean migration to Britain.

The chapter argues that the racialised and gendered construct of 'the family' is at the heart of inclusions and exclusions in the British nation. Thus, while there have been important changes in the positioning of black, and other minoritised, people in Britain since the Second World War, inclusions and exclusions from the nation continue to be gendered as well as racialised and ethnicised.

2. The Racialised Intersection of Family and Nation

One of the contradictions inherent in the treatment of 'the family' is that it is often seen as a matter of private taste and responsibility. Yet, it is a prime site for social policy intervention precisely because it is now, and has long been, constructed as the building block for the nation and integral to the nation's aims. Consider the following quotes from Margaret Thatcher, when she was British Prime Minister, and from the then Labour Home Secretary, Jack Straw.

> The family and its maintenance really is the most important thing not only in your personal life but in the life of any community, because this is the unit on which the whole nation is built (Margaret Thatcher interviewed by Julie Cockcroft, Daily Mail, 4 May 1989, quoted in Griffin, 1993).

> I don't agree with all Freud had to say but I do agree that 'bonding together' in family groups is both instinctive and necessary to human welfare and therefore essential to the health of a society.

> In our Manifesto we committed ourselves to strengthening family life. We promised to uphold family life as the most secure means of bringing up our children. Families are the core of our society. They should teach right from wrong. They should be the first defence against anti-social behaviour. The breakdown of family life damages the fabric of our society. (Home Secretary Jack Straw's speech at the launch of The Lords and Commons Family and Child Protection Group's Report 'Family Matters' Thursday, 23 July 1998).

That the family is the building block which is constructed as central to the nation is evident in political pronouncements from the 1940s and more recently. I want to argue that the importance of the family to the nation has always been racialised – as well as gendered (Lutz, Phoenix & Yuval-Davis, 1995; Yuval-Davis, 1997). Bhikhu Parekh (1995) demonstrates how nationalism draws on metaphors of the family.

Paul Gilbert (1999, pp. 136, 147) argues that:

> It is a clich (sic) that much nationalism draws, to a greater or lesser extent, on metaphors of the family (see Parekh 1995, pp. 33-35), which is seen as exemplifying the relationships of members of the nation in miniature [...]. The New Right espouses, I suggest, this romantic conception of the nation. It is an ethnic conception, in the sense that it makes membership of the nation, in normal circumstances, an ascriptive characteristic deriving from pre-political facts as to one's identity. In so far as these facts are taken to be biological facts of genetic relatedness like those that hold between members of the family, or rather between members of a supposedly natural family, then this ethnic conception can be described as a racist one. This, as we shall see, is a slight over-simplification, but the tendency to racism is inherent in the ethnic conception of the nation. For the attempt to demarcate a single people on the basis of a 'single national character', regarded as explicable naturalistically, is almost bound to lead to racial exclusiveness.// [...]. I suggest, the nationalism of New Labour shows that it has not sufficiently broken free from the assumptions of the New Right to embrace the consequences of a socialist communitarianism.

It is, of course, not the case that the ways in which 'race', gender, family and nation intersect are straightforward. Instead, (following Foucauldian theory) they set up a multiplicity of power relations and, hence, of resistances to these constructions. However, as Gilbert (1999) argues, the racialised and ethnicised conception of the nation legitimises a minimal welfare state. It is not surprising then that politicians so frequently invoke the family as the cornerstone of the nation.

The racialising of the nation is evident if we consider Eleanor Rathbone's pronouncements on this issue in the middle of the twentieth century. She was a remarkable woman, who is admirable in many ways. As Johanna Alberti (1996, p.1) has pointed out, she was a suffragist in the reign of Queen Victoria and became a(n Independent) Member of Parliament [1929-1945] at the first election in which all women could vote in Britain. She is the one feminist who was active in the Victorian women's movement and then in the parliamentary political arena within which that movement had sought to give women a place and power. Her campaigning was central to the establishment of family allowances. In the posthumous 1949 republication of her 1924 book (*The Disinherited Family*, republished as *Family Allowances*), Beveridge wrote an epilogue in which he attributed the preparation of the 1945 Family Allowances Act first and foremost to Eleanor Rathbone.

Eleanor Rathbone argued that the 'most fundamental necessity of the State' was 'its own reproduction' and that 'childrearing' was the 'most essential of all the services' to the state (1917, p. 116, quoted in Alberti, 1996, p. 38). Rathbone was patriotic and her patriotism was reinforced by her experience of living through two World Wars. She was also entirely against Nazi thinking and argued that the family allowance should be paid to 'aliens' (Alberti, 1996). However, she took for granted that the British were superior to other peoples as did most of her white middle class contemporaries who took it for granted that they had both the right and the responsibility to intervene in the affairs of those in the 'colonies'. Therefore, it is not surprising that she felt certain that she had a right to intervene in Indian gender relations in the 1920s and 1930s, arguing that Indian men should not expect freedom from white men until Indian women had achieved equality with Indian men. Rathbone was also preoccupied by what she termed 'wretched little brides' and 'child brides'. She appeared unable to understand why Indian women in the All India Women's Conference and the Women's Indian Association (both of which had been opposed to child marriage since their inception) were opposed to her imperialist manner of intervention. Yet, she had never, at that time, been to India, or ever asked if Indian women were campaigning against child brides, which they were (Alberti, 1996).

Rathbone has also been much criticised for her casual use of the term 'Turk complex' (1924, p. 343) to refer to men's assumption that they were superior as a result of being paid a 'family wage'. As was common in the 1920s and 1930s among the British middle and upper classes, Eleanor Rathbone engaged in some eugenic thinking. (So, for example, did William Beveridge, the 'architect' of the British welfare state, and Marie Stopes, the campaigner for contraception and a founder member of the eugenics society in Britain):

> I often think the day will come when the people of this country [...] will ask themselves whether a country with Imperial responsibilities such as ours can afford to look on and do nothing about the steady shrinkage of the white populations compared with the yellow, the brown and the black (Hansard, 25 March 1935, p. 299, col. 1649, quoted in Alberti, 1996, p. 139).

The reason for pointing out this aspect of Eleanor Rathbone's thinking is not to suggest that she was particularly reprehensible. Instead, it indicates how taken-for-granted was the racialising of family and nation at the beginning of the century. As a result, the intersection of the family and the nation provided a site for boundary maintenance between the British and those constructed as 'Others'. As Catherine Hall (1998, p. 15) points out „[...] nations are formed through processes of racial and ethnic inclusion and exclusion." Rathbone lived in the post-slavery, imperial period in which the empire began to clamour for freedom. Her views reflect those of her period, as is indicated by a consideration of how media and government reports of the introduction of the British welfare state demonstrate that many people assumed that it would help to unify the nation through supporting families around that time.

> The scheme as a whole will embrace, not certain occupations and income groups, but the entire population. Concrete expression is thus given to *the solidarity and unity of the nation,* which in war have been its bulwarks against aggression and in peace will be its guarantees of success in the fight against individual want and mischance. (Cmd 6550, 1944, para 8 – my emphasis) The first duty of Government is to protect the country from external aggression. The next aim of national policy must be to secure the general prosperity and happiness of the citizens ... to plan for the prevention of individual poverty resulting from those hazards of personal fortune over which individuals have little or no control (White Paper Social Insurance (Cmd 6550), 1944).

Today the British people join together in a *single national friendly society for mutual support during the common misfortunes of life* [...]. The main outlines of a social service State approaching maturity are now plainly discernible in a logical array: the assumption by the State of a positive duty to prevent avoidable idleness, ignorance, squalor, ill-health and want (The Times, first leader, 5 July 1948) (my emphasis).

Government policy has long aimed for a nation unified against outsiders so that the citizens are prepared to be loyal to the country in time of war. Quotes such as those above make clear that the introduction of the welfare state in 1948 was part of a pact between the government and people designed to forestall civil unrest following two World Wars. (See the trilogy by Pat Barker (1991, 1994, 1995) for illumination in a novel, of how ordinary citizens were disaffected after the First World War).

Fiona Williams (1989, xiii) was one of the first academics to point out that the „themes of *Family* (Work) and *Nation* have been central organising principles in the development of the welfare state." It is, therefore, not surprising that, as Gordon Hughes (1998, p. 29) argues, the British Welfare State was predicated on the notion of a racialised and gendered citizen: the white, married male worker with women having a specific supporting role.

Beveridge's welfare policies were firmly grounded in terms that related them to the advancement of national efficiency and racial supremacy: Housewives as mothers have vital work to do in ensuring the adequate continuance of the British race and British ideals in the world' (Beveridge, 1942, para. 117)[...]. The Liberals, whose programme of reforms [...] was the framework upon which Beveridge built his National Insurance system, integrated imperialism into welfare reforms in a particular form of social imperialism which stressed the necessity for social reforms, including provisions for mothers and children, to assist in breeding the Imperial Race in Britain to defend and maintain the Empire (Williams, 1989, pp. 125f).

What we may term the 'Beveridgean citizen' was thus effectively constructed as the fully employed, married, male worker who, through his taxes, supported the state, and the state in turn supported him through the provision of social welfare. Although this figure of the citizen emerges out of a quite specific politics of class compromise (between organised labour and capital), it is a profoundly gendered and ethnicised one. It is important to note that the British Nationality Act 1948 did confirm the rights of commonwealth and colonial citizens to enter and settle in the UK (although these rights were consistently and increasingly undermined in subsequent decades). However, radical social policy analysts such as Norman Ginsburg (1992) have also noted that racism was institutionalised in several ways in the administration of social welfare during this period (Hughes, 1998, p. 29).

The point then, is that 'race', nation, and family are interlinked. The Welfare State came into being in the same year when India won independence from Britain and partition of India and Pakistan occurred. It is perhaps ironic that it normalised white families where men are dominant.

The racialisation of the nation has been an important theme in the work of many academics. Paul Gilroy's (1987) evocatively titled book „There ain't no black in the Union Jack" demonstrated the ways in which nations are imagined through 'race' (a point also made by Barker, 1981). Gilroy argues that the politics of 'race' are inextricably linked with conceptions of belonging, so that there is a blurring of the distinction between 'race' and nation with Britain represented in both biological and cultural terms. Many academics have also pointed out how 'race' is inscribed in British Nationality Acts. As a result, it has long been easier for white people from Australia and the African continent with distant British ancestry to enter Britain than for black and Asian people who grew up as members of British colonies with no independent nationality. In addition, there is a contradiction between nationality as formal status and who is assumed to belong to the nation since black, Asian and Arab people with British passports are frequently treated as if they do not belong to the British nation. As a result, Britain is generally constructed as a 'multi-racial society', but not as a 'multi-racial nation' (e.g. Brah, 1996).

Black families and those from other ethnic minorities have long been socially constructed as 'other', rather than as normal. For African American families in the USA and African Caribbean families in Britain, relatively high rates of lone motherhood have been seen as problematic and resulting from cultural differences. The Swann report into the 'educational underachievement' of black children largely blamed this on single motherhood (Department of Education and Science, 1985). Lone motherhood and its concomitant 'father absence' have long been blamed for the 'criminality' of young men, particularly those who are black and/or working class (see the critique by Griffin, 1993).

3. Disrupting the Link Between 'Race' and Nation?

In the current New Labour government, it seems at first sight that there has been a major disruption of the link between 'race' and nation, particularly since the government's emphasis on social inclusion (rather than exclusion) seems to be lived out in a number of ways. Firstly, with the increase in rates of lone motherhood in the 1980s and 1990s, government and media linkages of single motherhood and African Caribbean families dropped into disuse. Secondly, there is now a number of black and Asian peers as well as nine black and Asian MPs – all Labour. Thirdly, the attention paid to Mark Leonard's (1997) argument that we need to 'renew' British identity in the light of socio-economic changes also seemed to mark a change in the racialisation of the nation. Leonard coined the term 'Cool Britannia' (which was picked up and used for a time by Tony Blair, other members of the British Labour government and the media). He argued that there was a pressing need to renew British identity and the stagnant image of Britain held in many other countries. Just as British identity was (re)constructed by the Victorians on the basis of its strengths at the time, so Britain needs to re-work British identity self-consciously. According to Leonard, the current strengths around which a new British identity can be forged include multicultur-alism and the major contributions made to the economy and culture by 'minori-ties'.

Finally, there have been some marked turning points in the racialisation of the British population since the New Labour government came to power. The 50th anniversary of the arrival in Britain, in 1948, of the troopship 'Empire Windrush' carrying Caribbean people is generally seen as an iconic moment in the history of significant numbers of African Caribbean people coming to live in Britain. The 1998 anniversary inspired both celebrations of, and reflections on, the meanings and experiences of Caribbean migration to Britain. (These cele-brations were initiated by the BBC). The very attention given to the Windrush in the British media underlined a crucial change in British society over the last 50 years: from the assumption of mono-ethnicity to being undeniably and inextrica-bly multiracial and multi-ethnic. More people began to give recognition to the fact that the Caribbean migration marked in the Windrush celebrations occurred in a context where black people and Asian people have been in Britain for cen-turies (Fryer, 1984; Visram, 1988). This appeared to constitute a turning point for the acceptance of black people as part of the British nation. That this was followed by programmes examining British slavery and the white and black de-scendants of slaves and slave-owners served to emphasise the inextricable link-ing of whiteness and blackness in the making of the British nation.

There have clearly been changes in conceptions of black people over the last 50 years. Those who were constructed as 'dark strangers' in the 1960s (and even in the 1970s) are now represented throughout British society and make crucial contributions both economically and culturally. It is the beneficial nature of these contributions that was a major impetus for the coining of the term 'Cool Britannia'. Mark Leonard argued that it was a more useful way to characterise British national identity than was the construction of Britain as old and tradi-tional. It makes central the recognition of British multi-ethnicity and that its mi-nority ethnic groups make important contributions to Britain's economy and culture.

Similarly, the establishment by Jack Straw in 1993 of the inquiry into the death of Stephen Lawrence and police failure to investigate it properly (which was reported in March 1999) also marked a turning point. For it appeared to dis-rupt a racialisation of black people as less valuable than white people are and as having no purchase on access to justice for themselves. Moreover, it focused on the niceness, normality and perseverance of a black family – the Lawrences, whose dogged determination and the support they fostered, kept Stephen Law-rence's murder on the agenda. As Home Secretary, Jack Straw clearly stated that 'race' was the most important part of his job (interview with Simon Hattenstone,

Guardian, 21 February 2000) and he was justifiably proud of having set up the Lawrence Inquiry. The post-Lawrence Inquiry Race Relations (amendment) Act represents an important change in race equality legislation. It does not include the outlawing of religious discrimination but does make organisations responsible for 'racial' equality within their organisations.

There are other examples which indicate that Britain may be addressing the implications of its multi-ethnicity and attempting to disconnect its history and nation from racism. For example, the establishment of the Holocaust gallery at the Imperial War Museum in 2000 brings Britain into line with what has been done in the US and puts modern Jewish history into mainstream British history. Similarly, in the light of the recent British football hooliganism in Belgium during the 2000 European cup, Jack Straw, the Home Secretary, has recognised that it is not just the odd person who engaged in football violence. Instead, he pointed out that it was white young men, performing a version of English nationalism, who engaged in it. As a result, he linked English racism with 'the baggage of empire' and argued that we must disconnect racism from national pride.

4. Contradictions to Inclusion /(Re) Production of Exclusions

Yet, while the 50th anniversary of the Windrush was appropriately cause for celebration and recognition of the dynamism of British society and peoples, it also allows an engagement with the contradictions in this optimistic and romantic story. For the children, grandchildren (and great-grandchildren) of the Windrush generation have not been engaged in straightforward progress from exclusion and being the objects of racism to inclusion, multiculturalism and celebration. Instead, their experiences are, and have been, driven with contradictions of what Phil Cohen (1988) has termed multicultures and multiracisms. It is, for example, clear that – far from normalising black families – the Stephen Lawrence case was one in which the Lawrences were repeatedly constructed as exceptional. The fact that Stephen was taking A' levels examinations and wanted to be an architect has been used to construct him as different from, and presumably, more deserving than other black young men. Duwayne Brooks – Stephen's companion on the night he was murdered – came from a different family background and received much less favourable treatment and no media sympathy for his Post Traumatic Stress. There has equally been media treatment of the Francisco and Menson families who campaigned for (and eventually obtained) justice for murdered black family members as exceptional and notably praiseworthy rather than as ordinary citizens. There continue to be racist attacks and racist murders throughout Britain.

A year on from the publication of the McPherson report, *The Guardian* produced a 16 page special supplement on 'Race' (Monday 21 February 2000). Most of those who wrote in the edition agreed that the McPherson inquiry was an important event in thinking about 'race' in Britain and that we are now in a position where it is unthinkable that Britain could ever be anything but multicultural. Yet, most also agreed that racism was still a major issue in British society. They were, however, divided as to whether or not the McPherson report was likely to lead to real change in British society. It is perhaps illuminating that the piece by Ian Katz, who commissioned the pieces for the 'Race' supplement, is entitled *'Tale of two nations'*. That being British continues to be racialised is well demonstrated by the current outcry against asylum seekers, particularly gypsies from Romania who beg. It is significant that the greatest outcry has been against female gypsies who take their children with them when they beg. The intersection of asylum seeking outsiders who are not behaving in ways constructed as conducive to 'good mothering' outraged the media so much that this form of begging was stamped out within weeks.

In March 2000, the then British Home Secretary Jack Straw was reported on the BBC *Today* radio programme (24 March 2000) as suggesting that British society had much to learn from Asian family values – such as respect for older generations. The rationale for this was argued to be because of the importance of the family and because Asian families are much more successful at staying together. This seems like a straightforward, and welcome, inclusion by a Secretary of State of Asian families as valuable to the nation. It apparently marks a difference from „ideological constructions of Asian marriage and family norms [...] as a problem for British society" (Brah, 1996, p. 74). However, this apparent inclusion is not so straightforwardly positive. The *Today* programme discussion counterposed Kumeera Khan and Tariq Modood as 'Asian intellectuals' who took contrary positions. Kumeera Khan explained that this was a patronising view which treated all 'Asian' families the same, when the term 'Asian' is itself a social construction. Constructions of 'Asian families' are constantly changing, and, like all other families, Asian families are varied. Tariq Modood contested this view on the grounds that Asian families do have something to offer to British society in general.

The important point here is that holding a group up for scrutiny, as an example, is not necessarily positive. Much has now been written on how admiration of black people's supposed sporting prowess can itself be oppressive. In a similar way, assumptions of the unitary, positive Asian family ignore intergenerational dynamism (e.g. Beishon et al., 1998) and those examples where women are subjected to the sort of violence documented, for instance, by Southall Black Sisters. Straw's admiration is, arguably, little different from the contrasting of black family forms with Asian families which was taken for granted in the Swann report as the explanation for the poor educational performance of African Caribbean students. This reminds us of the recursiveness of particular racialisations and ethnicisations of 'the family'; emphasising Lutz' (2002) argument that we need to understand the history of racialisation, ethnicisation and nationalism, Foucault's archaeological approach is of central importance. It also indicates that particular family forms can be used to support political claims without challenging the contradictions that serve to buttress racist notions and gendered inequalities in families from all ethnic groups.

In this context, it is not surprising that families are major sites of contestation so that Pragna Patel (1997, p. 262) argues that „the family has always been an important battleground for resistance [...]. Our demand is for the right of black and minority families to live undivided when they choose, but for women to have a real option of leaving an unhappy marriage without the state and community colluding to deny that choice."

In this context, it is noteworthy that there are marked contradictions between the Labour government's acknowledgement of racism and the necessity of eradicating it and their apparent hostility to asylum seekers while allowing white Zimbabweans freely to come to Britain. Far from being new, this contradiction is a well-established one – as is demonstrated by the following quote from *The Guardian* newspaper. Equally importantly, there are sometimes contradictions between people's own personal histories and their current practices as Guttenplan (2000) argues is the case for Jack Straw, whose grandmother was a German Jew who sought refuge in Britain, but who as British Home Secretary introduced restrictive policies for asylum seekers.

> This country has kept out asylum seekers for a century. DD Guttenplan on our exclusive past
>
> Compare the 500,000-6000,000 files on families and individuals seeking refuge in the archives of Britain's main Jewish organisations with the 80,000 refugees actually admitted.
>
> Even the Kinder-transports had their grim aspect. Of the 7,842 children given refuge here by the end of August 1939, (Louise) London writes (in Whitehall & the Jews 1933-48): Admission saved the children's lives. Exclusion sealed the fate of their parents.
>
> Last month's disclosure that MI6 knew about Nazi plans to 'liquidate' 8,000 Roman Jews, yet did nothing to warn them, made headlines. And the evidence, from documents declassified in the US, that decoded radio intercepts dealing with the deportations were circulated to Winston Churchill may well force a revision of the widely held view that, unlike some of his ministers, Churchill did what he could to help the Jews. But there were already many instances in the documentary record when Whitehall's reluctance to admit refugees is expressed in language whose brutal frankness crosses over from callous indifference to outright anti-Semitism.
>
> It is impossible to read London's book without a mounting sense of déjà vu. Take out the word Jews and put in its place Romanies or Ethiopians or Kosovars or Bosnians and you have the essence of New Labour's asylum policy.
>
> It is more likely that the government means to screen asylum seekers in their place of origin, with the same hostile intent that forced Austrian and Czech Jews to apply for visas.

> Why else would the Tories – though they object to Straw's (the Labour Home Secretary) willingness to work through European institutions – be so supportive? That his own grandmother, a German Jewish refugee, might have been kept out by such a policy is no more of a restraining influence on the present Home Secretary [Jack Straw] than it would have been on his (Conservative) predecessor, himself the son of a Jewish refugee (The Guardian, Saturday 22 July 2000, pp. 1-2).

What has become clear from the many leaked government memos that have been published in British newspapers is that the current Labour government is desperate to court popular support. As a result, the British Prime Minister, Tony Blair is anxious to follow Conservative policies' 'public opinion'. Both of these he sees as warranting exclusionary hostility to asylum seekers as well as to the euro.

> On asylum, we need to be highlighting removals and decisions plus if the April figures show a reduction, then a downward trend. Also if the benefits bill really starts to fall, that should be highlighted. Plus some of the genuine asylum claims should be given some publicity (from leaked memo published in all British newspapers on Monday 17 July 2000).

It is tempting to think that Tony Blair's anxieties are misplaced. However, it is the case that there has been much media and apparently, popular support for the Conservative opposition's harsh stance on asylum seekers. The following quote makes clear that the media can be extremely hostile to government statements on racism. I discussed earlier, as an instance of attempts to disrupt the racialisation of the nation. However, his pronouncement was not universally welcomed. The *Daily Mail*, quoted below, is a national paper that would be expected to agree with exclusionary constructions of the British nation:

Daily Mail Comment:

> Mr Straw's insult to our patriotism
>
> According to the Home Secretary, England has failed to develop a modern sense of identity because it is lumbered with the 'baggage of the Empire' and 'jingoism'. This failure, runs the bizarre theory, is the root cause not only of mindless football hooliganism, but of racism too. How very New Labour [...].
>
> And strangely, for one so keen to spot racism, Mr Straw cannot see that his sweeping remarks can themselves be described as racist [...] to link hooliganism with racism and then to allege, at least by implication, that Englishmen are peculiarly prone to such behaviour and feelings is both insulting and absurd. Countries with no significant, or recent imperialist past have football hooligans too [...] (The Daily Mail, Monday 17 July 2000).

The fact that Jack Straw had particularly been talking about young, white *men* was not commented on in the editorial.

It is, of course, not only governments which engage in contradictory thinking about inclusions and exclusions from the nation. Increasingly, politicians and the media are beginning to argue that 'developed' countries need labour from 'majority countries' if they are to maintain their economies. The French interior minister, Jean-Pierre Chevenement produced a document for a meeting of EU ministers in Marseille which was quoted in *The Guardian* (28 July 2000). It made the point that with declining fertility rates, the EU will need between 50 million and 75 million immigrants by 2050 and that this will leave the 'percentage of the population of non-European origin' unchanged. Germany, which has already called for the immigration of 20,000 Intermediate Technology specialists from India and Ireland, is considering inviting 200,000 skilled workers over the next seven years. The *Times* newspaper editorial of 17 July 2000 made a somewhat similar point about inviting unskilled fruit pickers into Britain.

> Millions of pounds worth of strawberries and cherries are rotting in the fields, as a buoyant labour market leaves farmers short of the fruit-pickers they need for their harvests [...].

> The seeds of a solution should be plain. As the farmers realise, if it is impractical to recruit within these shores, employers must turn elsewhere. Yet Britain's immigration policy [...] makes this all but impossible. The vast majority of those who seek to work here are resourceful, determined and industrious people who wish for nothing more than an honest living – and who can help the country to overcome its demographic dilemma. History shows that even skilled professionals happily take menial jobs, as a foothold in a liberal economy. They are at present kept out by an absurd asylum system, or forced into illegal entry and work. This situation is of no benefit to Britain. Clear channels for economic migration would better allow all concerned to enjoy the fruits of their labours (The Times, 17 July 2000).

This is, however, an issue which is far from being new. In Britain in the 1950s, for example, the British government encouraged migration from the Caribbean in order to fill jobs in transport and nursing that the white British population did not want to do in the post-war economic boom. It was also a period when more working class women than before were staying at home after marriage and were therefore not available for employment.

In summary, then, the racialisation of families and the nation have changed somewhat over the last 50 years. However, the contradictions inherent in current government pronouncements and policies mean that the white middle classes continue to be at the heart of national constructions of families. There are, thus, both continuities and discontinuities in historical treatment of the racialisation (and gendering) of the nation. It is this that leads Valery Small (1999, p. 1) to ask when she discusses black families: „The Government has outlined proposals to support the family. But which family?" This confusion how to draw boundaries around the family and the nation and who can/should be included within it has, arguably, worsened since September 11th 2001. For both Britain and the USA have had to recognise that one feature of globalisation (so often praised by multinational corporations) is that 'terrorism' is planned within, as well as outside, their national boundaries.

5. The Consequences of Racialisation and Ethnicisation of the Nation for Everyday Practices

If we consider the level of everyday practices, rather than political discourses, the racialisation of the nation is also apparent. Various surveys report that, while there is a substantial minority of white people who say that they would object to living next to black or Asian people. When asked, a decreasing percentage of the white population said that they would mind (47%) if a close relative married a black or Asian person. Yet, there are also vicious attacks on men whose partners are of a different colour (e.g. Guardian, 24 March 2000).

From research publications, it is striking that racialisation constitutes an important feature of everyday practices. For example, members of black and Asian families as well as those from white families tend to see themselves as different from each other and from the white majority, even in instances where there are overlaps between them (Beishon et al., 1998). In addition, for black and Asian families, as well as some white people who associate with black and other minority ethnic people, racism has an impact on how they live their family lives and engage in parenting. This is particularly the case when families are subject to racist victimisation because they are in 'mixed' relationships or from minority ethnic groups. Chahal and Julienne (1999) report a research project on 74 people from four locations in the United Kingdom who were given either focus group or 42 individual interviews with people who had experienced racist victimisation. Several reported that their children had suffered racist harassment or attack. In these cases, children were not allowed (and were reported not to want) freedom to move about their neighbourhoods by themselves:

> My children did not want to go out any more and they hated so much the area that they asked me all the time to move out from there. They could hardly sleep at night and I had to take them to school and bring them back in my car. They wouldn't go for themselves (p. 34).

> My child used to play downstairs with all the kids and she stopped of her own volition because they called her names. Things she couldn't understand being only five but in general frightening her and calling her names (p. 28).

> The children are not allowed to play outside. They have been chased and are afraid to go out. I have to wait for them at the bus stop when they come back from school [...] (p. 25).

It is not only black and other minority ethnic children who might be subjected to harassment as a result of racism. For example:

> The little boy my daughter plays with has been headbutted by their [perpetrators] older son and called a 'paki lover'. He is three-and-a-half years old. He starts crying when he sees them. Other kids used to come and play with us and they were getting victimised as well so their parents had to stop them coming. The parents told us that themselves (pp. 26-27).

Contrary to earlier beliefs, contact between young people in schools does not necessarily produce anti-racist discourses. Instead, it frequently sustains contradiction in racialised practices. This was repeatedly evident in a study of Social Identities carried out by Barbara Tizard and myself. Almost all the young people interviewed espoused a strongly egalitarian discourse, in which they argued that everybody was equal and should be treated equally, regardless of 'race', gender and social class. However, many also recognised that there was informal segregation in their schools, as is evident in the quote below from a group interview with ethnically mixed 16- and 17-year-old young women attending an all girls' school.

Q. Can I ask now about friendships ... and whether you have a wide range of friends?

A1. It doesn't matter what colour, race or religion your friends are. I mean you should be friends with them for that they are, not what they look like or (inaudible).

Q. So what colour are your friends in school?

A1. Everything. Someone's colour doesn't matter to me...

A2. Everyone has said that everyone has got black friends, they've got Turkish friends, they've got all sorts of friends, but when it comes down to it – when you are sitting in assembly, when you're sitting in a big room, there's always the people that stick together. There's the black people. There's the white people.

A3. Especially in school.

A4. That is true.

All speak simultaneously – loud and heated but not clear.

A. Like even in that room outside, there's like all one group sitting on one side and all the others sitting on the other side. I mean they'll talk to each other and they're friends. I'm not saying they don't talk to each other and ignore each other, but it's just there.

Q. Do you feel more comfortable with black or with white people?

A. It makes no difference. But when there is a group of black people I do feel, they seem to, they like, I do feel pressurised. I feel very uncomfortable because they seem to resent – not you being white, but I just think if they're in a group then they must feel pressurised, or I think to myself why do they all go round in a group? And sometimes I feel slightly threatened because they must be angry that they feel an outcast. I mean surely they must think of themselves and go – you know – go in a group with all black people and I resent that. And if you walk past you think, oh you know – I don't know – you just – you get vibes from them and you do feel threatened slightly. (Young white woman)

Informal segregation is not, of course, the only story to be told about racialisation in schools. A feature of 'multicultures' in Britain and the US is the marked increase there has been in the number of people of 'mixed-parentage' and in 'mixed' relationships and friendships – some of which are forged at school (Phoenix & Owen, 1996). However, informal segregation serves to highlight the differentiation of young people's racialised experiences. It also confirms that mixed schooling is no more guarantee to produce familiarity and understanding between different ethnicities than it has produced between genders.

Even less optimistically perhaps, years of mixed schooling can produce racist discourses designed to exclude all except white people from the British nation. For example, Roger Hewitt (1996) studied young white working class Londoners living on a disadvantaged housing estate renowned for its reproduction of racist discourses and racist attacks. The young white people he talked to asserted their disadvantage in ways that made clear the inextricable linking of 'race' and class position in the construction of their identities. They justified their anti-black discourses by blaming black people for white people's poverty as in the following account from a fifteen-year-old young woman, which was unusual because it was a discourse produced almost exclusively by young men in Hewitt's study:

> I don't like blacks full stop, right. We brought 'em over 'ere for slaves but now they're getting all the money and taking it all off out, our money, and then we can't pay for our water, tax or anyfing, (sic) so I think they should go back to their own country (Hewitt, 1996, p.16).

Discourses such as this require serious attention if we are to understand how it might be possible to shift racist discourses for young white people racialised in Britain. The contexts in which such discourses flourish are ones in which white working class young people find themselves disadvantaged educationally and with regard to employment, housing and other socio-economic resources. In these situations, it has commonly been found that young white working class people express resentment of black and Asian people. Phil Cohen (1997), for example, argues that the young white working class people he studied associated the deterioration of their circumstances and neighbourhoods with the black people who had increasingly come to live in the same neighbourhoods.

Therefore, it is perhaps not surprising that, in the US, where it is extremely easy to organise adoptions of babies if one has enough money, different values are ascribed to white, Asian and black babies. We know that intercountry adoptions in northern countries are most preferred from countries where children are most white and that intercountry adoptions from African countries are rarely sought (Tizard, 1990).

6. Back to the Future: Visions of Inclusion

Few people would now agree with the then Conservative politician, Enoch Powell's dramatic pronouncement in 1968 that black and Asian immigration to Britain would lead to streets running with 'rivers of blood'. While some people still view the fact that black people are now inseparably British with distaste, others, however, view this more positively:

> Over time, our rituals will catch up with the reality of our society. Hegel once said that 'the owl of history only flies at dusk', and the fact that there is so much talk of changing our costumes shows that dusk is near. Maybe the new millennium will be a chance for Britain to find a new vocation: as a modern multi-cultural creative nation that is at ease with its past and its future (Mark Leonard, The Guardian Saturday Review, Saturday 21 November 1998, p. 2).

Looking further into the future, some writers have more radical visions. Patricia Williams, who gave the 1997 Reith lectures on BBC Radio 4, for example, argues:

> I do think that to a very great extent we dream our worlds into being. For better or worse, our customs and laws, our culture and society are sustained by the myths we embrace, the stories we recirculate to explain what we behold. I believe that racism's hardy persistence and immense adaptability are sustained by a habit of human imagination, deflective rhetoric and hidden license. I believe no less that an optimistic course might be charted, if only we could imagine it. What a world it would be if we could all wake up and see all of ourselves reflected in the world, not merely in a territorial sense, but with a kind of non-exclusive entitlement that grants not so much possession as investment. A peculiarly anachronistic notion of investment, I suppose, at once both ancient and futuristic. An investment that envisions each of us in each other (Williams, 1997, p. 16).

In that spirit, Paul Gilroy has looked forward in time and come up with what seems like a more utopian view in relation to 'race': post-raciality or the end of imagining the world, society and each other in terms of 'race'. Paul Gilroy (1997, 1998, 2000) suggests that, in an era of molecular biology, it is time to imagine 'race' differently from how it was imagined in the modern era when it was an idea which 'knits together science and superstition' and which is now anachronistic. He suggests: „The skin may no longer be privileged as the threshold of identity. There are good reasons to suppose that the line between inside and out now falls elsewhere." (Gilroy, 1997, p. 196).

It is clearly important to try to find new ways to think about 'race' and it is conceivable that in the distant future 'race' itself will no longer be central to people's life experiences and understandings. Avtar Brah's (1996) notion of 'diaspora space' is potentially helpful here. As a concept, 'diaspora space' foregrounds both ethnicised and gendered identities. According to Brah, it constitutes the space in which all our genealogies are entangled, those with known histories of migration and those without. It articulates difference and is the site where diaspora, border and the politics of location intersect. It is, therefore, in 'diaspora space' that the contradictions of multicultures and multiracisms are played out and binarised categories of racialised and ethnicised belonging and outsider status are reproduced *and* disrupted (Brah, 1999).

7. Conclusions

There have been important changes in the positioning of black, and other minoritised, people in Britain over the last 50 years. However, it is clear that multi-cultures and multiracisms continue to be in contradiction. These contradictions as an inherent part of 'diaspora space' are part of politicians', the media's and the general population's social geographies, social histories and everyday practices. Constructions of those to be included and excluded from the nation are gendered as well as racialised and ethnicised.

Those like Patricia Williams, Paul Gilroy and Mark Leonard who have written of their future visions of 'race' and blackness are beginning to put the disappearance of 'race' on the agenda. By this, they do not mean the suppression of talking about it, but new ways of imagining and thinking about it. In a way, this is a new version of the Martin Luther King vision where racialisation and ethnicisation do not differentiate life chances and, therefore, are not the focus of national exclusion and inclusion: a vision of 'all of us'.

References:

Alberti, J. (1996). *Eleanor Rathbone*. London: Sage.

Barker, M. (1981). *The New Racism*. London: Junction books.

Barker, P. (1991). *Regeneration*. New York: Plume.

Barker, P. (1994). *Eye in the door*. New York: Dutton.

Barker, P. (1995). *The Ghost Road*. London: Viking.

Beishon, S., Modood, T. & Virdee, S. (1998). *Ethnic minority families*. London: Policy Studies Institute.

Brah, A.(1996). *Cartographies of Diaspora*. London: Routledge.

Brah, A.(1999). The Scent of Memory: Strangers, Our Own and Others. *Feminist Review*, 61, pp. 4-26.

Chahal, K. & Julienne, L. (1999). *„We can't all be white!" Racist victimisation in the UK*. Published for the Joseph Rowntree Foundation. York: York Publishing Services.

Cohen, P. (1988). Perversions of Inheritance: Studies in the making of multi-racist Britain. In Cohen, P. & Bains, H. (eds.), *Multi-Racist Britain*. London: Macmillan.

Cohen, P.(1997). *Rethinking the Youth Question: Education, labour and cultural studies*. London: Macmillan.

Department of Education and Science (ed.) (1985). *Education for All*. London: HMSO (The Swann Report).

Fryer, P. (1984). *Staying Power. The history of black people in Britain*. London: Pluto Press.

Gilbert, P. (1999). Family values and the nation-state. In Jagger, G. & Wright, C. (eds.), *Changing Family Values*. London: Routledge, pp. 136-149.

Gilroy, P. (1987). *There ain't no black in the Union Jack: The cultural politics of race and nation*. London: Hutchinson.

Gilroy, P. (1997). Scales and eyes: 'Race' making difference. In Golding, S. (ed.), *The Eight Technologies of Otherness*. London: Routledge, pp. 190-196.

Gilroy, P. (1998). Race ends here. *Ethnic and Racial Studies*, 21(5), pp. 838-847.

Gilroy, P. (2000). *Between Camps: Nations, Cultures and The Allure of Race*. London: Allen Lane.

Griffin, C. (1993). *Representations of Youth*. Cambridge: Polity Press.

Guttenplan, D. (2000). This country has kept out asylum seekers for a century. *The Guardian Newspaper*, Saturday July 22, 2000, pp. 1-2.

Hall, C. (1998). A family for nation and empire. In Lewis, G. (ed.), *Forming Nation, Framing Welfare*. London: Routledge, pp. 9-47.

Hewitt, R. (1996). *Routes of Racism*. London: Centre for Multicultural Education, Institute of Education.

Hughes, G. (1998). „Picking over the remains": The Welfare State settlements of the post-second World War UK. In Hughes, G. & Lewis, G. (eds.), *Unsettling Welfare: The Reconstruction of Social Policy*. London: Routledge, pp. 3-37.

Leonard, M. (1997). Britain™: *Renewing our identity*. London: Demos and Design Council.

Leonard, M. (1998). The Guardian Saturday Review, Saturday 21 November.

Lutz, H., Phoenix, A. & Yuval-Davis, N. (eds.) (1995). *Crossfires: Nationalism, Racism and Gender in Europe*. London: Pluto Press.

Lutz, H. (2002). The long shadows of the past: The new Europe at the Crossroad. In Lenz, I. et al. (eds.), *Gender and migration: Crossing borders and shifting boundaries*, vol. 2.

Parekh, B. (1995). Ethnocentricity of the nationalist discourse. *Nations and Nationalism*, 1, pp. 25-52.

Patel, P. (1997). Third wave feminism and black women's activism. In Mirza, H. (ed.), *Black British Feminism: A reader*. London: Routledge, pp. 255-277.

Phoenix, A. & Owen, C. (1996). From miscegenation to hybridity: Mixed parentage and mixed relationships in context. In Brannen, J. & Bernstein, B. (eds.), *Children, Research and Policy*. London: Taylor and Francis, pp. 111-135.

Rathbone, E. (1924/1986). *The Disinherited Family*. Bristol: Falling Wall Press 1924/1986.

Small, V. (1999). Mythmaking: Black families and parenting. *The Parenting Forum Newsletter*, 16, pp. 1-2.

Southall Black Sisters (1990). *Against The Grain: A celebration of survival and struggle*. Southall: Southall Black Sisters.

Tizard, B. (1990). Intercountry adoption: A review of the evidence. *Journalof Child Psychology and Psychiatry*, 32, pp. 743-56.

Visram, R. (1988). *Ayahs, Lascars, Princes: The story of Indians in Britain 1700-1947*. London: Pluto Press.

Williams, F. (1989). *Social Policy. A Critical Introduction, Issues of Race, Gender and Class*. Cambridge: Polity Press.

Williams, P. (1997). *Seeing a Colour-Blind Future: The paradox of race*. New York: The Noonday Press.

Yuval-Davis, N. (1997). *Gender and Nation*. London: Sage.

Part II:
Space, Cultures and Identities in Process

Claudia Schöning-Kalender

Gender, Dress and Nation – The Modernization Discourse in Turkey

The centrality of gender relations and sexuality in the cultural construction of ethnic or national identity has been pointed out at several instances during the *ifu* semester. There is indeed a worldwide discussion on this topic and a very rich literature. [1] Focussing on the modernization discourse in Turkey, already beginning in Ottoman times in the early 19th century, I want to look at the emphasis that is given to dress in this context. My argument is threefold: The ongoing discursive concentration on women's veil inside of Turkey neglects the fact that the change of men's wear had an important political impact on the cultural construction of a collective identity. Outside of Turkey this approach perpetuates the orientalistic gaze. And in the wider framework of a postcolonial approach the impact and the distinct character of the relationship between modernization and anti colonialism in the case of Turkey has to be historically developed.

In a comparative analysis of the political situation in Iran 1978 and in Germany in 1989 Valentine M. Moghadam states that „. . . women and gender issues figure prominently in political discourse, state ideologies, legal politics, and the construction of a national identity. [. . .] Cultural representations of women and legislation on family law, reproductive rights, and women's rights reflect the importance of gender in politics and ideology and signal the political agenda of revolutionaries and regimes. Whether political discourses support women's emancipation and equality, or whether they glorify tradition, morality, the family, and difference, the point remains that political ideologies and practices are gendered" (Moghadam, 1995, p. 354).

The Turkish sociologist Nilüfer Göle states that due to a very specific mode of modernization in almost all Islamic countries the women's question held a very prominent position in the modernization discourse (Göle, 1995). In fact, plenty of evidence exists in Algeria, in Egypt, in Afghanistan, in Iran, in Turkey. Still, it doesn't seem right to reduce the topic to an Islamic context. Referring to

---

1   See Malathi de Alwis in this volume.

the positioning of women in the prevalent Hindu context of Indian nationalism Rama Melkote coins the label „icons of modernity"[2]. And Nira Yuval-Davis also gives it a wider framework while referring to macho-trends in many anti-colonialist and black power movements: „The 'emancipation of women' has come to signify much wider political and social attitudes towards social change and modernity in a variety of revolutionary and decolonization projects, whether in Turkey, India, Yemen or China. It has been one of the important mechanisms in which ethnic and national projects signified – inwardly and outwardly – their move towards modernization. However, these changes did not lack ambivalence, as they have had to signify at the same time modernization and national independence. The process of mimicry was limited at best" (Yuval-Davis, 1997, p. 60).

The Turkish Case

The process of modernization as mirrored in the discourse on women's emancipation in Turkey is very outspoken and well documented. Starting in the Ottoman Empire, it is as old as the modernization discourse itself and it is still going on. In comparison with non-Islamic countries this discourse gains its uniqueness from the fact that it is the women's veil that has always been and still is at stake, it has become a manifestation of this discourse. Although clothing of women and men as well, has been a distinct signifier of revolutionary change in other countries (for example in India[3]), the Turkish case with an explicit orientation towards 'Europe' and the 'West' in the context of her Islamic history and culture is a very special example of the ambivalence Yuval-Davis is talking about. Turkey holds a special place in the Islamic world: it inherited the history of the Ottoman Empire, although a decisive step in the process of nationbuilding was the destruction of this empire, and it was the first and still is the only state in the Islamic world with a strict secularist regime.

At the EXPO 2000 in Hanover, Germany, Turkey presented herself with a pavilion that was supposed to mark Turkey's role as a bridge between Europe and Asia. This symbolic representation was certainly not one of the nation-state on first sight but rather that of an interface and a blending of cultures that have at different times in history existed in Anatolia.[4] Symbolically and explicitly, in

---

2   Rama Melkote was invited as lecturer to the project area „body" at ifu and held an evening lecture on „Nation, State – historical construction, contemporary meanings – implications for gender" (24. 07. 2000).

3   See especially the research of Emma Tarlo on dress and identity in India (Tarlo, 1996).

4   In a project group on „Gendered representations of the nation state at the EXPO 2000" a group of ifu participants analysed certain national pavilions at the EXPO-site.

the architecture and in verbal description, it is represented as the bridge between Western and Eastern civilizations, the region and landscape of Anatolia with all its historical richness. This richness is symbolized in the figure of King Anthiokhos I. of Kommagene born more than 2000 years ago in Eastern Anatolia at a moment when four planets met in the sign of the lion, which made him a god by birth. The historical landscape of Nemrud Dağ with the monuments of this kingdom in the Taurus mountains and close to the Euphrat river, which is a tourist attraction nowadays, was shown in a breathtaking computer simulation.

Towards the exit of the pavilion the female counterpart was positioned, a huge white woman figure rising out of the water, spreading her arms and her gown with wide long sleeves, almost resembling wings, falling down in soft waves. This piece of art by a Turkish artist was named „The Mediterranian Sea".

With these two figures, King Anthiokhos and „The Mediterranian Sea", a complex of binaries, like east and west, the mountains and the sea, culture and nature, male and female, was presented to the spectator in order to underline the wealth and depth of Turkey's culture and civilisation.

In another, much less spectacular corner of the pavilion, there was a computer terminal where one could sit, read and learn about different features of the modern Turkish Republic. [5] One of the texts was titled „Ideology, Fashion and the Winds of Change. " Following an introduction concerning modernization from the middle of the 19th century on, the implementation of the parliamentary system and the achievements of the Turkish revolution after World War I, the text goes on: „One of the proudest achievements of the Republic was the establishment of Women's Rights in the new social order. The Turkish woman has been exalted symbolically throughout history as the mother figure and the pillar of family. Since Atatürk's reforms, women's role in social, political and economic life has expanded dramatically. Since the early days of the Republic, well-educated women, particularly in the cities, have taken on active roles in the professions, government and business. "[6]

The argument of women's promotion in society, especially in the field of education, had been brought into discussion in the Ottoman Empire following the opening towards the West (the so-called Westernization – batılılaşma – and the Tanzimat period towards the middle of the 19th century), especially among the urban elites. Part of this westernization process of the Ottoman Empire was the participation in the world exhibitions from 1867 onwards. Girl's schools and the education of girls were touted, primarily by men with western education and experience, as a path for female advancement. The German political scientist

---

5   These texts are especially designed for the EXPO 2000 and as in all national pavilions are meant for a positive self representation of the nation, of course one would not expect any critical comment on political sites of everyday life in today's Turkey.

6   Unfortunately there was no reference concerning the author or the source of these texts. They should be accessible in the archives of the Turkish embassy.

Renate Kreile in her book on „Political Power, Gender Politics and Women's Power in the Near East" argues that the politicization of gender relations in this region was an act of colonial violence and the result of colonial desire (Kreile, 1997). Since she is referring to a region from Morocco in the West to Iran in the East this argument does not really go into the detail of the different regions and certainly not into the core of Ottoman power. Towards the end of the 19th and beginning of the 20th century the Ottoman Empire was still an imperial power, even if it was weakened and under growing economic pressure by the other imperial powers. Accordingly Deniz Kandiyoti, rather than focussing on footprints of colonialism, argues that the growing politicization of the gender discourse was a manifestation of the long overdue modernization of Ottoman patriarchy, i. e. the fight for more independence and privacy of the bourgeois family and it's 'pater familias' (Kandiyoti, 1991).

One significant facet of Ottoman society was the strict segregation of the sexes. This was true for the nobility and the Muslim urban upper classes as well as the well-to-do minority families (Christians, Jews). In this segregation women's dress had always played a crucial role as a textile borderline, mobile but not to be transgressed. Thus, women's dress from the very beginning of the modernization discourse was more or less the main topic on the agenda.

In fact, women's dress had been a topic of the sultans' orders (fermanlar) for centuries[7], but with the end of the 19th century it entered the political arena. And dress – that is, primarily the veil – had always been an object of curiosity for foreign travellers, one of the most famous being Lady Mary Wortley Montagu who accompanied her husband on his diplomatic mission to Istanbul in the years 1717/18. In her letters to a friend back home in England she described the indoor and outdoor clothes of the noble Ottoman women in all detail. [8] In the politicization of women's dress there might after all be some kind of rejection of the western orientalistic gaze that was represented in these letters as in many other comments on women's appearance by western travellers throughout the 18th and 19th century. [9]

One of the many layers of the modernization discourse on women's dress certainly was western fashion: Introduced by Queen Eugenie of France on her visit to Istanbul following the world exhibition in 1867, the dressmakers of the palace had a hard time learning the new cuts and finding the material. The high time for professional dressmakers among the minorities in the capital began, because they had better insight into „European stile". In the notebooks of a tailor

---

7   See Çakır, 1994, pp. 175-176.
8   The letters of Lady Mary, originally published in 1863, are today widely criticised as orientalistic, as "the Lady's Turkish Masquerades", see Kreiser, 1997, and Yegenoglu, 1995.
9   See Melman, 1992.

who was working for the palace, we find the proof for a radical change in material and design of women's dress between the years 1854-56 and 1873/74. [10]

Presumably as a reaction to the growing westernization of the elite women's outfit, the modernization discourse on women's dress gained more ideological features towards the end of the 19th century: A new black gown was imported from the Syria province, the so-called çarşaf, covering up and hiding all female shapes completely. We could call it an anti-elitist and anti-consumerist movement of the growing urban middle classes, very religious and anti-western. Although he was also known to be very religious, the sultan Abdulhamid forbade anyone to wear this cloth in the vicinity of the palace because he was afraid that someone could hide under it and get into the palace without being noticed. At the same time, fashion also influenced the fate of the çarşaf. It was out of the çarşaf that the so-called tango-çarşaf was created, a costume-like dress with a pelerine and a thin veil either drawn over the face or thrown back.

With the beginning of the second constitutional monarchy in 1908 and the rise of the national movement „unity and progress" (ittihad ve terakki) more facets were added to the dress discourse. The women's movement also grew rapidly, women became more visible through their (somewhat less restricted) presence in public spaces. The development of national dress became a topic[11], certainly influenced by the discussions on international meetings of the women's movements and the prevalent discussion on plain and natural women's dress in the United States and in Europe.[12] Although the abolishment of the veil and the visibility of women in public were hotly discussed, especially in the newly emerging women's magazines and magazines of the women's movement[13] this does not at all mean that women from then on went around bare headed. This was as much a question of religious belief and tradition as it was one of belonging to a certain social class, thus one of adequate and up to date dress.

Atatürk's Women

With the onset of the War of Independence and the final establishment of the Turkish Republic in 1923, Mustafa Kemal Atatürk, the leader and founder of the one-party regime, immediately took over his self ascribed task of a cultural

---

10 See Tezcan, 1988.

11 Women's national dress was the first topic on the programme of the first women's movement in the Ottoman empire, see Çakır, 1994, p. 178.

12 See Newton, 1974.

13 In a first attempt to get an insight into the scene of women's magazines in the Ottoman Empire in a publication project of the women's library in Istanbul lists 39 magazines in the period between 1869 and 1927, see Kadın Eserleri Kütüphanesi, 1993.

secularization of the new nation state. His aim was to achieve this secularization in one generation. The dress reforms were one important part of this project. This may be best exemplified with the example of „Atatürk's women".

Who were these women? Atatürk married once, and he stayed married for three years. He did not have own children, but adopted seven daughters, who lived with him during his marriage and after. He had also adopted sons, but they never lived in his house.

Atatürk's wife, Latife, became a symbol of the emancipated Turkish woman. Quoting Lord Kinross, the well known biographer of Atatürk: „Asked once why he had married, in the teeth of his often quoted Turkish proverb, 'to be a bachelor is to be a sultan', he had answered in terms of this very reform. How could he persuade the people to unveil their wives if he himself had no wife to unveil? He had married indeed as much for sociological as for personal reasons" (Kinross, 1964, p. 421) Actually Latife, the well-educated daughter of an influential Smyrnian family, was not a women to be unveiled. She was very self confident and dressed at the height of fashion for the upper-classes of that time. Again Lord Kinross: „This was no peasant women, but a lady of evident breeding, unveiled and wearing, with her Turkish headdress, sober but elegant clothes" (Kinross, 1964, p 327). By marrying her Atatürk married into the upper class of which he himself was not a member.

Atatürk formed his daughters, however, literally as prototypes of republican women; in their appearance one could read an „iconography of power" (Kandiyoti, 1991). Two of them became very famous, Afet Inan as the first female professor of history in Turkey. She lived with Atatürk up to his death in 1938. She was the woman at his side after his divorce from Latife. Sabiha Gökçen was the first female pilot of Turkey and the first female military pilot in the world. These women are almost never photographed with their heads covered and the dresses they are wearing are, one can tell, made by Ataturk's tailor. The costume which Afet Inan was wearing for her first speach at an international conference of historians was especially designed by Atatürk himself and it very much resembled his own outfit with the tie and a long tailor jacket. [14]

Although these women in their modern dress were the real icons of the Turkish republican modernity and although Atatürk travelled throughout the country with the neverending story of the emancipation of women and the abolishment of the veil on his lips, he definitely never officially forbade the veil. This is very often wrongly reported. He always stuck to propaganda, commented on women's outfit and headdress wherever he travelled in the country suggesting modesty and modernity as the adequate guidelines. In fact, when the young

---

14 One has to be careful not to overinterpret this outfit. If we look at western European fashion of those days we find that to a certain extent crossdressing was very much en vogue.

actor Bedia Muvahhit appeared on the stage without any headdress he suggested that she should wear a light fashionable scarf in order to acquaint the people in the provinces with the new look step by step (Akçura, 1993, p. 36). Atatürk was the leading force in this modernization discourse, but definitely more in an educative than in an executive role.

The picture becomes much different when we take into account that Atatürk had not only cast an eye towards women's dress but also to men's dress as well, especially on the headdress. On a propaganda tour in 1925 he publicly wore a hat and from then on he promoted the hat as the only decent headwear for a modern man. Furthermore, with a law of November 1925 men were literally forced to wear a hat. In her memoirs the author Halide Edib-Adıvar, a combatant of Atatürk during the War of Independence and, for a while, his close companion, draws a very critical picture of the meaning and effects of the so-called Hat Law. „The continuation of reforms in Turkey under the dictatorial regime from 1925 to 1929, and especially their nature, are more interesting than the terrorist methods by which they were supposed to be made possible. This process of reform has been going on for nearly a century, but within the last twenty years it has moved with tremendous rapidity." (Edib-Adıvar, 1930, p. 223) She is also very critical on the western press and it's view on Turkey "usually the outcome of the most superficial and hurried observation after a pleasant Mediterannean trip, is that Turkey was changed overnight from an eastern to a western country. This is worse than superficial, this is false. "(ibid.) In the nature of the leading reforms she sees the continuation of earlier tendencies to westernization in a tradition of change, and not departures from the fundamental line of progress that the Turks have taken. „The first and most spectacular of these reforms was the 'Hat law' passed in 1925. It was also the most futile and superficial in comparison to the others which followed. But it was the only one which accomplished an external change overnight. In a week it made the Turks don European hats (the only part of the city dwellers' outfit which had not been westernized) and made them look like westerners, although the manner in which it was accomplished was utterly un-western. The westernization of Turks is not and should not be a question of mere external imitation and gesture. It is a much deeper and more significant process. To tell the Turk to don a certain headdress and get 'civilized' or be hanged or imprisoned, is absurd, to say the least. The opposition of individuals among the men in the street, really much more westernized than those who carried the measure through, had a note of wounded self-respect rather than of objection to wearing hats. Among all the recent measures, this was the most seriously opposed in the country itself. Any opposition to the 'Hat Law' was labeled reactionary. The interesting fact connected with the substitution of the hat for the Turkish fez is that it attracted the greatest attention in the western world. Other more fundamental changes taking place in Turkey were either entirely unnoticed, or criticized, or neglected as unimportant items of foreign news in the western papers. But the moment the Turks put hats on their heads, the general cry in the West was, 'At last the Turks are civilized; they wear hats. ' Hence those who enacted the 'Hat Law' *might* say: We have killed a few and imprisoned a large number, but it was good psychology, has anything in the past brought the Turks so much into the limelight? Has anything brought them nearer to the European mind?' The chief result of the 'Hat Law' was that it enriched European hat factories at the expense of the already impoverished Turks. Broadly, one can say that it could not have been passed without a regime of terror. The Islamic reactionaries, the liberals, the people who understood the spirit of the West, were all opposed to it for different reasons. What would have happened was this: The very small number of Turks who wore hats in the summer in Constantinople would have increased gradually and in a generation hat wearers would have been in a majority in the cities. But the Turkish peasant would have stuck to his old headdress. " (Edib-Adıvar, 1930, pp. 225f.) There were upheavals throughout the country and some opponents (mostly out of religious reasons) were even sentenced to death or put in prison.

With this reform Atatürk documented his absolute dictatorial and patriarchal power towards the men and at the same time left it to them (the men and family fathers) to decide over the dress of their wives and daughters. This was not only a discoursive but in fact a very violent turn in the modernization of patriarchy in Turkey (Kandiyoti, 1991).

On first sight it seems that the Hat Law had no background in the modernization discourse, it was only prepared in a very short and intense campaign by Atatürk on a trip through the most conservative (in terms of religion) regions of Turkey. However, looking through Turkish literature we find quite a few instances of very overt change in men's clothing, especially in the vicinity of the palace and as far as the military is concerned, which precipitated later changes in the urban population. These changes in men's clothes, actually beginning at the same time as the discourse on modernization and its connection to women's clothing have obviously not made their way into public discourse.

This could have two reasons, both closely connected to the ambivalence of modernization in a postcolonial context as Yuval-Davis pointed out. In the transnational reception of modernization in this context, it is again the women and their public appearance that are recognized as signifiers of the self and the other. And in the superficial uplifting of women's position in 'modern' society beyond the wife, the mother and the housekeeper, this position obviously has to be kept up discursively, otherwise it breaks down in mere ideology.

The text in the computer corner of the Turkish pavilion at the EXPO continues, promoting the vitality of today's young generation, a „can do generation of entrepreneurs". „The possibilities of breaking all ties with both the past and the landscape, on which the future depends, has never been so real as it is today. For example, the ongoing process of agricultural industrialization is taking away the apricots, cherries and the rest of the Anatolian natives, along with the happy chickens, sheep and the cows, all marching in a parade which will eventually transform them into tasteless uniformity and miserable existence. Our hopes lie with the wise Turkish woman, who knows better and listens to her palate, searching out vegetables without hormones at the local market. Will she be able to pass this wisdom on to her ambitious daughter who prefers wearing Levi's?"

References

Akçura, G. (1993). *Bedia Muvahhit. Bir Cumhuriyet Sanatçısı.* Istanbul.

Çakır, S. (1993). *Osmanlı Kadın Hareketi.* Istanbul.

Durakbaşa, A. (1988). Cumhuriyet Döneminde Kemalist Kadın Kimliğinin Oluşumu. In *Tarih ve Toplum,* vol. 9, 51, pp. 39-43.

Edib-Adıvar, H. (1930). *Turkey Faces West.* Yale University Press (USA).

Göle, N. (1995): *Republik und Schleier. Die muslimische Frau in der modernen Türkei.* Berlin.

Kadın Eserleri Kütüphanesi ve Bilgi Merkezi Vakfı (Ed.) (1992). *Kadın Dergileri Bibliyografyası 1869-1927.* Istanbul.

Kandiyoti, D. (1991). Patriarchalische Muster. Notizen zu einer Analyse der Männerherrschaft in der türkischen Gesellschaft. In Neusel, A./Tekeli, S./Akkent M. (Ed.): *Aufstand im Haus der Frauen. Frauenforschung aus der Türkei.* Berlin, pp. 315-330.

Kreile, R. (1997). Politische Herrschaft, Geschlechterpolitik und Frauenmacht im Vorderen Orient. Pfaffenweiler.

Kreiser, K. (1997). Lady Mary und das Elend der Okzidentalistik. In Bode, C. (Ed.): *West Meets East: Klassiker der britischen Orient-Reiseliteratur.* Heidelberg, pp. 31-48.

Lord Kinross (1964). *Atatürk. The Rebirth of a Nation.* London.

Melman, B. (1992): *Women's Orients. English Women and the Middle East, 1718-1918. Sexuality, Religion and Work.* London.

Montagu, Lady Mary Wortley (1962). *Briefe aus dem Orient.* Stuttgart (first London 1763).

Moghadam, V. M. (1995). Gender and Revolutionary Transformation: Iran 1979 and East Central Europe 1989. In *Gender & Society,* vol. 9, 3, pp. 328-358.

Newton, S. M. (1974). *Health, Art and Reason. Dress Reformers of the 19th Century.* London

Scarce, J. (1987). *Women's Costume of the Near and Middle East.* London.

Schöning-Kalender, C. (2000). Republik ohne Schleier. Kleidung als Symbol im nationalen Diskurs der Türkischen Republik. In Decker, T./Helslot, J./Wijers, C. (Ed.) Roots & Rituals. *The Construction of Ethnic Identities.* Amsterdam, pp. 565-577.

Schöning-Kalender, C. (2001). Textile Grenzziehungen. Symbolische Diskurse zum Kopftuch als Symbol. In Schlehe, Judith (Ed.) *Zwischen den Kulturen – Zwischen den Geschlechtern.* München (Münchner Beiträge zur Interkulturellen Kommunikation Bd. 8), pp. 187-197.

Tarlo, E. (1996). *Clothing Matters. Dress and Identity in India.* London.

Tezcan, H. (1988). Osmanlı Imperatorluğu'nun son yüzyılında Kadın Kıyafetlerinde Batılılaşma. In *Sanat Dünyamız,* 37, pp. 44-51.

Yeğenoğlu, M. (1995). Haremdeki Leydi: Montagu'nun Mektuplarında Feminizm ve Orientalizm. In Defter, vol. 8, 24, pp. 115-138.

Yuval-Davis, N. (1997). *Gender and Nation.* London.

Aysegül Baykan

The Performative Vernacular: An Approach to City and Gender

"The act of walking is to the urban system what the speech act is to language or to the statements uttered. At the most elementary level, it has a triple 'enunciative' function: It is a process of *appropriation* of the topographical system on the part of the pedestrian (just as the speaker appropriates and takes on the language); it is a spatial acting-out of the place (just as the speech act is an acoustic acting-out of language); and it implies *relations* among differentiated positions, that is, among pragmatic 'contracts' in the form of movements (just as verbal enunciation is an 'allocution,' 'posits another opposite' the speaker and puts contracts between interlocutors into action). It thus seems possible to give a preliminary definition of walking as a space of enunciation" (de Certeau, 1984, pp. 97-98).

1. Characterizations of 'Public' Space

The concepts of space in general, and of city and public space in particular, are interconnected complex articulations, which, depending on the context, may be concrete, metaphorical, figurative or representational. Viewed from the perspective of city space, the emphasis on spatiality originates from the premise that everyday routine activities take place in space whereby particular individual or group presences are intertwined with spatially organized social structures. Space contextualizes and grounds the ways of life, politics, power, and ideology of different groups and subject positions. Therefore a discourse on the idea of a public domain also needs to consider space an integral element to its constitution. However, whereas the space of the city is heterogeneous, hybrid, and embodied, more often than not characterizations of the 'public' space, as argued by feminist scholars, are exhaustive and universalist, repress differences, and assume that agency is homogeneous and disembodied. Today, with new interventions to theories about the public realm, the spaces women occupy (and other groups subject to domination and discrimination) are viewed as contested fields of representation where they explore and practice their differences publicly rather than in private domestic places (Rose 1993, Massey 1994).

It is now widely recognized in gender studies that the public-private distinction is problematic, and always shifts in meaning. To give an example, Weintraub suggests four different organizing principles for the „theoretical languages or universes of discourse" on this binary: 1) The liberal model within which 'public' stands for the state administration and 'private' for the market economy. 2) The republican approach to political community and citizenship, a realm of collective decision-making, where public is often a synonym for the political. 3) The social history perspective, as reflected by the works of Ariès for whom the public realm is a domain of sociability for different groups with corresponding cultural and dramatic conventions. 4) A range of feminist approaches that question the views on the private (domestic) sphere versus the domain of the masculinist universal space of the political, the public, and the civil realms of society (Weintraub, 1995, p. 284).

What concerns us here is specifically the third approach since it has further implications for feminist theory as well. Weintraub argues that Ariès' sociability approach characterizes a historical period prior to the rise of the private realm of face-to-face inter-personal relations and does not address the status quo of contemporary societies within which the vitality of the streets, plazas, and public meeting places have disappeared. Sennett, whom Weintraub places in the sociability school as well, has similarly argued that modernity, with its realm of bureaucracy, the welfare state, work and organizations, has contributed to and enhanced the privatization of the individual life (Sennett 1978). More recently, Sennett proposed the concept of the 'power of place' that counteracts this historical process of privatization (Sennett 2000). His argument is as follows: Simmel, contrary to Kant and Hegel before him, found the civil society as experienced through the practice of city life impersonal and rational. His rationality implied a social construction, a sense of abstract visual connectedness with which people in interaction were able to keep their distance in the over-stimulating environment of their encounters in the city. According to Sennett, as a first response to Simmel, Arendt and Habermas have similarly privileged an impersonal public realm, but with emphasis on the domain of speech rather than the visual. The second response to Simmel, Sennett suggests, has come from the school of *teatro mundi*, as exemplified by the works of Goffman and Geertz. Sennett locates his own system of thought within this school, but with certain reservations. To be specific, he is concerned with the political dimension of the theatrical language of the „self-dramatizing" acts of people and their differences in the public realm (Sennett, 2000, p. 386). He asks how politics might be brought into the *teatro*. The answer is that it is found in places „at the edge" where, he claims, people will most likely meet others „*unlike* themselves" (Sennett, 2000, p. 386). We can conclude from Sennett's argument that politics pertain to the space of the city only where differences encounter each other – only at the very edge, in dramaturgic language and speech. Consequently, politics of difference are excluded from the center, the visual sphere, and from the physical touch of the crowds of the street. In short, the public space of the city becomes a political drama where differences speak to each other at the edge, based on a normative order of the stage where civic intercourse takes the form of sociability.

Contrary to Sennett, Deutsche (1998) has argued that the public space of the center is as much a space of exclusions and evictions as it is a shared space, and hence political. In many instances, places such as parks, plazas, and atriums, even when they are the result of collaboration between private and public agencies, become privatized for certain groups and deny access to others (Deutsche, 1998, p. 57). Furthermore, the rhetoric on 'public' space and the demand for harmony of differences are means to justify exclusions and homogenized spaces. According to Deutsche, 'public' is not a real category as 'city' is, but an ideological artifact and a contested and fragmented terrain (Deutsche, 1998, p. 59).

Urban ecology and urban planning, based on naturalizing and universalizing epistemologies, seek to impose coherence, order, and rationality on space. But this is a political act and an exercise of power. At the ground level, in the city streets, parks, plazas, and neighborhoods, the politics of space are about the embodied, inhabited encounter of the powerful and the powerless. This is not merely a normative structure of sociability and civility. Politics, therefore, have to be located at these encounters of power, enunciating acts, and performative presences of different groups, not merely at the edge, but everywhere. To explain this last point, I develop a theoretical framework of the encounters between different groups of power, based on the concepts of the vernacular and performativity.

2. Defining the Vernacular

The concept of the 'vernacular' in conventional use refers to naturalized, localized, a-historical, and nativist modes of knowing and practice. It ranges from language dialects to architecture, to a variety of socio-cultural practices attributable to a specific sub-group, as in the example of African American English. Vernacular, as opposed to the standard, has a pejorative connotation. The term 'Ebonics' for example (as coined by Robert Williams in 1973), refers to the rhetorical devices, phonology, and other aspects of the Black vernacular especially as a performance of solidarity, resistance, and identity – in other words, as insubordination to the dominant culture (Green, Smart, 1997, Lippi-Green, 1997). In other usages vernacular has stood for various forms of 'tradition' as opposed to the 'modern' (Wright, 1998). According to Wright, since the late eighteenth century the West located the vernacular on the one hand in nature's rural terrain and folk culture, and on the other, in the lands of exotic places, among the 'primitive'. Behind the romanticized construction of the vernacular in these modes there is a disguised authoritarian essence. Furthermore, as Wright argues, when the vernacular is close to home, spatially and in time, it is viewed in disdain, as it then stands for the various different practices of several groups who do not conform with the universal modern sound and outlook. Following Wright's thinking, I oppose the form of modernist framing of the vernacular. Instead, the vernacular is deliberately appropriated as a general concept that refers to the totality of different agencies, their practices, meanings, and groups in resistance to appropriation of the power by both the disciplinary regimes of knowledge and socio-economic and political interest groups.

Sharon Zukin is a notable theorist who reflects on the impact of the appropriation of the city on the vernacular. She sees the role of space in the postmodern city in the dynamics of power, and defines the vernacular as an articulation of powerlessness against the cultural appropriation of space by capital. According to Zukin, postmodern urban landscapes are constituted by turning modern localities into liminal spaces that mediate between nature and artifice, public use and private value, global market and local place (Zukin, 1992, p. 222). Through gentrification, the places of daily activities and social rituals of the powerless vernacular are turned into 'landscapes' for the powerful, thus eroding their living space. Zukin's approach is political and oppositional, and therefore powerful in its own right. However, its intention is to show the mechanics of cultural appropriation of space by the power of capital interests in today's world where investment and production has become global, cultural meaning is abstracted from material work, and a shift has taken place from production to consumption. The vernacular, in Zukin's approach, refers to the group of people and the context of their lives prior to these processes, and at whose expense these processes take place. Beyond that, Zukin does not specifically aim at a conceptual and theoretical articulation of the vernacular. For her, the vernacular exists before the becoming of the postmodern landscape she defines. In other words, in Zukin's approach the vernacular is traditionalized.

The vernacular, as it is defined and used in this paper, refers in general to the agency of the enunciative presence of the subordinated. As defined above, it might refer to the individual agency of a singular woman/man, to group agency (as in class or a particular ethnic or religious group), and/or to a particular position of a spatial community, such as the squatter housing of Turkish cities, the *gecekondu*. Either way, the vernacular is constituted at the crossroads of alternative spaces of enunciating acts: at the level of the bodily presence of the agent, *vis-a-vis* citizenship (economic/political/social agency), or within the distributive/re-distributive mechanisms of the contemporary (global) city. This mode of using the vernacular helps to shift the emphasis away from a subject of mere consciousness, a state of mind, or a set of pre-determined cultural values as it is embodied in space. It enables us to refer to lives as material, symbolic, and political practices situated at the junction of negotiations within regimes of power. Henceforth, in daily activity the vernacular has to negotiate different levels of class, patriarchy, hegemonic nationalisms, religious fundamentalisms, global capitalism, and so forth. The discourses on nationalism, modernization, globalization, authenticity and religiosity, among others, present themselves as the medium through which the defined vernacular operates. In addition, as the vernacular acts within this space, it also affirms its difference and negotiates for power.

3. Defining the Performative

Recently social and cultural analysis has become more cognizant of the necessity for a performative approach to study contemporary circuits of capital, information, modes of representation, history, and politics as they affect the subordinated groups of people of the world (Coplan, 1993, du Toit, 1997). Accordingly, ahistorical reductionist approaches to identity and presence have been replaced by studies where agents (the vernacular as proposed in this paper) assume a mimetic relation to power/regimes. For example, in reference to culture Bhabha claims that it is an enunciative function rather than an epistemic one that affirms a sense of self and identity (Bhabha, 1994). In the case of gender differences, enunciation of difference through a practice of signification is especially important according to Judith Butler (1990), with whom the theory of performativity has become associated. Other theorists in feminism have also followed the same line of thought. For example, Moi claims that according to Irigaray, woman under patriarchy often use the strategy of mimicry „to *undo* the effects of phallocentric discourse simply by *overdoing* them [...] Irigaray's undermining of patriarchy through the overmiming of its discourses may be the one way out of the straitjacket of phallocentrism" (Moi, 1993, p. 140). Similarly, according to Moruzzi (1993), women assume the feminine role deliberately and as an imitation of a constructed feminine essence so that they transform subordination into corroboration. „Feminine mimicry, or masquerade, may allow a (female) subject to acknowledge the genealogy of her victimization and her practical experience of its constraints without becoming immobilized within the identity of the victim" (Moruzzi, 1993, p. 262). To put it differently, the vernacular agent affirms itself in multiple ways without being appropriated by hegemonic spaces by mimicking and masquerading symbolic constructions so that it can negotiate its presence within alternative discourses of truth and authenticity within which it is situated. In this way, the vernacular agent moves from one corner of the hybrid self to the other, a (dis)location in metaphorical, symbolic and physical spaces. This ought to show us the ambivalence in the vernacular's position *vis-*

à-vis the expectations and the definitions of the situated domains, be it public or private, rural or urban, traditional or modern, Eastern or Western, and so on. As confronted by the vernacular, these locations, distinguished and reified by the center, are not separate domains. Each performance is a political enunciation of self, sexuality, the body, labor, and family, all of which take place in these very spaces. It must be noted that approaching the biography of an agent in this manner is different than the usual approach to 'identity.' The former is embodied, unlike the disembodied self-consciousness of the latter. The body, by contrast, is situated within the larger body-politic. On the one hand, the body's movements, day in and day out, take place within contradictory, heterogeneous and hybrid regimes of hegemonic interpretations and economies of desire, performing as woman, peasant, migrant, worker, transvestite, and so on. On the other hand, the vernacular agent asserts agency, desire, and the power of resistance against hegemonic articulations. As they exist within dialogic relations of power configurations between different groups sharing a given space, these assertions for presence are *performative*, as identity is performatively situated in the 'now and here'.

4. Space-Making in Istanbul

The city of Istanbul is an overlapping space of micro-geographies. It is commonly referred to as 'village-city'. In this way, a crisis situation is implied to exist between the 'urban-elite culture' and the 'peasant-culture' of the immigrants. In various narratives, from the social sciences to the media, the immigrant 'people' *(halk)* who come and create places in their squatter-neighborhoods *(gecekondus)* become a generalized construct of people with a pre-modern, localized culture. In this way, a generalized space of people, as founded on an 'authentic' folklore of Anatolia, is situated in opposition to westernized citizens. Hence, very similarly to the former conventions of defining the vernacular that Wright has criticized (as we discussed above), culture is reified in terms of fixed sets of beliefs, values and religion, and power and difference are reduced to a single binary of modernity versus authentic culture. This paper aims to oppose these forms of binaries and reifications by constructing and using the concept of the performative vernacular in reference to the majority of the inhabitants of Istanbul.

The immigrants to Istanbul encounter hardships in relation to various domains of economic, social, and political articulations. Migration takes place as a result of landlessness, joblessness, war, or maybe for the desire for the diversity of spaces the city can offer. As large numbers flock to the city, they become the post-modern flaneurs for survival in the city. They search for familiar practices, language, shared experiences of the past – spaces – that may help them find work or a home to live.

The existing popular culture reveals the ethics and aesthetics of these vernacular identities of the city and functions as the encounter with the vast complexity of the city in place-making. Meanwhile, the hybridity and complexity of the urban landscape call for new spaces of self-expression from the vernacular. According to Swiss et al. (1998, p. 17), for example, the effect of music (which can be economic, political, bodily, or emotional) is bound to the material practice of space, whereby the realm of aurality creates a sense of place – a practice of spatial imaginary. Different aural spaces, in this manner, correspond to wider differences. The ethnography of the audiences articulates to the popular culture as it is expressed in particular meanings. In this way communities enunciate their presence.

Yet at the same time, in strolling in the streets, promenading along the Bosphorus, in public concerts and/or picnics in the park, women and men of different backgrounds from different origins, with different dialects, patterns of life and religiosity, and different economic status are brought together. These city-spaces constitute and offer sociability, but also privacy and a diffused sense of agency outside of the communitarian structures of home and neighborhoods. They are emancipatory as they allow for transgression and subversive modes of action, which defy authoritarian forms of the community structures that are binding and de-personifying. In general, the literature points to the authoritarian and alienating dimensions, especially for women, of the public space. I will argue here for another possibility. As discussed above, Weintraub (1995) has presented how the dualist construction of the private-public separation is ambivalent and slippery, and often refers to multiple spheres. This paper aims to emphasize these aspects of sociability as lived in public, yet individually, because, paradoxically, for large segments of the population the private sphere of intimacy that allows for individual expression of desire is in fact possible only within and through the complexity of the city that is a network of interwoven lives of many people.

As explained above, a large city such as Istanbul is made up by layers of different spaces. Some are places within themselves, small familiar communities to cope with the complex outside world and a refuge in the struggle against the hardships and the power of the dominating forces of the center, with a political emphasis on locality. Others are contested, diffused, and overlapping networks of interests – cultural, economic, or political. In contemporary cities such as Istanbul there are several spatial forms beyond the simple binary of the private-public distinction. In these overlapping spaces, resistance to everyday operations of power, from patriarchy to (global) economy and the authoritarian state, take place. Women resist patriarchal conventions, Kurdish music is heard beyond the legal restrictions on the language, the poor sit on benches in wealthy neighborhoods. This co-presence is not simply an arena for sociability, but also a domain of *political* enunciation of presence within the public space, as a woman, as a worker, and so on.

In conclusion, the arguments presented above point to a need for new concepts and categories of analysis to study the life of cities of societies that encompass large marginal populations. The claims of the denizens of these cities define public space in new ways. In enunciating their presence, possibly in subversive ways against the hegemonic structures of the center, they also contribute to the possibility of a more sociable and democratic co-existence.

References

Bhabha, H. (1994). *The location of culture*. London: Routledge.
Butler, J. (1990). *Gender trouble: gender trouble and the subversion of identity*. London: Routledge.
Coplan, D. B. (1993). History is eaten whole: consuming tropes in Sesotho Auriture. *History & Theory*, 32, pp. 80-105.
de Certeau, M. (1984). *The practice of everyday life*. Berkeley: University of California Press.
Deutsche, R. (1998). *Evictions: art and spatial politics*. Cambridge: The MIT Press.
du Toit, L. (1997, August). Cultural identity as narrative and performance. *South African Journal of Philosophy*, 16, pp. 85-94.
Green, C. & I. I. Smart. (1997, December). Ebonics as cultural resistance. *Peace Review*, 9, 521-527.
Lippi-Green, R. (1997, Summer). What we talk about when we talk about Ebonics: why definitions matter. *Black Scholar*, 27, pp. 7-12.
Massey, D. (1994). *Space, place, and gender*. Minneapolis: University of Minnesota Press.
Moi, T. (1993). *Sexual/textual politics*. London: Routledge.
Moruzzi, N. C. (1993). Veiled agents: feminine agency and masquerade in the battle of Algiers. In S. Fisher & K. Davis (Eds.), *Negotiating at the margins*. New Brunswick: Rutgers University Press, 255-277.
Rose, G. (1993). *Feminism and geography*. Minnesota: University of Minnesota Press.
Sennett, R. (1978). *The fall of the public man*. New York: Vintage.
Sennett, R. (2000). Reflections on the public realm. In G. Bridge & S. Watson (Eds.), *A companion to the city*. New York: Vintage, pp. 380-387.
Swiss, T. , Sloop, J. & Hermann, A. (1998). *Mapping the beat*. Oxford: Blackwell.
Weintraub, J. (1995). Varieties and vicissitudes of public space. In P. Kasinitz (Ed.), *Metropolis*, New York: NYU Press, pp. 280-319.
Wright, G. (1998, October). On modern vernaculars and J. B. Jackson. *Geographical Review*, 88, pp. 474-482.
Zukin, S. (1992). Postmodern urban landscapes: mapping culture and power. In S. Lash & J. Friedman (Eds.), *Modernity and identity* (pp. 221-247). Oxford: Blackwell.

Neela Karnik

Displaying the Other. Tribal Museums and the Politics of Culture in India[1]

1. Tribals in the New Nation-State

As a group of indigenous people with distinct cultural and social identities, the tribals in India have had a turbulent history in the new nation-state. The focus of intense ethnographic scrutiny in the colonial period, they were the subject/object of extensive painting and photographic collections, which were commissioned in the hey-day of anthropology. Indeed India was regarded as the museum of mankind. Various Land Acts and Forest Acts enforced in the colonial period made inroads into their already fragile culture.

The tribals are scattered all over India, and they are marginalized: They are 'tribals' in the sense that they have no easy access to stable vocations, loans, education, health care or advantages of a modern welfare state. In independent India their status under a new Constitution was listed as Scheduled Tribes, and the government was committed to the preservation of their unique culture and way of life. This had a paradoxical effect: They were subject to what James Clifford calls the 'narratives of salvage', and at the same time they were occluded from the effects of development discourses and denied agency. Their claims to land are mired in legalese, or under litigation. In some cases the land has been pledged for a handful of grain to unscrupulous land grabbers or acquired by the government for railroads, dams, roads, or other developmental projects.

From colonial times to the present, various forces have combined to threaten the fragile identities of the tribal people, foremost among them Hindu hegemonic ideology and practices, evangelism (via the missionaries) and developmental discourses, as a result of which tribal people have perforce had to surrender land claims and natural prerogatives. They have been 'displaced', and their associations with land through which tribals communicate with their pasts,

1   Late Neela Ashok Karnik had been officially invited as an *ifu* lecturer in the project area „Migration". She had turned in her papers but unfortunately her health condition made it impossible for her to take part in *ifu*. Neela Ashok Karnik died in January 2001. To honour her and her scientific work we include her projected contribution to the ifu curriculum in this book. We thank Mr Karnik for his kind support in editing the paper (editor's note).

communicate with their sense of mortality and fertility, and from which they derive their myths, are ignored. In the interest of national development such people have been dislocated – forced to migrate, to lose belief in the sacred and become morally diminished. Yet it is tribal culture, which is evoked most emphatically at national spectacles to retrieve the sense of ethnicity so crucial in an era of globalization. In other words, tribal art and culture from various parts of the country are showcased as being distinct from a national culture (in terms of high culture) or are proffered as a national culture in an era of globalization when boundaries of national art become porous, and are blurred by a universal aesthetic – a global standard as it were.

Tribal culture and tribal art museums have been established all over the country. Museums play an important role in shaping the cultural and intellectual legacy of a nation as it emerges out of a colonial past, and they are vitally implicated in the narratives of a nation in a post-colonial era, implications which raise questions about the politics of representation, the hegemony of cultural interpretations and about global forces as cultures are plugged into leisure, travel and market economies.

While the primary task of museums is collecting, studying, interpreting and exhibiting, museums are also implicated in the shaping of knowledge by constructing material things as objects and classifying these in systems that are socially constructed rather than through concepts – of the 'rational', or the 'truthful'. As a signifying practice such a mode implies inclusions and exclusions to determine which objects can form collections that are complicit in creating systems of knowledge.

With the disappearance of class as an analytical category and the arguments of post-structuralists on the constructedness of communities, modern systems of knowledge become crucial in creating difference – difference which is mired in inequities or shifts in local and global economies.

This paper attempts to analyse how the practice of museumizing produces a certain knowledge about tribals by looking at the category 'tribal' as it is displayed within some of the tribal art museums and staged as spectacle in various cultural displays or public events. It argues that the beginnings of such displays emerged from the attempt to collect, classify and build repositories of facts and objects as a strategy for knowing India, and points out that the emphasis on the 'exotic' diversity within ethnographic accounts of colonial India continued into the spectacles staged by the nation state after Independence. Increasingly patterns and motifs of tribal art and *Warli* painting[2] in particular, appear on handmade paper, tea-towels and sari borders proffered as examples of indigenous transpositions or appropriations to create 'ethnic chic'. The popular Hindi film

---

2   The *Warli* were a food gathering tribe in western Maharashtra whose paintings are usually figures and animal motifs painted on the walls of their houses.

casts the tribal culture as idyllic: pastoral, non-urban, innocent and therefore occluded from modernization and progress. Tribal music, dances, dress (contextu-
ally costume) form a vital feature of what is termed as 'colourful India' or
'authentic India' in the various cultural shows put up in five-star hotels for foreign tourists.

These representations deployed by the state for the construction of a nationalist narrative are reproduced by tribal museums in what appears to be an aesthetic of unchanging pasts, stable identities and persisting traditions. Such a
view obliterates the ruptures and the violent dislocations which tribal cultures
have experienced, and negates the radical alterations which have taken place
within tribal societies. Do these representations reflect processes of transformation? Or do they stratify the category 'tribal' as an essence culled out of ethnography and orientalist discourses?

While tribal cultures are *visually* present, they are absent from discursive
space and function in contesting ways within and against dominant national orders, implicated either with narratives of 'cultural disappearance and salvage' or
with the narratives of 'revival, remembrance and struggle'[3] Can there be a simultaneous social and historic reading of these tribal displays to resuscitate this
category? This paper will raise these issues through a brief discussion of some
broad typologies of tribal displays: ethnography, spectacle, and museum collections of tribal art and culture.

2. Museumizing Tribals

The term 'museumizing' indicates the presence of a range of problems implicated with the category tribal. It emerges from the politics of viewing and from a
contradiction at the heart of ethnic museums: that ethnic cultures lack the potential for transformation and therefore need to be preserved, and, that the irresisti-
ble forces of modernity have radically altered tribal cultures. The paradox requires both a historicizing and unpacking in museum discourses so that tribal
museums stay aware of the paradox, and display or narrate it at all times. Another long standing paradox which is inherent in post-colonial ethnographic
writing informs the contouring of this problematic: How does one speak of the
Other, without essentializing, appropriating or falling between representation
and appropriation? This is the classic 'predicament' of representing cultural dif-

---

3   For an extended discussion of the consequences of the art-culture system for non-western
     cultural artifacts and other complex problems of representations of ethnographic objects,
     see Clifford, 1991, p. 214.

ference so well theorised by Francois Lyotard[4] and others who speak of a post-modernist turn, which loosened the authority of grand narratives and revised ethnography in important ways.

This created awareness from within which to speak, to try and draw out theoretical and experimental styles in which to discourse others' cultures, to be critical about one's own position thereby to open up a conceptual space for a contested category even as one speaks or writes it.

To conceptualize in writing the category 'tribal' is in fact to transgress. It means marking a culture primarily unmarked by literacy, always already bracketed out from the written and characterized by the oral. The 'tribal' is a category, which has fostered writing and othering, and is always written about, never writing.

The notion of museum used here extends from the liberal idea of museum as *'ajab-ghar'*, a cabinet of wonders to a broader, metaphorical use. The museum idea involves the expository gestures of showing and telling like „look", „see", „that's how it is", which are analogous to speech acts and generate a subject – object relation, a frame through which an object is made to speak to a viewer or reader. [5] The object, though mute, is present and recedes before what is said about it, creating a discrepancy between the thing and what it stands for. That discrepancy is filled in by the narrative which impels the subject to connect the 'present' of the object to the 'past' of its making while moving through the museum or having the museum move past while signs on display are being read.

As a metaphor 'museumizing', the act of presenting like in a museum is tied up with museum as a paradigm of a cultural practice, and with museums as sites of discourses that are deployed in and through them. Museums resonate with powerful, paradigmatic myths of primitivism, barbaric tribes, ideas of the noble and the savage, evolution, technological advance and so forth often in a combination of binaries: civilization vs. primitivism, culture vs. nature and so on. Besides things in a museum are ordered, explained and evaluated for aesthetic or historical knowledge.

Exposition or museumizing is a representation with an undeniable persuasion of a 'truth', it is „a power that museums have", as Carol Duncan says, „to define and rank people, to declare some as having a greater share than others in

---

4   In this often cited work on the ‚post-paradigm' Lyotard speaks of the contemporary incredulity towards metanarratives, a „crisis of narratives" resulting in the collapse of grand theory, and consideration of contextuality, ruptures and discontinuities. „Postmodernism ... refines our sensitivity to difference and reinforces our ability to tolerate the incommensurable."(cf. Lyotard, 1984) See also Marcus and Fischer, 1986.

5   I have drawn on Mieke Bal's idea of the rhetoric of persuasion and ‚truth-claims' that acts of exposure involve. See Bal,1996, p. 14.

the community's common heritage". [6] Museumizing, or exhibiting means putting something on display, implying the publicizing of deeply held convictions about a subject, making an exposition of a certain point of view and also (ex)positioning oneself within a discourse. Museumizing, is also an attempt to negotiate for a slippery category, 'tribal'.

Drawing on the practices of narratology – the act of showing and telling implied in museums – I shall attempt to read this category on display.

3. The Nomenclature 'Tribal'

In his once influential ethnographic survey of the province, R.E. Enthoven clarifies his use of the term tribal. „Broadly [...]the term tribal is used in these pages for a unit based on common descent as opposed to the term caste which is applied to a social unit that is founded on common occupation, residence or language." (Enthoven, 1920) His report is a collection of details of tribal rituals and practices of tiger-worship, stories about *bhagats*[7], the medicine man, or witchcraft, hunting habits, music (generally the drum, pipe and the flute) and liquorbrewing customs.

Contributions of ethnographic interest emerged from the directives issued by the Board of Directors of the East India Company 1807 that the Government of Bengal undertake a statistical survey. Thus *The Joumal and the Proceedings of the Bengal Asiatic Society* (1784-1884), the *Calcutta Review* (1843-1883), Francis Buchannan's surveys, census records, tribes and castes handbooks, linguistic surveys, archaeological surveys, travelogues and missionary accounts and monographs were the repositories of lore about the tribals. This focus on the exotic and the strange in many of the reports, travel narratives and missionary tales reinforces the desire to preserve tribal societies as curiosities.

In 1935, under the Government of India Act, entire belts with predominantly tribal populations were declared „excluded" and „partially excluded" areas under the direct administrative control of the governor of the province. In 1947 the Indian Constitution passed the order for the 'Schedule of Tribes', but without proffering any enabling, liberating practices. The term tribal coming now from the declared Schedule of Tribes has a salience evoking both an anthropological category and a metaphorical marginality. In India the category is framed in a

---

6   Carol Duncan argues that heritage museums belong to the realm of secular knowledge and are implicated in producing political meaning, and conferring citizenship by means of ritualized viewing. (Duncan 1991, pp. 88-103).

7   Bhagats are religious men in tribal societies who performed all the relious ceremonies. They were basically disciples of god and derived from the word „*bhakt*" meaning devotion .

paradox: the tribal and tribal culture is visually present but discursively absent; a silenced category since there is no comprehensive definition of what constitutes tribal identity. Yet there is the overwhelming presence in terms of cultural residue, which, despite hegemonic pressures, resists the homogenization processes unleashed by a modern nation state. Two questions arise: First, does this presence-as-resistance imply that older modes of domination still prevail? Second, more importantly, does the category need to be re-examined?

The category, caught between the Nationalist's fear of being marshaled into yet another distinct group within a community as yet only imagined, and the colonial government's anxiety to preserve tribals as they were, as museum 'survivals', led to an existence in a singular gray zone.

During the late colonial period Verrier Elwin – intrepid traveler, clergyman, Gandhian, and finally renegade[8], who befriended the tribals all over India – shaped Nehru's policy for tribal welfare well into the years after Independence[9]. Most ethnographic knowledge of tribal cultures within India in the early years of the century goes back to his work. Elwin's approach stemmed from his missionary and evangelical strain and was to turn into the civilizing mission to give impetus to his work and writings – an impressive collection on customs, dress, physiology, magic, marriage customs, food habits, songs, weapons, sacred rights, myths and stories. Curiously, his writing further 'exoticized' tribals as colourful, picturesque people engaged in headhunting, sexual orgies in the 'ghotuls'[10], and in human sacrifices. Typically in the ethnographic traditions the frontispiece of his book *Philosophy for NEFA*[11] shows a map in the cartographic tradition of the great age of discoveries with icons depicting the essentializing characteristics of head dress, weapons, masks, images of head-hunting *Nagas*[12], totem-poles, and so on. Elwin's proposal to intern various tribals in national parks held unfortunate connotations; despite his protestations that he wished to preserve them as they were not as „museum specimens for the benefit of anthro-

---

8   In his later years Elwin became a sustained critic of government policies (both British and independent Indian) towards the tribes.

9   Elwin shared Nehru's confidence and was appointed Advisor for Tribal Affairs in the 1950s. He instituted the Tribal Research Institutes with the attachment of a museum to house collectibles. There are now fourteen institutes located in tribal belts all over India. His controversial views on the protection of the tribals caused a furore among nationalists who saw his attempts as a strategy to keep them out of nationalist politics in view of the colonial government's directive preventing Congress workers from entering tribal areas. For details of Elwin's controversies with the sociologist Ghurye and Baba Thakkar see Guha, 1996, pp. 2375-2389.

10 Ghotuls are dormitories or educational centres of the Gond tribes of Central India. These dormitories may be bi-sexual or mono-sexual.

11 North-East India Frontier Agency (special territory, since 1987 the state of Arunachal Pradesh).

12 Tribe in North-East India

pologists" but as a means „to preserve the good taste of the tribals, the arts – the beautiful textiles, the music and the dance", his views were vehemently attacked. [13]

Elwin was severely criticized by a man who had worked tirelessly for the *Bhil Seva Mandal,*[14] A. V. Thakkar, a staunch Gandhian who joined the *Servants of India Society* founded by G. K. Gokhale[15] and adopted the „khadi and temperance"[16] programme. In his memorial lecture at the Gokhale Institute of Economics and Politics in Poona in 1941 Thakkar criticized Elwin's policy of 'isolation' and proffered 'assimilation' through a rigorous temperance propaganda to deliver tribals from the „drink- devil"; he endorsed the opinion of the Dutch Catholic missionaries who blamed the God's love for the karma dance for sexual profligacy among their women[17]. Thus a moral economy, Hindu hegemony, the christianizing efforts, and an incomprehensible system of law and justice worked to nearly devastate the fragile culture of the forest (i. e. tribal) people and alienate them thoroughly from the agendas of a new nation state.

4. Tribal Displays

Historicizing the modes of representing the Other in ethnography one finds that in museums, as in anthropology, the major contribution is one that recognizes and acts upon the need to capture the cultural diversity of tribal and non-western peoples. Central to ethnography and to the museum enterprise, both contiguous

---

13 Many of Elwin's ideas form part of his work A Philosophy for NEFA (Shillong, 1960) and New Deal for Tribal India, (New Delhi, 1963).

14 The Bhil Seva Mandal was an organisation which worked for the upliftment of the Bhils – a tribe in Madhya Pradesh or Central India. In 1927, an enquiry committee under the chairmanship of Thakkar was constituted for looking into the problems of tribals.

15 G. K. Gokhale was the leader of Indian National Congress until 1915. Mahatma Gandhi considered Gokhale his political guru.

16 Khadi is hand-woven rough cloth, often prepared at home /in the villages. This was the method used to generate self-reliance and employment opportunity to local population. This also generated nationalistic feelings as against mill-made textiles often produced by English mills and imported. Temperance was used as a measure of frugal living i. e. shunning imported luxuries.

17 In his lecture Thakkar said, „anthropologists like Elwin might even countenance adultery, witchcraft, human sacrifice in the belief that the „original" culture of the tribal should not be tainted by the so-called alien culture of the Indian nationalists". He later remarked that the [Gond] women desert their husbands because of the excessive sexual excitement caused by frequent singing and dancing of karma dance with its obscene song and drink throughout the night" (cf. Thakkar, 1941, pp 23-26). Thakkar's Gandhian injunctions against meat-eating (ahimsa), and liquor were alien to the tribal way of life as was charkha spinning a symbolic activity for the nationalists.

activities in most ways, is the urgency to maintain Europe's nineteenth century „grand vision" of the science of man: to catalogue, measure, classify in that powerful Linnéan paradigm which provided Europe with an influential ideational and ideological apparatus with which to scale the human. Supportive to this attempt is the axis operative from the age of capital, namely, the Nature to Man axis which determined the notion of transformation, evolution and progress along the axis, taking the distance between the two tropes as a measure of things, articulated as noble and savage in the Romantic, Rousseauesque spirit of pre-industrial society; and as displaced and disenchanted in the wasteland discourses of modernity.

Post-coloniality privileged identity and cultural politics and the business of reinventing identities. The study of marginalized people was inflected by the analytical categories of race, class, gender and in a multi-layered Indian caste society, and riddled with ironies about multiple representations, which engendered a subversion of the subject of ethnography.

Writing about cultural difference was moving either towards hard political and economic facts or a liberal humanism – both reductive. What needed to be examined were the consequences of increasing globalizing pressures on that residual category „culture", its display in spectacles and in its repository, the museum.

5. In Spectacles

The West has a long tradition of exhibiting humans for their performative or curiosity value and steering these towards spectacles: The chamber of horrors, circus, as a part of zoological collections, and of course as living ethnographic displays. By the mid nineteenth century in the wake of interest in „missing links", evolution and racial types, the great expositions and the world fairs featured „displays of mankind" with a quasi-scientific bias to lend legitimacy to many of the 'specimens' displayed.[18]

To impress upon the people of India the dignity, diversity, industry and progress it had made under British rule, and to proclaim the Queen's authority over the Indians, an Imperial Assemblage[19] was celebrated in early 1877. As Bernard

---

18 For an excellent discussion of the ethnographic artefacts see Kirshenblatt-Gimblett, 1991. See Altick, 1978.
19 During the period of 1855-1915, Delhi had been the scene of three great Imperial Assemblages or Durbars (as they were more popularly known). The first was summoned by Lord Lytton on 1st January 1877 to announce Queen Victoria as the new Empress of India. The second was the Coronation Durbar of 1902-03, held during Lord Curzon's Viceroyalty to proclaim the accession of King Edward VII. The last – the greatest of the

Cohn has pointed out in his classic essay *Representing Authority in Victorian India,* the goal was to convey the idea of British social order to the Indians. „The British conception of Indian history thereby was realized as a kind of 'living museum'", he says; Lord Lytton declared that if one wanted to understand the meaning of empire, all one had to do was to look at „the multitudinous in its traditions, as well as in its inhabitants, almost infinite variety of races which populate it, and of the creeds which have shaped their character" (Cohn, 1983, pp. 193-194).

It was an event, which was to be repeated in 1903 as the imperial *Durbar* and in 1911 for Edward V's proclamation as emperor. Most importantly, as Cohn points out, „it became for Indians and Europeans a kind of marker. It became a standard by which public ceremony was to be measured" (ibid. , p. 208).

The nation state, however, has chosen to adopt Lytton's 'ritual idiom'. The congress meetings were very much like the *Durbars* as Cohn suggests, but so is the present Republic Day Parade. That grand spectacle reiterates the fantastic diversity of India's people more so by inscribing some of its most marginalized groups, the tribals, in the state's elaborate ritual as citizens.

The Republic Day Parade on January 26th each year is a state ritual. It commemorates the past in pageants and spectacles of the INA[20] forces, the sepoy's revolt[21], the emergent nationalist forces, the present day armed forces in sumptuary and regalia-marching (in much the same ceremonial order adopted for the great *Durbar*). They are followed by the bands, the array of latest arms and gadgetry, polished guns, ram-rod straight soldiers, sleekly groomed horses, elephants and camels in ceremonial trappings, and the tribals in colourful clothes and head gear, with bows, arrows, swords, spears, drums, pipes and bells, singing, and dancing.

They are followed by the state flotillas – one for every state in the Indian union. Each is elaborately decorated with the defining characteristic of that state. So, *Kerala* will stage its spectacle of progress with models of the hydroelectric power stations, scenes depicting coffee and pepper plantations and so forth. *Himachal Pradesh* shows off its apple-cheeked lasses, and load carriers. The states with the tribal belts unerringly (re)present their tribals – the *Bhil, Gond, Naga, Warli, Koli,* and so on in their obligatory colourful, ethnic clothes, with their drum, flute or timbrel, singing or dancing. The women are shown weaving, at

---

three durbars, was held in 1911, depicting the splendours of India's imperial capital before the visiting Sovereign and his Consort.

20 Indian National Army.

21 This pertains to the „Mutiny" of 1857 against the British Rulers of India. It is now referred to as the First war of Indian Independence. During this revolt Indian sepoys (soldiers) rose against the British Forces. The Ruler of Jhansi (a kingdom-state in Central India at that time) who was a woman and who was renowned as the „Rani of Jhansi" , played a prominent part to lead the revolt.

the potter's wheel, or gathering forest products. Around these representations are the many symbols of progress – transmission towers, factory produced goods, aluminum, several steel machine parts amidst which the 'tribal' stands quite forlorn.

This precisely is the image of the tribal in the sub-continent, marginalized and museumized in a spectacle, which legitimizes the representation and constructs authority by deploying the spectacular in the service of a gesture. It sanctifies the image of the nation state. The 'museumized' people-as-signs (and, signs-as-people), strive to communicate their cultural status and the social context of their represented reality, but their self-consciousness, embellished with costume, music, dancing, their staging, in fact projects them as pure signs, objects of the gaze. Rehearsed gestures enhance their mannequin-like identity, frozen as it were forever in a tableau. Sometimes the formal space of the spectacle moving at an orderly pace and bounded by the formality of the military parade is carnivalized by the costumed, stiffened, effigy-like models who transgress the limits of ordered behaviour and shout, wave, mouth things at the crowds in an attempt to step off the display ramp and assert a common humanity. The crowds gape as the flotillas roll by and fold the present into itself; the tribe-person moves away only to be staged another day.

This occasion is the Folk Dance Festival at the National Stadium, New Delhi. It sustains the carnival mood engendered by the Republic Day celebrations in the capital. In the 1950s Nehru, a great impresario, would don a *Naga* shawl, a *Rajasthani pagdi*[22], and dance to a *Madia* drum[23] in a benevolent gesture indicating his desire to assimilate tribal culture via dancing and singing.

The colonial dance is essentially a mediation, the tribal's communion; with the rhythm his cosmos is now turned into an entertainment in a public sphere. The tribals dance for the sake of dancing, or for some religious or magical significance; three generations in tandem, they dance in sameness (which becomes monotonous on the proscenium stage), because the dance is part of a social heritage and does not reflect an individual talent. Conceptually, too, the tribal is museumized.

Perhaps the most subversive use of the representation of tribal culture as a tribe thing has been in popular Hindi cinema or the Bombay *masala*[24] film. The state's patronage of cinema in the years after Independence is well documented. It is reflected in the inauguration of the International Film Festivals and by visits of film delegations abroad. Nationalist leaders like Misra, the M. P congress president, K. N. Munshi, and Sawarkar's close associate Niranjan Pal, recognizing the power of this media, began to either write scripts or direct film productions which would effectively project the idea of nation and its agenda through cinema.

---

22 A type of turban particular to Rajasthan, a state in India.
23 A drum used by the Madia tribe of Central India.
24 Masala means all the ingredients that a Hindi film would have, i. e. song, dance and thrills typical of Bombay life which the back-benchers enjoy.

Films increasingly began to represent the marginalized sections of society in a deliberate attempt to harness, through cinematic representations Gandhi's program – for the rehabilitation of *Harijans*[25] and marginalized people like the scheduled castes and tribes. Most of these early films depicted exploitation of tribals in parables: the rape of a girl and the rape of the forests, usually forest officials, rapacious landlords, and timber merchants even as they portrayed the tribals' fierce, celebratory love for nature. *Izzat* (1936)[26] was about the exploitation within the picturesque *Bhil* community and set the pattern for most tribal depictions. Commercial considerations compelled the producers to represent and package tribals as colourful, attractive, dancing and singing. Soon more exotic and erotic elements were included and images of tribal life and culture as simple, pastoral, but infinitely desirable pervaded the screen. These representations, barring a few exceptions, were stereotypical, undifferentiated and uncritical in their adoption of a mélange of design, style, colour and accessories – essentially „gaudy" tribal attire. No specificity of region or culture was shown, except their love of singing, story telling, gaiety, love for forests.

In tribal India sex was perceived to be the man's obligation and the women's right, and the popular film appropriated this notion to stage the spectacle of the 'primitive' woman's sexuality in the tribal-song sequence; the heroine in tribal costume, generally scanty tribal clothes, sings to provoke the hero to make romantic overtures, or sings folksongs about forest lore, myths and riddles, accompanied by drums, pipes, and flutes. It is generally a group song, sung at a village *mela* (gathering). Primarily it creates a libidinous space, in which to inscribe a representation of the tribal woman who sings to seduce, distract or entertain the urban hero or villain, the *pardesi*. Most popular are the „gypsy" dance – Helen's *meheboba, meheboba* – in the blockbuster, curry western *Sholay*[27]; the *bichoowa* dance in *Madhumati*[28]; *jooth bole kawa kate* in *Bobby*[29]; *mana dole* in *Nagin.*[30]

---

25 Untouchables or scheduled tribes

26 scripted by Niranjan Pal, directed by Osten starring Ashok Kumar and Devika Rani

27 The film Sholay (Embers) was the biggest blockbuster of the seventies – an Indian western where two ex- prisoners are hired by a retired jailor to nab the local gangster who terrorises the villagers. Helen is a gypsy girl who entertains the gangster. The word meheboba means „lover".

28 Madhumati is another popular film of the fifties where the heroine is a tribal girl who wants to gain the attention of the hero through a dance sequence which will sting his heart. The word bichoowa means scorpion.

29 Bobby is a teenage love story and a runaway success film in which Bobby, the heroine, in a dance sequence threatens her lover by singing a ditty that she will go away to her mother's house if he lies to her anymore and as a punishment the crow will bite him.

30 Nagin was another film depicting tribal culture. The word nagin means a female „nag" (cobra snake). Here the tribal girl takes on the role of a snake-charmer and regales the audience. The words mean „the body is swaying to the rhythm of the heart".

At any rate what seems easily transferred from tribal cultures into public spectacles are folkloric, superficial elements like dress, jewelry, arts and crafts, motifs, foods, designs, and entertainment, which offer an antidote to a homogenized, nationalized culture, to effect a revival of subjugated knowledges.

6. 'Tribe Things'

The idea of tribal museums emerged from the anthropological museums first established in 1814 and 1874 by the Bengal Asiatic Society. However, the model was one of the first heritage museums in *Bombay Presidency*[31], namely the Victoria and Albert Museum and Botanical Gardens. At the foundation ceremony in 1865 *Bhau Daji Lad*, one of the founders, characterized it as „a temple of science containing the wonder of ages, of literature, science, and arts", in fact a western construct. „It shall be a College of Inquiry as distinguished from a College of Reading."[32] The model was assiduously followed in the making of tribal museums.

The critical terrain of the tribal museum is marked by two contradictory strains: One serves to establish a hegemonic interpretation of a specific culture and ethnic identity, and the other a globalizing strain which negates difference and promotes a universal aestheticism. This tends to obliterate the localism of the artifacts – the materials used, the design, the use in everyday life – and privilege instead an 'effect. ' The objects torn from their environment are fragments of a culture; by nature multiple in use and as products not of the excess of art-as-play but labour. In display ethnographic objects become singularly curious, more detached from their context and therefore more easily classifiable as art. In museums the context, the intangible is lost-the-life-world and the cosmology – whatever cannot be taken away – is textualized as another fragment, the ethnographical fragment as label.

One of the first measures taken to mediate the notion of tribal for a new nation state was that culture approach, the patronage of handicrafts. The first Five Year Plan established six boards for the promotion of handicrafts and what were called village industries, among them the Khadi and Village Industries Board, the All-India Handicrafts Board, the All India Handloom Board, the Central Silk Board, and the Choir Board. These function as agencies to procure tribal artifacts, which could easily be subsumed.

While this cannot be a complete list, it is fairly representative of how tribals are represented in Hindi films. Among exceptions are representations in middle cinema and art films, including Ray's cinema especially his *Aranya din Ratri* and S. Paranjpe's *Papiyha.*

31   British Military province since the early 19th century.
32   Quoted in Birdwood, 1964, p.16.

Between 1959 and 1981 the Indian Government held a series of meetings about permanent tribal collections. The everyday life of ten different tribal cultures were to be recreated and exhibited, among them *Warli, Gond, Agria, Madia, San-thal, Toda, Naga* – some of the most colourful. The objects were proffered as art objects rather than objects of everyday use; this seemed strange to those who produced them, since they could not make a distinction between craft, a collective community production of functional objects, material culture and art.

Those fragments of culture found in the cabinet of a museum or in a place of pride in an urban home, were transformed by that very display into rare, aesthetic objects; in museums under boutique lighting they were minimally labeled – a *Madia* figurine, a bird, deer, a comb, a *Mizo* spear, *Gond* pipe, *Naga* shawl, *Bhil* bow or *Warli dev chowk* (marriage square), a *Bohada* mask and so on.

Typically such objects form the core collection of the Tribal Research Museum in Pune, to be read as replica of other tribal museums. Established in 1962 as an extension of The Tribal Research and Training Institute, it was mooted as a site „committed to preserve the artistic and poetic impulses of tribals". (Tribal Research Institute and Museum, 1989) It published statistics on the production and sale of tribal handicrafts (during the Tribal Arts Festival it holds annually), and details of the artist, the number of *(Warli)* paintings sold, the reputation abroad, and the status of the artifacts in a market economy.

The museum itself is housed in a multi-storied complex, shabby and dimly lit. The artifacts are displayed behind glass, and no indication is given of their artistic or practical value – in fact the distinction is subverted. The labels are didactic – the connection and their dependence on ecology are not explained. The diorama of a market place with life-size mannequins, things in use, and costumes dominates the meager space of the museum. It is exhibited in the style of a natural history museum. The representations of the hunters and the food-gatherers are shown alongside foraging animals to reiterate the tribal's closeness with and affinity to nature. Objects are crammed together under inadequate lighting. Certain artifacts are placed for effectiveness as pure forms. The collection is devoid of any signs of the vital social reality in which they are produced.

Representing the symbolic ceremonies, the daily chores and the simple social realities of *Warli* life, *Jhiva Soma Mhase's*[33] work depicts the unchanging rhythms of tribal life. They are plugged into global notions of taste through the aesthetics of charm and austerity, which suggests persistent tradition. Yet, tribal lives and cultures are being subjected to violent new contexts: displacement, the desacralizing of traditional spaces, loss of forestland and the pressures of commercial patronage and mass production. The ideology of progress within a nation state has compelled changes without offering a possibility for reinvention.

---

33   A well known *Warli* painter.

When displayed in public museums or exhibitions of contemporary art, „tribal art" is used to distinguish the art of the metropolis which is Eurocentric in its aesthetic orientation, from „ethnic" art implying a „primitive" or „folkloristic" way of seeing or imagining, by itself a distinctly Western practice which served to make logical some of the choices the modernist painters made at the turn of the century. Artistically arranged tribal objects are violently decontextualized. The *mundhas* (marriage pillars) in the museum are displayed with only a vestigial reference to its complex religious and cultural potency. The concern is with how the state deploys a secular ritual to inscribe tribal culture within a homogenizing, multicultural, pluralistic culture; and, at the same moment stresses its difference from it.

The museumizing of the tribal is part of that impulse which seeks to establish, unconsciously perhaps, positions of authority, dominion and social imperialism over the „collected other" in the service of the state. While the history of museums shows a gradual movement towards greater awareness of the public, it is only recently that self-conscious reflections about the political implications of exhibitions and what these imply about the cultures on display, has been seriously undertaken.

7. Conclusion

In this paper I attempted to tease out a conceptual space in which tribals could have agency in control of the space/time in which to realize themselves creatively. The processes of wresting agency require access to resources, which are indispensable for this process. In this sense it is vital to examine whether tribals have been left with any of these resources in order to continue to retain a way of life and eventually an identity.

From precolonial times, and indeed in myth and legend, we find references to how the tribal has been exploited. In modern history in a shaming way laws, rules and acts have destroyed the very fabric of tribal life-world – human, natural and material resources of tribals everywhere have been taken away. They have been caught as it were in a spiral of impoverishment, and thereby denied the means of gaining agency.

Colonial historiographies represented the tribal in terms of law and order as the abject/object of law, the rebellious body, the member of a „criminal tribe" always in revolt. Yet historiography maintains that many of these revolts took place without any outside agency; in this sense were the tribals, as rebellious bodies, not making their own history? Did they not have a sense of their own historiography, even from the periphery? Like their cosmologies – distinct for each tribal group, their historiography, the stories of their origins were author(ized) on a different plane and authenticated by a belief, which, despite the appropriation of aspects of tribal culture, had no major impact on the dominant cosmology.

In spectacles there is a valorization of the singing, and dancing tribal body. „Dance" is their life but do they mean a cultural performance when they dance? Is there an epistemic rupture here? Like „painting" which we insist is what they do of the images of their life-world? In a spectacle they are drained signs rearranged as dancing bodies, they are our 'other' performing selves whom we appropriate through dance. Only in obliterating the specificity of their origins, culture, and their life-world can we impute onto the tribal body, our deepest nostalgia for the unfettered spirit.

It is intriguing that nowhere has any tribal group expressed anxiety about its isolation (isolated from whom, or what? Our civilisational norms?). Perhaps it is that we cannot come to terms with the degree of cultural difference represented. Perhaps that difference is not negotiable for them, which is precisely why we tremble at the edge because they can do without us. Their notion of heaven as a forest without boundaries, and hell a life without forests can never be ours. Yet their life-world remains a mote in the eye; since that cultural difference cannot be negotiated, it is appropriated in order to reach the last libidinal space of creativity and wholeness. That is the object of our nostalgia, a nostalgia that offers no real challenges except in terms of the imaginary, which needs to be tamed and consumed in recognizable forms – in art, music, and dance. I realize that this discourse belongs to another realm towards a psychoanalytical discourse of our civilizational identity – something quite beyond the purview of the paper. But this line of inquiry needs to be pursued if only to explore the need for this other, our need for his invention. Why do we want to possess a *Warli* painting? What part does it play in our ritual of citizenship? That tribal artifact is not just a cultural commodity, but a vital part of the paraphernalia required as baggage for cultural valence, to justify selfhood and identity. We create a lie called a *Warli* painting, the lie of the state (a la Derrida), as part of the paraphernalia (Derrida, 1996).

In the museum-as-state, excesses have to be curbed, especially nostalgia and sadness for what is represented. It is expected by the museum as a complicitous condition for viewing. The function of curbing excesses is partially performed by the museum catalogue, which tells us „here is the object, treat it like a spatial text placed in the glass case". As such it disciplines the gaze, holds and manipulates it, often at the cost of the object.

One must wonder about the object then, not just at it. In tribal museums there is the hidden, repressed narrative about the value of the thing, for tribals and their things, distance is a crucial measure of their identity, and in museums the distance is measured along the axis from man to nature. Museums push the frontiers of nature up towards man to accommodate tribals and their things at the bottom of this axis.

Here lastly, perhaps one can raise questions, think aloud, and take a risk: is the resourcelessness of the tribals a matter of choice or a matter of subjugation? Why in a post-modern era does border crossing and hybridity constitute advance? Why is the normlessness of tribal societies a mark of imbalance via discourses of development? And finally: is the nation-state willing to share and transfer natural, material and human resources back to the tribal belts and sustain that life-world, that mode of life? Nehru brought about a transfer only in terms of culture, untainted culture, authenticated by the very existence of this schedule of tribes, not in terms of community needs required to keep them as they were. What was put on show, museumized always, was tribal art and culture wrested out of its context as art and culture, when in fact for the tribal there is no art, but only the shapes in which he moulds his needs.

Besides, 'tribes' also collect things – plastic pins, buttons, aluminium buckets, polyester dresses, transistors – the paraphernalia of modern commodities, and museumize these perhaps?

Tribe things in a museum have a melancholy about them, perhaps because tribals are compelled to make their things for display. The little *Warli* girl who cries for crayons has no choice. She has to use rice flour and red mud to paint. We need the *Warli* painting at any(ones) cost. Unless this category tribal is allowed a discursive space, even this space, in which it can explore the terms required for its realization, unless the category is continuously negotiated as an open-ended one, the thorny question of why the tribal is museumized and why his/her displacement is so displayed will stay with us.

References

Altick, R. (1978). *The Shows of London.* Cambridge, Mass. : Belknap Press.

Bal, M. (1996). *Double Exposures: The Subject of Cultural Analysis.* New York, London: Routledge.

Birdwood, G. (1864). *Report on the Government Central Museum and on the Agricultural and Horticultural Society of Western India, for 1863, with Appendices being the History of the Establishment of the Victoria and Albert Museum and Gardens.* Bombay: Education Society Press.

Clifford, J. (1991). Four Northwest Coast Museums. In Ivan Karp and Steven Levine (Eds.), *Exhibiting Cultures: The Poetics and Politics of Museum Display.* Washington, London: Smithsonian Institution Press, pp. 212-254.

Cohn, B. S. (1983) Representing Authority in Victorian India. In Hobsbawm, E. and T. Ranger (Eds.), *The Invention of Tradition.* Cambridge: Cambridge University Press, pp. 193-208.

Derrida, J. (1996). *The Lie of the State and the State of the Lie.* A talk delivered at the Asiatic Library. Mumbai.

Duncan, C. (1991). Art Museums and the Ritual of Citizenship. In Ivan Karp and Steven Levine (Eds.), *Exhibiting Cultures: The Poetics and Politics of Museum Display.* Washington and London: Smithsonian Institution Press, pp. 88-103.

Elwin, V. (1963). *New Deal for Tribal India.* New Delhi.

Elwin, V. (1960). *A Philosophy for* NEFA. Shillong.

Enthoven, R. E. (1920). *Tribes and Castes of Bombay.* Bombay.

Guha, R. (1996). Savaging the Civilized: Verrier Elwin and the Tribal Question in Late Colonial India. *Economic and Political Weekly.* xxxi, 35, 36 & 37 (special issue), pp. 2375-2389.

Kirshenblatt-Gimblett, (1991). The Objects of Ethnography. In Ivan Karp and Steven Levine (Eds.), *Exhibiting Cultures: The Poetics and Politics of Museum Display.* Washington, London: Smithsonian Institution Press, pp. 386-443.

Lyotard, J. F. (1984). *The Postmodern Condition. A Report on Knowledge.* Minneapolis: University of Minnesota Press.

Marcus, G. E. & M. J. Fischer (1986). *Anthropology as Cultural Critique: An Experimental Moment in the Human Sciences.* Chicago: University of Chicago Press.

Thakkar, A. V. (1941). *The Problem of the Aborigines in India.* Poona.

The Tribal Research Institute and Museum (1989). Poona.

Saskia Sassen

Analytic Borderlands: Economy and Culture in the Global City

What happens to place in a global economy? And how is globalization inscribed – in the spaces of the economy and of culture, in built form, and generally in space? I want to use these questions to argue that the dominant narrative about economic globalization is a narrative of eviction. Key concepts in the dominant account – globalization, information economy, and telematics – all suggest that place no longer matters. And they suggest that the type of place represented by major cities may have become obsolete from the perspective of the economy, particularly for the leading industries as these have the best access to, and are the most advanced users of, telematics.

It is an account that privileges the capability for global transmission over the concentrations of built infrastructure that make transmission possible; that privileges information outputs over the work of producing those outputs, from specialists to secretaries; and the new transnational corporate culture over the multiplicity of cultural environments, including re-territorialized immigrant cultures, within which many of the „other" jobs of the global information economy take place.

The overall effect is to lose the place-boundedness of significant components of the global information economy. This loss entails the eviction of a whole array of activities and types of workers from the account about the process of globalization which, I argue, are as much a part of it as is international finance. And by evicting these activities and workers, it excludes the variety of cultural contexts within which they exist, a cultural diversity that is as much a presence in processes of globalization as is the new international corporate culture. The terrain within which the dominant account represents economic globalization captures, I argue, only a fraction of the actual economic operations involved. It reconstitutes large portions of the city's economy in „cultural" terms – the spaces of the amalgamated other, the „other" as culture. My purpose is to reframe the terrain of the economy, incorporating the discontinuity between what is represented as economic and what is represented as cultural in the broad sense of the term – the „center" as economy and the „other" as culture. In so doing I reconstitute „the" economy as a multiplicity of economies with distinct organizational patterns. It also invites a re-reading of the notion of a unitary economic system, a notion central to mainstream economic thought and encapsuled in the notion of „the" economy.

How do we reintroduce place in economic analysis? And secondly, how do we construct a new narrative about economic globalization, one which includes rather than evicts all the spatial, economic and cultural elements that are part of the global economy as it is constituted in cities.

For me as a political economist, addressing these issues has meant working in several systems of representation and constructing spaces of intersection. There are analytic moments when two systems of representation intersect. Such analytic moments are easily experienced as spaces of silence, of absence. One challenge is to see what happens in those spaces, what operations (analytic, of power, of meaning) take place there.

One version of these spaces of intersection is what I have called analytic borderlands. Why borderlands? Because they are spaces that are constituted in terms of discontinuities; in them discontinuities are given a terrain rather than reduced to a dividing line. Much of my work on economic globalization and cities has focused on these discontinuities and has sought to reconstitute them analytically as borderlands rather than dividing lines. This produces a terrain within which these discontinuities can be reconstituted in terms of economic operations whose properties are not merely a function of the spaces on each side (i. e., a reduction to the condition of dividing line) but also, and most centrally, of the discontinuity itself, the argument being that discontinuities are an integral part, a component, of the economic system.

Methodologically, the construction of these analytic borderlands pivots on what I call circuits for the distribution and installation of economic operations. These circuits allow me to follow economic activities into terrains that escape the increasingly narrow borders of mainstream representations of „the" economy and to negotiate the crossing of discontinuous spaces. It also underlines how the particular distribution and installation of economic operations over a variety of terrains is but one possible form of the materialization of economic activity.

These are the instruments through which I want to re-read the city's economy in a way that recovers organizational, spatial and cultural dimensions that are now lost in the dominant representation of that economy. I do this in three sections. The first is a brief discussion as to why cities are useful arenas within which to explore the limitations of this narrative. Secondly, I explain why crucial aspects of the most advanced sectors of the economy are place-bound, a fact disregarded in the mainstream account of the information economy, and especially its global dimension. Why does this matter? Because recovering place in the analyses of the economy, particularly place as constituted in major cities, allows us to see the multiplicity of economies and work cultures in which the global information economy is embedded. It also allows us to recover the concrete, localized processes through which globalization exists and to argue that much of the multi-culturalism in large cities is as much a part of globalization as is international finance. The third section examines how space is inscribed in the urban economy, and particularly how the spaces of corporate culture, which are a representation of the space of power in today's cities, are actually contested spaces. The overall purpose is to bring these various elements together in an effort to move from an economic narrative of eviction to one of inclusion.

1. Why focus on cities in this inquiry?

These questions can be usefully explored in large cities such as New York and Los Angeles, Paris and Amsterdam, and any of the other major Western European cities, for at least two reasons. First, cities are the sites for concrete operations of the economy. For now we can distinguish two forms of this. One is about economic globalization and place. Cities are strategic places which concentrate command functions, global markets, and, I add, production sites for the new advanced information industries. The other form through which this concreteness can be captured is by an examination of the day to day work in the leading economic complex, finance and specialized services. Such an examination makes it clear that a large share of the jobs involved in finance, for example, are lowly paid clerical and manual jobs, many held by women and immigrants. These types of workers and jobs do not fit the dominant representation of what the premier economic complex of our era is about.

Secondly, the city concentrates diversity. Its spaces are inscribed with the dominant corporate culture but also with multiple other cultures and identities. The slippage is evident: the dominant culture can encompass only part of the city. And while corporate power inscribes non-corporate cultures and identities with „otherness," thereby devaluing them, these are present everywhere. This presence is especially strong in our major cities which also have the largest concentrations of corporate power. We see here an interesting correspondence between great concentrations of corporate power and large concentrations of „others." It invites us to see that globalization is not only constituted in terms of capital and the new international corporate culture (international finance, telecommunications, information flows) but also in terms of people and non-corporate cultures. There is a whole infrastructure of low-wage, non professional jobs and activities that constitute a crucial part of the so-called corporate economy.

I now want to move to a rather straightforward account of the distinct ways in which place, and particularly the type of place represented by large cities, matters in today's global economy.

2. Place in the global economy

We can begin this inquiry by asking whether an economic system characterized by pronounced concentration of ownership and control can have a space economy that lacks points of intense agglomeration. Elsewhere (2001) I have argued at great length that the territorial dispersal of economic activity made possible by global telecommunications creates a need for expanded central control functions – if this dispersal is to occur under conditions of continued economic concentration. Globalization has engendered a new logic for agglomeration, a new spatial dynamic between dispersal and centralization. The neutralization of distance through telematics has as its correlate a new type of central place.

One way of capturing this is through the image of cities as *command centers* in a global economic system. The notion of command centers is actually one that lacks content. In the specialized literature it is usually thought of in terms of the power and global reach of large corporations. I have sought to give it content, to capture the „production" of global command functions, the work of global control and management.

Focusing on production rather than simply on the enormous power of large corporations and banks brings into view the wide array of economic activities, many outside the corporation, necessary to produce and reproduce that power. An exclusive focus on the power of corporations and banks would leave out a number of issues concerning the social, economic and spatial impact of these activities on the cities where they are located.

The domestic and international dispersal of loci of growth and the internationalization of finance bring to the fore questions concerning the incorporation of such growth into the profit-generating processes that contribute to economic concentration. That is to say, while in principle the territorial decentralization of economic activity could have been accompanied by a corresponding decentralization in ownership and hence in the appropriation of profits, there has been little movement in that direction. Though large firms have increased their subcontracting to smaller firms and many national firms in the newly industrializing countries have grown rapidly, this form of growth is ultimately part of a chain in which a limited number of corporations continue to control the end product and to reap the profits associated with selling on the world market. Even industrial homeworkers in remote rural areas are now part of that chain (Beneria, Roldan, 1992).

This is not only evident with firms, it is also evident with places. Thus, the internationalization and expansion of finance has brought growth to a large number of smaller financial markets, a growth which has fed the expansion of the global industry. But top level control and management of the industry have become concentrated in a few leading financial centers, especially New York,

London, Tokyo, Frankfurt, Paris, and other such cities. These account for a disproportionate share of all financial transactions and one that has grown rapidly since the early 1980s.

The fundamental dynamic posited here is that the more globalized the economy becomes the higher the agglomeration of central functions in global cities. The extremely high densities evident in the downtown districts of these cities are the spatial expression of this logic. The widely accepted notion that agglomeration has become obsolete when global telecommunication advances should allow for maximum dispersal, is only partly correct. It is, I argue, precisely because of the territorial dispersal facilitated by telecommunication advances that agglomeration of centralizing activities has expanded immensely. [1] This is not a mere continuation of old patterns of agglomeration but, one could posit, a new logic for agglomeration.

Information technologies are yet another factor contributing to the new logic for agglomeration. These technologies make possible the geographic dispersal *and* simultaneous integration of many activities. But the distinct conditions under which such facilities are available have promoted centralization of the most advanced users in the most advanced telecommunications centers. Even though a few newer urban centers have built advanced telecommunications facilities, entry costs are increasingly high, and there is a tendency for telecommunications to be developed in conjunction with major users, which are typically firms with large national and global markets. Indeed there is a close relationship between the growth of international markets for finance and trade, the tendency for major firms to concentrate in major cities and the development of telecommunications infrastructures in such cities. Firms with global markets or global production processes require advanced telecommunications facilities. And the acceleration of the financial markets and their internationalization make access to advanced

---

1   In the case of the financial industry I argue that this dynamic is central as well but that there are two distinct phases. Up to the end of the 1982 third world debt crisis, the large transnational banks dominated the financial markets both in terms of volume and the nature of firm transactions. After 1982, this dominance is increasingly challenged by other financial institutions and the major innovations they produce. These lead to a transformation in the leading components of the financial industry, a proliferation of financial institutions and the rapid internationalization of financial markets. The marketplace and the advantages of agglomeration assumed new significance in the 1980s and led simultaneously to a) the incorporation of a variety of markets all over the world into a global system which fed the growth of the industry after the 1982 debt crisis and b) new forms of concentration, specifically the centralization of the industry in a few leading financial centers. Hence, in the case of the financial industry, a focus on the large transnational banks would exclude precisely those sectors of the industry where much of the new growth and production of innovations has occurred and it would, again, leave out an examination of the wide range of activities, firms and markets that constitute the financial industry in the 1980s and 1990s.

telecommunications facilities essential. The main demand for telecommunication services comes from information intensive industries which, in turn, tend to locate in major cities which have such facilities.

Besides being command points, I see two additional ways in which major cities are strategic places in the global economy. One is as production sites for finance and specialized services, and the other as transnational marketplaces for these products.

2.1. Production Sites

Centralized control and management over a geographically dispersed array of plants, offices, and service outlets does not come about inevitably as part of a „world system." It requires the development of a vast range of highly specialized services and of top level management and control functions. These constitute the components for „global control capability".

By focusing on the production of this capability, I am seeking to displace the focus of attention from the familiar issue of the power of large corporations over governments and economies; or the issue of supracorporate concentration of power through interlocking directorates or organizations such as the IMF. I want to focus on an aspect that has received less attention, what could be referred to as the *practice* of global control: the work of producing and reproducing the organization and management of a global production system and a global marketplace for finance, both under conditions of economic concentration. This allows me to focus on the infrastructure of jobs involved in this production. Furthermore, while it is typical to think of finance and specialized services as a matter of expertise rather than production, the elaboration of, for example, a financial instrument requires inputs from law, accounting, advertising. There is a production complex in the advanced service economy that benefits from agglomeration. In addition, the actual production process includes a variety of workers and firms that are not usually thought of as being part of the information economy.

The growth of advanced services for firms along with their particular characteristics of production helps to explain the centralization of management and servicing functions that fueled the economic boom beginning in the 1980s in cities such as New York, London Tokyo, Amsterdam, Toronto, and so on. The face-to-face explanation needs to be refined in several ways. Advanced services are mostly producer services; unlike other types of services, they are not dependent on vicinity to the consumers served. Rather, economies occur in such specialized firms when they locate close to others that produce key inputs or whose proximity makes possible joint production of certain service offerings. Moreover, concentration arises out of the needs and expectations of the people likely to be employed in these new high-skill jobs. They are attracted to the amenities and life-styles that large urban centers can offer. The accounting firm can service its clients at a distance, but the nature of its service depends on proximity to specialists, lawyers, programmers. In this sense then, one can speak of *production sites*.

2. 2. Transnational marketplaces

Globalization does not *only* consist of instantaneous transmission around the globe; much of it takes place in markets and these are situated in particular places. Cities are the location for market transactions in global finance and specialized services. These are markets where firms, governments and individuals from all around the world can engage in transactions that often bypass the „host" country.

Multi-site forms of organization in manufacturing, services and banking have created an expanded demand for a wide range of specialized service activities to manage and control global networks of factories, service outlets and branch offices. While to some extent these activities can be carried out in-house, a large share is not. High levels of specialization, the possibility of externalizing the production of some of these services and the growing demand by large and small firms and by governments, are all conditions that have both resulted from, and made possible, the development of a market for freestanding service firms that produce components for what I refer to as global control capability.

This in turn means that small firms can buy components of that capability, such as management consulting or international legal advice. And so can firms and governments from anywhere in the world. In brief, while the large corporation is undoubtedly a key agent inducing the development of this capability and is its prime beneficiary, it is not the sole user.

This focus on the *work* behind command functions, on *production* in the finance and services complex, and on market*places* has the effect of incorporating the material facilities underlying globalization and the whole infrastructure of jobs typically not marked as belonging to the corporate sector of the economy: Besides the already mentioned work of secretaries and cleaners, there are the truckers who deliver the software, the variety of technicians and repair workers, all the jobs having to do with the maintenance, painting, renovation of the buildings where it all is housed.

This can lead to the recognition that there are multiple economies involved in constituting the global information economy. It allows for a valorization of types of activities, workers and firms that have never been installed in the „center" of the economy or have been evicted from that center in the restructuring that began in the 1980s and have therefore been devalorized in a system that overvalorizes the „center. " Globalization can, then, be seen as a process that involves several economies and work cultures. Yet it is in terms of the corporate economy and the new transnational professional work culture that economic globalization is represented. How can we expand the terrain for this representation to incorporate those other conditions and actors? And how can we make a new reading of the locations where corporate power is now installed, a reading that captures the non-corporate presences in those same sites?

3. Globalization and Inscription

Once we have recovered the centrality of place and of the multiple work cultures within which economic operations are embedded, we are still left confronting a highly restricted terrain for the inscription of economic globalization. Sennett (1991, p. 36) observes that „the space of authority in Western culture has evolved as a space of precision." And Giddens notes the centrality of „expertise" in today's society, with the corresponding transfer of authority and trust to expert systems (Giddens, 1990, pp. 88-91).

Corporate culture is one representation of precision and expertise. Its space has become one of the main spaces of authority in today's cities. The dense concentrations of tall buildings in major downtowns or in the new „edge" cities are the site for corporate culture – though as I will argue later it is also the site for other forms of inhabitation, but these have been made invisible. The vertical grid of the corporate tower is imbued with the same neutrality and rationality attributed to the horizontal grid of American cities.

Much has been said about the protestant ethic as the culture through which the economic operations of capitalism are constituted in the daily life of people. Sennett (1991) opens up a whole new dimension both on the protestant ethic and on the American city by suggesting that what is experienced as a form of rational urban organization, the grid, is actually a far more charged event. It is „the representation in urban design of a protestant language of self and space becoming a modern form of power" (Sennett, 1991, p. 36).

We can recognize that the neutralization of place brought about by the modern grid contains an aspiration to a modern space of precision. This same aspiration is evident in the self-inscription of corporate culture as neutral, as ordered by technology, economic efficiency, rationality. This is put in contrast to what is thought of as the culture of small businesses, or, even more so, ethnic enterprises. Each of these is a partial representation, in one case of the city, in the other of the economy.

The dominant narrative presents the economy as ordered by technical and efficiency principles, and in that sense as neutral. The emergence and consolidation of corporate power appears, then, as an inevitable form that economic growth takes under these ordering principles. The impressive engineering and architectural output evident in the tall corporate towers that dominate our downtowns are a physical embodiment of these principles. And the corporate culture that inhabits these towers and inscribes them is the organizational and behavioral correlate to these ordering principles.

Authority is thereby „divorced from community" (Sennett, 1991, p. 37). „The visual forms of legibility in urban designs or space no longer suggest much about subjective life. . . " (Sennett, 1991, p. 37). Subjective life is installed in a multiplicity of subjectivities, and this undermines the representation of the advanced modern economy as a space of neutrality, the neutrality that comes from technology and efficiency, the ordering principles of a modern economy.

We can easily recognize that both the neutralization of place through the grid in its aspiration to a modern space of precision, *and* the self-inscription of corporate culture as neutral, as ordered by technology and efficiency, are partial representations of the city and of the economy. This inscription needs to be produced and reproduced, and it can never be complete because of all the other presences in the city which are inscribed in urban space. The *representation* of the city contained in the dominant economic narrative can exclude large portions of the lived city and reconstitute them as some amalgamated „other. " The lived city contains multiple spatialities and identities, many indeed articulated and very much a part of the economy, but represented as superfluous, anachronistic or marginal.

Through immigration a proliferation of, in their origin, highly localized cultures now have become presences in many large cities, cities whose elites think of themselves as cosmopolitan, that is transcending any locality, yet cannot recognize the immigrant cultures right there in their city as being part of that broader dynamic of transcending the national. An immense array of cultures from around the world, each rooted in a particular country or village, now are reterritorialized in a few single places, places such as New York, Los Angeles, Paris, London, and most recently Tokyo[2].

The space of the amalgamated other created by corporate culture is constituted as a devalued, downgraded space in the dominant economic narrative: social and physical decay, a burden. In today's New York or Los Angeles, this is the space of the immigrant community, of the black ghetto, and increasingly of

---

2   Tokyo now has several, mostly working-class concentrations of legal and illegal immigrants coming from China, Bangladesh, Pakistan, Philippines. This is quite remarkable in view of Japan's legal and cultural closure to immigrants. Is this simply a function of poverty in those countries? By itself it is not enough of an explanation, since they have long had poverty. I posit that the internationalization of the Japanese economy, including specific forms of investment in those countries and Japan's growing cultural influence there have created bridges between those countries and Japan, and have reduced the subjective distance with Japan (see Sassen, 2001, chapter 9).

the old manufacturing district. In its most extreme version it is the space of the „underclass, full of welfare mothers and drug addicts".

Corporate culture collapses differences, some minute, some sharp, among the different socio-cultural contexts into one amorphous otherness, an otherness that has no place in the economy, the other who holds the low wage jobs that are, supposedly, only marginally attached to the economy. It therewith reproduces the devaluing of those jobs and of those who hold the jobs. By leaving out these articulations, by restricting the referent to the centrally placed sectors of the economy, the dominant economic narrative can present the economy as containing a higher order unity.

The corporate economy evicts these other economies and its workers from economic representation, and the corporate culture represents them as the other. What is not installed in a corporate center is devalued or will tend to be devalued. And what occupies the corporate building in non-corporate ways is made invisible. The fact that most of the people working in the corporate city during the day are low paid secretaries, mostly women, many immigrant or, in US cities, African American women, is not included in the representation of the corporate economy or corporate culture. And the fact that at night a whole other work force installs itself in these spaces, including the offices of the chief executives, and inscribes the space with a whole different culture (manual labor, often music, lunch breaks at midnight) is an invisible event.

In this sense, corporate architecture assumes a whole new meaning beyond the question of the economy of offices and real estate development. The built forms of the corporate economy are representative of its „neutrality" – of being driven by technology and efficiency. Corporate architectural spatiality is one specific form assumed by the circulation of power in the economy, and specifically in the corporate economy. Wigley (1991) notes that the house is not innocent of the violence inside it. And we now know that the design of different types of buildings -homes, factories, „public" lobbies – is shaped by cultural values and social norms.

The supposedly „rational" organization of office space illustrates certain aspects of Foucault's microtechnologies of power (Rakatansky, 1992). But the changes in the details of inhabitation – institutional practices, the types and contents of buildings – indicate there is no univocal relation between these and built form. I agree with Rakatansky's observation that the play of ideologies in architectural form is complex. And I would add that this conception is essential if we are to allow for politics and agency in the built environment. Yes, in some sense, buildings are frozen in time. But they can be re-inscribed. The only way we can think of these towers now is as corporate, *if* located downtown (and as failed public housing project if they are in poor ghettos). Can we re-inscribe these corporate towers in ways that recover the fact that they are also the workplace of a large non-corporate workforce?

Another dimension along which to explore some of these issues is the question of the body. The body is citified, urbanized as a distinctively metropolitan body (Grosz, 1992, p. 241). The particular geographical, architectural, municipal arrangements constituting a city are one particular ingredient in the social constitution of the body; Grosz adds that they are by no means the most important ones. She argues that the structure and particularity of the family and neighborhoods is more influential, though the structure of the city is also contained therein.

„The city orients perception insofar as it helps to produce specific conceptions of spatiality. " (Grosz, 1992, p. 250). The city contributes to the organization of family life, of worklife insofar as it contains a distribution in space of the specific locations for each activity; similarly, architectural spatiality can be seen as one particular component in this broader process of the organization of space. I would add to this that the structure, spatiality and concrete localization of the economy are also influential. In these many ways the city is an active force that „leaves its traces on the subject's corporeality".

But it is citified in diverse ways: it is inscribed by the many socio-cultural environments present in the city and it, in turn, inscribes these. There are two forms in which this weaves itself into the space of the economy. One is that these diverse ways in which the body is inscribed by the diverse socio-cultural contexts that exist in the city, works as a mechanism for segmenting and, in the end for devaluing, and it does so in very concrete ways. For example, research by the anthropologist Philippe Bourgeois shows us the case of an 18 year old Puerto Rican from East Harlem who gets a job as a clerical attendant in an office in downtown Manhattan. He tells us that walking over to the copying machine, past all the secretaries, is humiliating. The way he walks, the way he is dressed, the way he moves presents him to the office staff secretaries and managers as someone from the ghetto. Someone who „doesn't know the proper ways".

The other way in which this diversity weaves itself into the space of the economy is that it re-enters the space of the dominant economic sector as merchandise and as marketing. Of interest here is Stuart Hall's observation that contemporary global culture is different from earlier imperial cultures: it is absorptive, a continuously changing terrain that incorporates the new cultural elements whenever it can. In the earlier period, Hall (1991) argues, the culture of the empire, epitomized by Englishness, was exclusionary, seeking always to reproduce its difference. At the same time today's global culture cannot absorb everything, it is always a terrain for contestation, and its edges are certainly always in flux. The process of absorption can never be complete.

One question is whether the argument developed earlier regarding the neutralization of space brought about by the grid, and the system of values it entails or seeks to produce in space, also occurs with cultural globalization. As with the grid, „global" culture never fully succeeds in this neutralization; yet absorption does alter the „other" that is absorbed. An interesting issue here that emerges out of my work on the urban economy is whether at some point all the „others" (at its most extreme, the informal economy) carry enough weight to transform the center. In the case of culture one can see that the absorption of multiple cultural elements along with the cultural politics so evident in large cities, have transformed global culture. Yet it is still centered in the West, its technologies, its images, as Hall argues. Thus absorbed the other cultures are neutralized. And yet ... they are also present. We can perhaps see this most clearly in urban space, where a multiplicity of other work cultures, cultural environments, and culturally inscribed bodies increasingly inhabit a built terrain that has its origins visibly in another culture, the culture lying behind the grid. Here again, I ask, at what point does the "curve effect", as social scientists would put it, take hold and bring the center down.

4. Conclusion

We cannot restrict our account of the global information economy to global *transmissions* and information *outputs*. Likewise, we cannot restrict our representations of economic globalization to the new transnational corporate culture and the corporate towers it inhabits. Globalization is a contradictory space; it is characterized by contestation, internal differentiation, continuous border crossings. The global city is emblematic of this condition. In seeking to show that a) these types of cities are strategic to economic globalization because they are command points, global marketplaces and production sites for the information economy, and b) that many of the devalued sectors of the urban economy actually fulfill crucial functions for the center, I try to recover the importance of cities precisely in a globalized economic system and thereby to make a countervailing argument. It is all the intermediary sectors of the economy (such as routine office work, headquarters that are not geared to the world markets; the variety of services demanded by the largely suburbanized middle class) and of the urban population (i. e. , the middle class) that can and have left cities. The two sectors that have remained, the center and the „other" find in the city the strategic terrain for their operations.

Select references

Beneria, L., Roldan M. (1992). *Unequal Burden: Economic Crises, Persistent Poverty and Women's Work.* Boulder, CO: Westview Press.

Bourgeois, P. (1996). *In Search of Respect: Selling Crack in El Barrio*. Structural Analysis in the Social Sciences Series. New York: Cambridge University Press.

Cordero-Guzman, H. R., Smith, R. C. & Grosfoguel, R. (Eds) (2001). *Migration, Transnationalization, and Race in a Changing New York*. Philadelphia, Pa: Temple University Press.

Fincher, R. & Jacobs, J. M. (Eds) (1998). *Cities of Difference*. New York: Guilford Press.

Grosz, E., Bodies-Cities. In Colomina, B. (Ed.) (1992). *Sexuality & Space*. Princeton Papers on Architecture. Princeton: Princeton Architectural Press, pp. 241-253.

Hamilton, N. & Stoltz Chinchilla, N. (2001). *Seeking Community in a Global City: Guatemalans and Salvadorans in Los Angeles*. Philadelphia: Temple University Press.

Hall, S. (1991). The Local and the Global: Globalization and Ethnicity. In Anthony D. King (Ed.), *Current Debates in Art History 3. Culture, Globalization and the World-System: Contemporary Conditions for the Representation of Identity*. Department of Art and Art History, State University of New York at Binghamton.

Harvey, D. (1985). *The Urbanization of Capital*. Oxford: Blackwell.

Holston, J. (Ed) (1996). Cities and Citizenship. A Special Issue of *Public Culture*. Vol. 8, nr. 2.

Rakatansky, M. (1992). Spatial Narratives. In Whiteman, J., Kipnis, J. & and Burdett, R. *Strategies in Architectural Thinking*. Chicago: Chicago Institute for Architecture and Urbanism, and Cambridge: The MIT Press, pp. 198-221.

Sassen, S. (2001). *The Global City*. (2nd Edition). Princeton: Princeton University Press.

Sennett, R. (1991). *The Conscience of the Eye: The Design and Social Life of Cities*. New York: Norton.

Valle, V. M. & Torres. R. D. (2000). *Latino Metropolis*. Minneapolis, Mn: University of Minnesota Press.

Wigley, M. (1992) Untitled: The Housing of Gender. In Colomina, Beatriz (Ed.). *Sexuality & Space*. Princeton Papers on Architecture. Princeton: Princeton Architectural Press, pp. 327-390.

Part III:
Transnational Gender Democracy:
Difference and Equality

Ilse Lenz, Helen Schwenken

Feminist and Migrant Networking in a Globalising World
Migration, Gender and Globalisation[1]

Globalisation promotes the movement of people, but migration is also a basic process of globalisation. In the last decades women's and men's migration was largely motivated by the pull of global or transnational labour markets. For example, while Turkish and Korean men migrated to Germany in the 1960s and 1970s to work in car factories or mines, Turkish women migrants worked in the electronics industries or as domestic workers, and Korean women migrated as trained nurses. Migrants are also forced out of their countries by environmental degradation, which, for example, increases the stress for women to provide food and water, or by the numerous wars and conflicts, which are increasing in the shadow of the new global world order. Whereas older people, women and children tend to stay in the refugee camps close to conflict areas, younger men and women search for opportunities for global migration. Political and gender repression by dictatorships, military regimes and some fundamentalist patriarchal rulers, have also led to increasing numbers of refugees. Finally we have the global intellectuals, scientists, business people, writers, artists or filmmakers who simultaneously live in Bombay and New York or Moscow and Berlin. Migrants take the initiative to realise their wishes and visions of their future. They are actors (not victims) – often moving in difficult environments – and therefore we want to focus on their agency in this article. Despite their active involvement, they still tend to have less power than the dominant autochthonous strata in immigration societies, and female migrants especially experience the interlinkage of gender, ethnicity and class as restrictive.

Globalisation is a moving force of the new migration. The dominant discourse on globalisation characterises it mainly as an economic process based on the deregulation and expansion of the capitalist market. In this article we aim for

---

1 This article is based on long going cooperation between the authors – also in the *ifu*-curriculum on migration. We want to thank the *ifu*-colleagues, researchers and the *ifu* project group „International feminist and migrant's networking" for stimulating discussions. We are very grateful to Verena Schmidt for her suggestions and to Heike Alberts for her sensible language editing.

a more complex and integrated perspective. First, we will develop a broader framework of globalisation, which focuses on economic, political and communicative processes, and we will locate migration in this context. Starting from this framework we will investigate options for new ways of social regulation in globalisation: While deregulation is a dominant current promoted and pushed by global institutions such as the IMF and the WTO, new social regulations have also been negotiated between supranational institutions such as the UN, states and civil society, and social movements, especially feminist networks. The international gender regimes, which are emerging from the decades of women (1975-1995), are a fascinating example.

The issue whether migrants from their disadvantaged position can also open up and use these new options is highly relevant. We want to consider it from looking at the women migrants' organisations and networks in Germany as they establish new transnational spaces of political and social meaning, and fight for new opportunities and renegotiate social regulations. Our contribution is about the Western European case, specifically the German. Western Europe is a migrant and refugee receiving region with distinctive repressive policies against refugees and migrants (see Lutz in this volume). Therefore we focus on opportunities for and restrictions of refugee and migrant women in order to articulate some of their concerns in this specific environment.

1. A Working Definition of Globalisation

Looking at gender and globalisation means to trace complex inequalities and the ways these interlink. In dramatic ways gender is mediated by world region, race and class. Globalisation processes are contradictory and uneven. The global economy has grown, but participation in it as well as the results have been different in different places. For example, the UN showed in 1985 that women perform two thirds of all the work in the world, but receive only 10% of the income generated by this work and have access to only of 1% of the productive resources. The first gender-sensitive World Population Report points out that one in every three women has experienced sexual violence or other forms of violence. Four million women and girls are sold annually into marriage, prostitution or slavery (Süddeutsche Zeitung October 19, 2000).

New sociological approaches have broadened the narrow economic focus of the first rounds of debates on globalisation. Without neglecting the crucial role of the globalising economy, they highlight the new quality of interdependence on a global scale (Giddens, 2001) opening new options as well as creating new risks. Giddens considers globalisation as a „two way flow of images, information and influences", "a 'decentred' and reflexive process characterised by links and cultural flows which work in a multidirectional way", and as „the product of numerous intertwined networks" (Giddens, 2001, pp. 59-60). These new forms of information and interdependence result in new reconfigurations of time and space, which transcend the order of the nation state, thus leading to transformations in which „established boundaries between 'internal' and 'external', 'international' and 'domestic'" are breaking down (ibid.).

In these approaches, globalisation appears as a „dynamic and open process that is subject to influence and change" (Giddens, 2001, p. 59), and the crucial factors are information and communication as well as flexible network organisations. Thus globalisation can be interpreted as opening new horizons of new opportunities, while simultaneously creating new risks. But we are wondering from a gender perspective how to relate these technology- and information-centered concepts to embodied subjects, i.e. persons with minds, emotions and bodies who want to live, work, reproduce and migrate in the context of globalisation. Looking at female migrants creating feminist movements and networks can open up new perspectives on globalisation and make women visible as actors.

Sylvia Walby emphasises the connections between modernization and globalisation. Both trends work towards a public gender order, integrating women in work, social movements, and politics (Walby, 2001). In the wake of both interrelated processes, the former hegemonial gender orders are eroding or changing. A critique of globalisation, however, which turns to the protected space of the nation state with a nostalgic gaze, tends to neglect its underlying neo-patriarchal gender order. The Western hegemonic national gender orders for example were characterized by the division of public and private and the allocation of women to the domestic sphere. While including men and women of the dominant cultural or ethnic group, they exclude minorities or migrant groups (Lenz, 1999).

Basically, globalisation emerges less in the form of a new deterministic structure, but rather as a set of interlinked, often contradictory and open processes. As globalisation processes lead to increasing economic and political interdependence and create new spaces of cultural and informational exchange, these fields are extending from the global to the national and local spaces. Globalisation processes are changing the following four fields of action and imply increasing interdependence:

1. Politics: growing international political interdependence
2. Economics: growing economic interdependence
3. Information, communication and mobility: increasing information and communication by new and old media and by personal mobility (migration, tourism, scientific exchange/conferences)
4. Ecology: ecological interdependence with new risks and chances.

Three of these global fields of action[2] will be briefly discussed now from a gender perspective:

1.1 The Political Field: Increasing International Political Interdependence

The importance of global or supranational organisations such as the UN or the EU has grown. The EU is becoming crucial for gender policy because for example about two thirds of the political decisions relevant for states are predicated or preinfluenced on the EU level. Gender mainstreaming[3] was introduced in the 1997 Amsterdam Treaty and is being transposed into some national legislation.

Whereas the nation state is changing its functions, but by no means disappearing, the regional and local levels of decision-making become more important within the EU multilevel governance. Especially the region turns into a space of negotiation and intersection, while global enterprises and regional strategies attempt to build clusters of economic innovation, science and technology transfer, and human capital development. Regional disparities and new demands on „flexible personalities" who are dissociated from providing care relationships are linked to these trends.

Political globalisation is marked by a dual democratic deficit: Accountability and representation become diffuse or non-existent in view of non-elected supranational political decision-making organisations. The gender democratic deficit is also dramatic as women are pervasively excluded: In the UN only 13% of the leading positions were filled with women in 1995. Women's membership in the European Parliament grew from 16,1% in 1979 to 31% in 2002 (IPU, 2002). Parallel to globalisation, women's political participation on the global, supranational and national levels has increased with the exception of the post-socialist countries in Eastern Europe. While only a few countries have reached the 30% target[4] of the Fourth World Conference on Women in Peking (1995) for female

---

2   Due to limited space it is not possible to discuss the field of ecology in which feminist networking has been important.

3   The European Commission formulates the main idea of gender mainstreaming as the „systematic consideration of the differences between the conditions, situations and needs of women and men in all Community policies and actions [...]. This does not mean simply making Community programmes or resources more accessible to women, but rather the simultaneous mobilisation of legal instruments, financial resources and the Community's analytical and organisational capacities in order to introduce in all areas the desire to build balanced relationships between women and men" (European Commission, 1996).

4   Only eight countries reached the target of a 30% share of women in parliament, set at the Fourth World Conference on Women in Peking 1995, among them five countries from Northern Europe, Germany, the Netherlands and South Africa (Unifem, 2000, p. 76).

parliamentarians and there are severe setbacks in some Eastern European and Sub-Saharan African Countries, in large parts of the world empowerment of women has increased, as is evidenced by the growing share of female members of parliament and of female administrators and managers (Unifem, 2000, pp. 76-84; UNDP, 2000, p. 165).

1.2. The Economic Field

Economic globalisation has been at the centre of the debate. The most dynamic and dramatic interdependence has emerged in the deregulation of financial markets from national controls. A parallel move is the globalisation of the stock markets and the increasing importance of shareholder value. The financial markets have been divorced from their national contexts and regulatory institutions and are publicly perceived as anonymous flows without the intervention of human agency. Research about new institutional frameworks is therefore crucial.[5]

Transnational corporations (TNCs) become visible as relevant global actors. On the one hand, their number has multiplied nearly ten-fold from about 7,000 in 1969 to about 60,000 with 800,000 affiliates abroad in the year 2000 (UNCTAD, 2001, p. 1; Lenz, 2000a, p. 28). Ninety of the largest one hundred TNCs are headquartered in the Northern Triad of the United States, the European Union (EU), and Japan. In the industrial sector, they concentrate in electrical and electronic equipment, and motor vehicles (UNCTAD, 2001). The top ten TNCs from developing or newly industrialised countries originate mainly from East Asia and focus on motor vehicles, electronics, diversified industries (South Korea, Hongkong) and petroleum (Venezuela, Malaysia) (UNCTAD, 2001).

The impact of TNCs on gendered labour markets has been contradictory and unequal. Whereas the quantitative impact of transnational employment has been highlighted, less attention has been given to its qualitative effects, especially the increment of TNCs' power due to their global organisational capacities and their contribution to the modernization of gender segregation.[6] Mass production industries like electrical and electronics or the car industry have made extensive use of the strategy of offshore production based on a continuation of their stereotypical division of labour. Whereas new models of flexible organisation

---

5   A widespread concept proposed e.g. by the *Attac* network is the so called Tobin tax: A light tax amounting to some percents should be levelled on all short term currency investments thus discouraging speculation.

6   The world's largest TNCs in 1999 employed an estimated 5,82 million persons (UNCTAD, 2001, p. 6). But one should keep in mind that the labour force in OECD countries was an estimated 372 million in 1995, and in East Asia and the Pacific an estimated 963 million (Filmer, 1995, p. 18), so only a minority is employed by TNCs. Also many dynamic TNCs are much smaller.

may have contributed partially to eroding or diffusing gender segmentation lines in the North, segregation has been reconstituted in the Free Production Zones and offshore plants especially in the South. As these plants employ educated women, often with high school degrees, for simple jobs without upward mobility, rigid gender segregation patterns have been globalised as well.

In some highly qualified service or knowledge industries such as in software as well as in call centres, men and women with tertiary training are employed, thus contributing to mixed fields or more blurred forms of a gender divisions of labour.

Whereas a modernization of gender roles can be observed in the middle ranges of management and skilled work especially in parts of the service and knowledge sector, segregation and retraditionalisation of sex stereotyping has characterised offshore production in the South and parts of the East. Also, many large TNCs have adopted affirmative action or diversity schemes to mobilise and effectively utilise a transnational workforce, including skilled women in middle management. Therefore, contradictory trends of both a reconstitution of gender segregation at a large scale and desegregation can be observed. The polarisation between different groups of working women, however, may increase.

A marked global trend is the flexibilisation of the labour force which set in with women, but in some regions is slowly spreading to men. Part time work, self employment or new forms of contract work have been increasing, involving less skilled as well as skilled women.[7]

The general impact of economic globalisation on the gender division of labour extends beyond the roles of TNCs for labour markets, however, because it also strongly influences the welfare states in their regional context. It may be surmised that this influence on the welfare states will lead to rearrangements of paid, unpaid and voluntary or civic work. Diane Elson designed a useful scheme to outline the relationships between gender and work in the global economy (cf. diagram 1; Unifem, 2000, p. 30).

---

[7] For an overview of the literature cf. Wichterich, 2000; Lenz, 2002.

Diagram 1: Globalisation and the Changing Gender Division of Labour

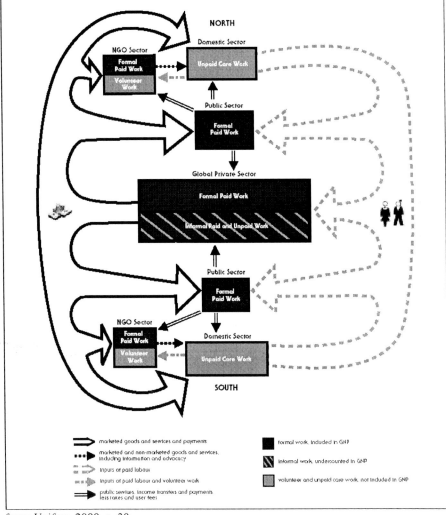

from: Unifem, 2000, p. 30

The global private sector is positioned at the centre; it is based on formal paid work as well as on informal paid or unpaid work, such as subcontracting or unpaid family work. The public sector undertakes paid care work, but relies on unpaid care work mostly by women in the domestic sector in the North and South. The NGO sector is contributing volunteer and unpaid work. Financial restructuring, especially in form of IMF measures, exerted strong pressure on public sectors in the South. Public health and education expenditures were cut back, and the services were partially or largely relegated to unpaid work in the domestic sector and some NGOs. In the North, the reorientation of welfare states from subsidies to promotion of employment, neglects the issue of who will do unpaid care work now. New evidence shows some success of integrating women into the new dual career working patterns as well as problematic trends as that many women join the 'working poor', and that some women become 'welfare drop-outs', now concentrating on informal work and unpaid care work. Unpaid and care work may become invisible again in view of the political priority of wage work.

Elson's diagram also renders visible the permanent transfer of persons with their capacities, experiences and wishes from the South and the East to the North in the form of migration. In the North migrants are being relocated mostly into labour market segments with less pay and security, and migrant women are often pulled into reproductive work such as domestic, health or sex work. Some authors assume that a redistribution of housework is taking place between white middle class women who now enter careers, and migrant women who have to accept household and care work for low pay and with little security. Thus, at the detriment of migrant women, a redistribution of care work between men and women is supposedly avoided (Lutz, 2000). German data, however, point to a special configuration of a rather limited group of upper class and upper middle class women with migrant houseworkers but no broad replacement of German former housewives and female employees by migrant women. In Germany, 15,9 million women were economically active in 2000 (Statistisches Bundesamt, 2002). In 1999, 12 million women were employees (3,58 million among them working part time), and 11,3 million of them had a German passport. This large group cannot primarily have relied on female migrant care workers as female migrants in 1998 numbered about 3,3 million (2,3 million among them in the main working age groups between 18 and 61) (Beauftragte der Bundesregierung für Ausländerfragen 2000). Furthermore, the total number of households which employ someone for domestic work on a regular basis or from time to time are three to four million. Part time work by women is another important strategy by which a large scale redistribution of care work with fathers or male partners is avoided (Klammer et al., 2000).

To allow some insight into the socio-economic situation of migrant women living in Germany we will now present some general data.[8] In Germany there are currently about 7,3 million registered, and up to one million unregistered, migrants, about 45% of whom are female migrants. Germany thus has a migrant population of about 9%. Most migrants came in the 1960s from Southern Europe or Turkey as so called guest workers or later due to family reunification. Since 1990 migration from Middle and Eastern Europe became more important.

---

8   For more detailed information and for the following data cf. BMFSFJ 2000; Bundesaus-
    länderbeauftragte 1997; Beauftragte der Bundesregierung für Ausländerfragen 2001,
    2002.

About 2,6 million foreign nationals have jobs integrated into the social security system. For most, the wage gap is growing between Germans and foreign nationals, except for certain groups of highly skilled ones. Among German employed women 22% are industrial workers and 65% are white collar workers, but among foreign women the shares are 53% to 37% respectively. As German and EU nationals have to be given priority in job recruitment according to state regulations, it is also difficult for non EU-nationals and especially refugees to apply successfully for a job. The unemployment rate for migrants, especially women, is more than double that of German nationals (about 20% for migrants and 33% for female migrants in 1997). Informal employment of migrants (undocumented migrants as well as those having a residence permit but no working permit, or having both but working without reporting it to the social security institutions), is widespread. These female migrants are mostly found in urban regions in personal services, cleaning jobs, domestic work or prostitution.

1.3 The Field of Information, Communication and Mobility

Three aspects are especially relevant:

1. Global Communication
The globalisation of communication and media make it possible to be informed about major developments on the global level in „real time". The image of the reconfiguration of time and space is strongly relying on these new opportunities of 'simultaneous ubiquity' or the representation of getting access to information „all over the place all the time". The Internet is a current symbol for the new global modes of communication. But to use these new options, organisations and individuals need access, resources and power. Existing evidences suggest large, but complex patterns of inequality in access according to world region, development level, class, and gender. According to the UN Human Development Report 1999 the world region is crucial: In 1998 „industrial countries – home to less than 15% of people – constituted 88% of Internet users. By contrast South Asia is home to over 20% of all people but had less than 1% of the world's Internet users" (UNDP, 1999, p. 63). Furthermore „current access to the Internet runs along the fault lines of national societies, dividing educated from illiterate, men from women, rich from poor, young from old, urban from rural" (UNDP, 1999, p. 63). The largest groups of Internet users are well educated, white, under 35 years old – and male (cf. UNDP 1999, p. 63). The billions of poor people with little access to education, especially poorer and older women, tend to be excluded.

But whereas access is still largely limited to groups which are also global or national elites, one example may illustrate that access to and use of global communication is not determined solely by world region, class or gender: In the

Philippines, less than one per cent of the entire population has Internet access, but women make up 43% of the users compared to 35% in Germany (UN, 2000, p. 96; UNDP, 1999, p. 63). Whereas women were initially hesitant about using the Internet, their participation increased fast at least in the North. Feminist networks all over the world have increasingly, and often enthusiastically, used the Internet as a medium of information, exchange and strategy coordination during the UN decades of women. Global networks are forming based on decentred plurilocal forms of communication and organisation, and feminist networks have played the role of pioneers.

2. Transnational migration

Global communication is not limited to technology transporting information, but migrants with their minds and bodies are also on the move. The new mobility and patterns of migration promoted the formation of transnational migrant networks and communities (Pries, 2001). Furthermore, migration has become feminized: the share of women has increased, and women take an active role in migration networks.

Especially two groups have new potentials and capacities for developing new approaches to transnational communication and networking: Some groups of second generation migrants develop complex and flexible identities and search for newly integrated perspectives on gender democracy.[9] As we will show later, they have important positions in communicating international perspectives to the women's movement and play crucial roles in transnational antiracist and feminist policy networks. The second group are transnational diaspora intellectuals who have proposed creative and very influential feminist approaches towards economic, political and cultural globalisation.[10]

3. Discourses on Human/Women's Rights and Global Democracy and the Formation of Feminist Networks and Action Groups

People and ideas on the move have met in global or transnational feminist networks. These networks experienced an opening of political opportunities during the UN decades of women from 1975 to the present. They grew rapidly in scope. By discussing the issues which they brought from local or national contexts or from global developments, and by learning through „conflicts in sisterhood", they have placed a multifocal set of issues on an expanding transnational agenda. In a process of communicating and network organising, feminist net-

---

9   Research on the migrant women's movement in Germany found out that about in half of the groups migrant women from different countries of origin were active; cf. Schwenken, 2000. These studies also show that trends towards fixed national identities or cultural nationalism are also present, but that transnationalism is an influential approach. Cf. Gutíerrez Rodríguez 1999.

10 One fascinating example is the special issue of Signs on globalisation; cf. Signs Vol. 26, 4, Summer 2001.

works were able to raise consciousness about and develop discourses on in-equality in work and education, violence against women, ecology as a gender is-sue, and the equal participation of women in politics and decision making. For this they had to find shared or common concepts in which their differences could be respected. For example, women's movements from different socio-cultural backgrounds came to share concepts like equality in work or lobbying for women's empowerment on a global level; but they give different meanings to and develop different strategies for realising these concepts in their contexts. The approach of women's/human rights proved very productive in finding a shared language. This approach made it possible to bridge differences and to develop convergent strategies of women's movements in the South, East and West, and allowed it to be translated into the global discourses of human rights and social issues. Thus global feminist and transnational networks and women's movements could influence the UN processes around the decades of women and the UN social conferences from the Rio conference on ecology in 1992 to the world social summit in 1996, as well as put pressure on governments.

Taking into account all these developments related to globalisation we argue for a broader understanding of globalisation and for overcoming its narrow eco-nomic focus. We propose to define globalisation *as an ensemble of interlinked processes with possibly open results characterised by*

- *increasing economic, political, social and ecological interdependence*
- *increasing global communication and mobility and*
- *increasing influence of new actors – especially supranational organisations, transnational enterprises and Civil Society Organisations (CSOs) or NGOs.*

These new actors can expand and promote the range of their options according to their material, organisational and power resources, as well as their capacity and potential for orientation, reflexivity and learning in the new complex global games. Global orientation and communication capacities become crucial for or-ganisations in globalisation. Some transnational networks of migrants have proved rather fruitful in that they have a long experience in inter- and transna-tional cooperation which they now benefit from. Besides these capacities of po-litical actors we have to consider unequal political opportunity structures which we will explain in the next section.[11]

---

11 In social movement theory these issues have been discussed as structural approaches ("political opportunity structure"), but closely connected to the nation state. Therefore one has to modify them due to new constellations. But the assumption that social move-ments develop and act in a political and social context that restricts or enables their pos-sibilities, and on which the movements only have a limited influence, is still important. Among scholars there is a broad consensus concerning the following four dimensions of political opportunity structure: 1. "The relative openness or closure of the institutional-ised political system; 2. The stability or instability of that broad set of elite alignments

The globalisation of communication, discourses and social movements, especially women's movements, suggests that new actors besides nation states and corporations enter the international stage to create an unprecedented diversity. Whereas the first international feminist networks before 1940 consisted of professional or upper class women and were centred on the West (Rupp, 1997), now representatives of working women, female farmers or students and „everyday feminists" or lesbians without a large bank account have joined international meetings. Feminists developed agency on a global and transnational level; they are opting for empowerment, and forming new network organisations. They participated in the emergence of international gender politics and gender policy networks by negotiating with or entering into strategic coalitions with supranational organisations such as the UN or the ILO, with state institutions such as the women's offices established during the UN decades of women, and with NGOs in global civil society.

2. New Inequalities and New Options in the Emerging Global Multilevel System

Options of actors are changing parallel to globalisation processes: Some actors can enlarge and differentiate their options, playing at the same time in many fields and spaces. Other actors experience shrinking options with the decreasing relevance of the nation state and its corporatist forms of regulation, or with the stronger impact of market forces. This dynamisation in the range of options is related to the interchanges of the new forms of communication/information which extend into 'simultaneous ubiquity' and the concurrent increasing potential of organisations. Manuel Castells suggests that flexible network organisations can develop and use these options especially well, as they tend to show reflective potential by rapidly and effectively processing knowledge and reflecting changes in their own set-up as well as in their environments (Castells, 2001).

The options which actors can envision and realise in the global game relate to their resources, power and capacities.[12] Of course, financial resources are im-

---

that typically undergird a polity; 3. The presence or absence of elite allies; 4. The state's capacity and propensity for repression" (McAdam et al., 1996, p. 10).

12   The focus in social movement theory on the ability of social movements to mobilise human and financial resources (Zald, 1992; McCarthy & Zald, 1994) is useful to analyse certain potentials, but it argues within the bounded rationality of economy. Therefore one has difficulties in explaining the strong compassion and voluntary engagement of activists which is often combined with high individual costs. The approach of resource mobilisation focuses on "social movement organisations" (McCarthy & Zald, 1994, p. 20), which means the well-organised and equipped parts of a social movement. In this respect

portant in globalisation, but the capacities for communication/information bridging global times and spaces and organisational capacities are also crucial factors. For example, TNCs as powerful enterprise organisations could claim their leading role in globalisation in view of their financial assets, their organisational efficiency and their global information management. Women's movements, like other social movements, have less access to resources (cf. Frerichs & Wiemert, 2001). Their networks tend to function in horizontal flexible ways which may provide specific advantages such as flexibility, intensive communication and creativity, but may also pose special problems of organisational efficiency and resource mobilisation.

Furthermore, women's movements' access to resources is also dependent on class, ethnicity or cultural environment. In local projects in poor regions it is very difficult or impossible for feminist migrants' groups to finance their activities, to find an office of their own, and even more to pay for internet access and computers, or for their transportation to international meetings. These differences between women according to class, ethnicity or cultural milieu also raise questions of new emerging hierarchies and of accountability. The professionalisation and specialisation of activities were very important to increase efficiency and to influence global gender policies. But the danger of feminist jet-setting without clear representation or accountancy to grass roots movements cannot be ignored (Wichterich, 2001).

To sum up our argument: Globalisation processes do not simply reinforce and carry on existing power relationships in deterministic ways. Even from asymmetric positions, actors can develop capacities for international orientation, communication and organising, which can support them in entering global games. International orientation in this sense means knowledge of global economic, political and cultural structures and institutions, and of global or transnational communication. As the global feminist networks and women's movements have shown, negotiating in asymmetric power relationships can bring incremental results.

These negotiating processes also suggest that the global and the national level should not be dualistically juxtaposed to each other in discussing globalisation. Rather the former monopolistic regulatory power of nation states is receding, whereas other levels of action are gaining in importance. The saying „Think globally, act locally!" reflects this emerging global multilevel governance. The most important levels are

- global level
- supranational (EU, Southern Africa, East Asia, NAFTA, Mercosur)
- nation state

---

more informal groups of action and looser parts of a movement are not well represented in this theoretical approach.

- local community
- household

Globalisation means not a simple top-down process, but rather processes of interplay in this multilevel system. The contribution of Jae-Soon Schauen and Behshid Najafi in this volume illustrates well some of these multilevel interplays concerning the fight against trafficking in women. International and supranational regulations, such as common definitions of trafficking or certain parts of the Programme of Action of the Beijing Conference, provide a framework for national and even local state and non-state activities in combating the trafficking in women. Watching the same processes from a bottom-up perspective one has to recognise that these global agreements came into being only with the contribution of women's and human rights' NGOs. They cooperated continuously and professionally while drawing their argumentative power from their experiences at a grass-root level, e.g. from their counselling work with trafficked women and local round tables. Because of this articulation of the global and the local, some authors speak of 'glocalisation' (Robertson, 1995). As the local level is the space of everyday experience and interaction for many women, it is comparatively open to feminist organising. Feminist migrant networks build bridges between these levels, opening up transnational spaces.

3. The UN Processes: Searching for Global Gender Democracy and Egalitarian Regulations

The UN process of women for equality, development and peace can be seen as a pioneer experiment in developing flexible modes of regulations sensitive to different cultural contexts. Therefore it is highly relevant to think about strategies for egalitarian regulation, as well as their limits. The UN decades of women and the social UN conferences provided spaces for communication and a highly visible agenda setting which was influential for the formation and development of international feminist networks. They opened arenas for changing norms, but did not have the power to follow up their implementation.

The UN processes also contributed to the establishment of gender policy institutions and new legal instruments or measures; they led to new global norms (like CEDAW[13]) and the selective integration of femocrats into national and supranational governance institutions. In other words, the results were norms

---

13 The *Convention on the Elimination of all Forms of Discrimination against Women* (CEDAW) from 1979 is the result of a long process, which has taken place within the UN system to incorporate equality between the sexes and principles of women's rights in the provisions of international laws. Up to now, 168 state parties ratified the convention (www.un.org/womenwatch/cedaw).

(some of them with the force of international law) on gender equality. These norms, of which CEDAW is the most important, were established in global negotiations with the world's nation states and supranational governing bodies. At the same time women's political machineries – women's offices or ministries, Equal Opportunities (EO) departments etc. – were enlarged or established following these negotiations in order to implement these norms (Unifem, 2000). From the first stage of the decade of women (1975-1985) onward, these norms, institutions and organisational structures contributed to an expansion of the political opportunity structure as femocrats were established in state and supranational bodies as potential allies.[14]

Building on this groundwork, the women's movements in South Africa, East Asia, Latin America, as well as in Europe and North America, were able to influence the UN *Fourth World Conference on Women* in Beijing 1995 (UN, 1995; Wichterich, 2000). The Beijing conference resulted in a declaration which established basic norms for and steps to achieve gender equality in a process of international negotiating between governments and feminists from very different regions and approaches. Its goals of empowerment and autonomy including the body and sexuality, equality in work and society, development and structural change, peace and non-violence (including in personal relationships) and political participation, can be seen as a feminist formula for global gender democracy.[15] Feminist networking thus put on the agenda the issue of developing concepts of inclusive global gender democracy, which respect gender and international justice, the differences between women and women's movements, and link up to a non-violent and sustainable development based on the empowerment of women and marginalised people.

Mainstreaming is a further strategy evolving since the Beijing declaration. It is based on the image of gender-free organisations routinely including gender equality in their work, and has two simple basic principles: 1) All programmes and issues of organisations should be checked for their gender impact and 2) women should have an equal participation in decision making. The responsibility for realising gender mainstreaming lies with supranational institutions such as the UN, the EU, and with governments of nation states who signed the Beijing declaration.

---

14 The first UN conference in Mexico 1975 and the World Action Plan passed at the conference contributed to the establishment of women's policy machineries in the nation states. The *Research Network on Gender, Politics and the State* (RNGS) does comparative research on the relations between women's movements and women's offices (or women's policy machineries) in Western post-industrial countries on a number of crucial issues (see Mazur, 2001).

15 See UN, 1995 and Unifem, 2000, pp. 47-60 for a brief overview of developments since the Beijing conference.

Refugee, ethnic minority and migrant women often chose the human rights channel to gain influence in the UN system as their representation within women's networks was sometimes difficult. But with the increasing presence of migrant women's organisations in national and international networks of women like the Women's Caucus at UN level, the issue of multiple discrimination was established. At the *World Conference against Racism, Racial Discrimination and Related Intolerance,* which took place in Durban/South Africa in September 2001, the common goal of migrant and women's groups was to lobby for a more complex understanding ('intersectionality') of discrimination related to gender and race. Further recommendations were made to improve the situation of refugee and migrant women like the inclusion of undocumented migrants in the documents, which was, however, strongly opposed by most migrant receiving countries. As the UN Conference as well as the NGO Forum were dominated by the Israel-Palestine conflict it was hardly possible to draw attention to gender issues.

However, the UN experiences show that the development of a global programme and vision for gender equality is different from its incorporation into the national and local contexts which will be selective and will be shaped by the national or local relationships of interest and power, by the political opportunity structure, and by political culture. Selection and incorporation is negotiated, and the approaches will be re-evaluated during these processes by the femocrats and gender politicians as well as by women's movements. The results are by no means as uniform as has been suggested in the catchword of 'McDonaldization' in globalisation (Ritzer, 2000). Rather, we would like to speak of national or local regulation. Regulation is not seen as a top-down state action, but rather as the outcome of social negotiations by state governments, interest groups (as enterprises and other organisations) and social movements (Lenz, 2001a).[16]

4. Achieving Global Regulations in the Field of Migrant Workers?

The mobility of workers, whether irregular migrants or those with legal contracts, relates to our definition of globalisation in more than one way: Economic globalisation goes hand in hand with ethnically segregated and gendered labour markets. Migrant workers themselves are part of transnational social networks and communications, which often lead to family reunification or trigger chain

---

16 By focussing on negotiations and various actors in developing international norms in globalisation, the concept of regulation is similar to 'global governance' (Held, 1999). But it is has a clearer focus on power relations and actors' interests (Lenz, 2001a).

migrations. Nation states often fear mass migration from the global South and East to the global North, and try to stem it by implementing restrictive migration policies. As the issue of migrant workers has an obvious global dimension, there have been some attempts of finding global regulations or at least some minimum standards for the treatment of migrant workers. Irregular migrant workers constitute the most vulnerable group of migrants, but national governments usually do not strengthen their rights. Is it possible to develop new regulations for migrants as in the case of gender? To focus on this research issue, we shall now present some regulations which may be important for future developments and serve as reference for migrant organisations. Firstly we will look at existing regulations in the framework of the International Labour Organisation (ILO). Secondly we will draw the attention to a political campaign of migrants, women's and other social movements which is lobbying for the adoption of a UN-convention which promotes the rights of migrants.

The International Labour Organisation (ILO) ratified conventions in which social standards are formulated. The two main ILO conventions to protect migrant workers are the *Migration for Employment Convention* (Revised) (ILO, 1949) and the *Migrant Workers (Supplementary Provisions) Convention* (ILO, 1975), but only valid for „workers lawfully resident". Only in the first part of Convention 143 all migrant workers „whether they are illegally employed migrant workers on its territory and whether they depart from, pass through or arrive in its territory" (Art. 2, 1., Part I. of Convention No. 143) are covered. At the international level it was the first attempt to secure certain rights for undocumented workers. Due to the inclusion of undocumented workers it is not astonishing that only eighteen countries ratified Convention No. 143, most of them so called sending countries. The ILO faces major problems as the convention was ratified only by a minority of states, and the ILO conventions are not part of international law, so that their relevance tends to be symbolic. Trade unions and NGOs argue that social standards should be included into the regulatory framework of the World Trade Organisation (WTO) in order to make them compulsory. The WTO replied that the ILO would be the adequate place, even though they were aware of the weak position of the ILO.

The United Nations' *International Convention on the Protection of the Rights of all Migrant Workers and their Families* (adopted in 1990) will form part of international law if enough countries will have ratified it (UN, 1990). The coverage and scope of the convention is wider than the above-mentioned ILO conventions, as it extends the protection of fundamental human rights to all migrant workers and their families, irrespective of their legal status. Lawful resident migrants are ensured equality of treatment with nationals of the host country in a number of legal, political, cultural and social areas. Since its adoption by the General Assembly it has been ratified by only nineteen countries (until February 2002), most of them again sending counties. The convention will only go into effect after it has been ratified by at least twenty countries, but it may turn out that migrant employing countries are not willing to take that step. In the current set-up NGOs cannot hold states to the convention, but encourage them to ratify the convention.

In 1998 a global campaign for ratification was launched by several NGOs like Migrants' Rights International (MRI), Human Rights Watch, International Commission of Jurists, Women's International League for Peace and Freedom or as an International Governmental Organisation of the Office of the UN High Commissioner for Human Rights (Migrants Rights International, 2000). The campaign adopted the slogan „Migrants' Rights are Human Rights," which is obviously borrowed from the women's struggle for human rights. Raising awareness about the existence and content of the convention as well as lobbying activities for the ratification of the convention and monitoring its implementation are major goals of the global campaign. Conceptually the campaign tries to build up inter-sectoral alliances between trade unions, International Governmental Organisations and NGOs. Only in recent times an increasing number of local and nation-wide working migrants' organisations started lobbying more intensively for these regulations. Margaret Keck and Kathryn Sikkink have called this kind of constellation of actors 'transnational advocacy networks' in their path-breaking publication „Activists beyond borders: advocacy networks in international politics" (Keck & Sikkink, 1998). As we shall illustrate later, transnational social spaces and activities seem to be a key element of migrants organising themselves.

5. Self-Organisation of Migrant Women in Germany

At the beginning of this article we asked whether migrants – especially female migrants – are only victims of globalisation or whether they can also open up and use new options and negotiate new social regulations even if they are starting from a disadvantaged position. This issue is of course linked to their power potential as global players. As main sources of this power potential were identified: The capacity for global orientation and communication, the organisational flexible capacities in order to fully mobilise members' potential, and the access to material resources such as money or time. Therefore we want to present selected results of an empirical study on the self-organisation of migrant women in Germany to look at this problem.[17] First we will consider basic characteristics of this self-organisation such as their goals, their activists, transnational constituency, and their activities. Then we will present some examples how they were

---

17 The findings in this part of our contribution are based on empirical research carried out by Helen Schwenken. The sample consisted of 224 migrant women's organisations, projects and groups located in Germany (Schwenken, 2000).

able to negotiate new regulations for example regarding the permit to stay by entering strategic alliances with feminist and other social movements. Finally we will consider how female migrants create transnational spaces in their networking.

5.1. Actors and Organisational Structures

Most activities by migrant women's organisations in Germany focus on the local level, but the transnational element is also crucial. Most striking in this respect is that the widespread assumption of the segregation of migrant women along ethnic or national lines is not true for large parts of self-organised migrant women who are often active in groups or organisations consisting of women from different origins. Among the most active women, migrants with a relatively secure legal status and women who have been involved in political and women's organisations before coming to Germany are to be found predominantly. Most of the active women were migrants who had achieved a fairly good legal and social status, even though more than half of the migrants who use counselling centres had problems with their legal status. Thus a secure legal status seems to make involvement in social and political organisations easier. Those migrant women who had a half time or full time job in autonomous counselling institutions or projects were often overqualified (as psychologists, lawyers or social pedagogues), or they tried to earn their living by giving language courses or working as free-lance translators in the non-profit sector. Their precarious socio-economic situation is related to the fact that some migrants, mostly from the second generation of the so called guest workers, benefited from the expansion of higher education which was implemented by the Social Democrats since the 1970s, and graduated from universities. However, they could not get jobs commensurate with their qualifications. Despite the influx of migrants, the recruitment for leading segments of German society continued to take place predominantly within certain social classes with the effect that many (second generation) migrants were excluded. Some of the intellectual migrants also dedicated their competence to groups which predominantly work theoretically or in political representation. Due to their intellectual competence and experience they took over a function as 'organic intellectuals' (Gramsci), which means as speakers and representatives of migrant women in Germany.

The internal structure of self-organised migrants' groups is interesting in so far as in about half of the researched groups active migrant women came from different countries of origin. This is quite astonishing as one seldom questions the image that migrants live in worlds clearly separated along national and ethnic belongings. Reasons for the international composition may include that migrant women face similar problems in Germany and therefore have similar po-

litical goals. There are also tendencies that migrant women in Germany built up
an identity as 'foreigners in Germany', which is the common tie to other migrant
women. Another reason might be that some communities are quite small, and
there are not enough women from one country of origin who might be interested
in forming their own group. In fifteen percent of the groups migrants organise
who come from different countries, but from one continent or world region. Especially women from Africa or Latin America chose this form of organisation. It
could be related to long-time effects and shared colonial contexts in certain
world regions. About one third of the organisations in the sample were groups
and projects in which migrants of the same national origin participated. Migrant
women with a Turkish or Kurdish background were the most represented, but
also women who fled from Iran or Filipino women are still very active.

A growing number of organisations of migrant women in Germany build up
different types of transnational networks and cooperation with women's organisations in their countries of origin besides the form of classical exile politics
(e.g. in form of a party or mass organisation) of, for example, Kurds or Iranians.
More and more organisations inform potential migrants in their countries of origin about the situation in immigration countries like Germany, e.g. in the sex industry. The organisation *Ban Ying* (which means in Thai: Women's Shelter) in
Berlin, for example, publishes a newsletter in the Thai language which is send to
women's organisations in Thailand. In Recife, Brasilia, a counselling institution
for girls and women who are working in the sex industry *Colectivo Mulher da
Vida* ("Collective Women of Life") distributes information with addresses of
autonomous counselling institutions for migrant women in different European
countries.

5.2. Main Activities of Self-Organised Migrant Women

In social movement theory the analytical division between self-help and political
organisations is very common (Raschke, 1987). But this does not fit in our case,
as it is a characteristic of the self-organisation of migrant women to combine individual counselling for migrants as well as develloping political statements.
Among the groups analysed, four types of activity can be observed: (1) political
initiatives, (2) meeting points for migrant women, (3) autonomous counselling
institutions, and (4) capacity building projects. About half of the groups, projects and organisations are involved in more than one main activity. Especially
political organisations also offer different types of counselling (legal, social,
health etc.) or capacity building courses. The courses range from alphabetisation
and language courses to job training, political seminars, dancing or cooking
courses. The participation in such courses could have an important function for
migrant women in the sense of self-determined time and independence. The

counselling institutions need to have a broad offer of competency as most of the clients do have more than one problem. For example, a serious problem with one's legal status or experiences of discrimination could cause related chronic diseases like allergic reactions, loneliness or depression. Counselling in different mother tongues is very important as especially experiences of violence or socio-cultural problems can be dealt with more adequately than in German language counselling. Many migrant women also have more confidence in women from their own national or ethnic context, but on the other hand German counsellors are also valued by many migrant women as they are thought to be more neutral, and there is less fear that sensitive and intimate information are given to members of the same national or ethnic community. For all these reasons most teams in counselling institutions for migrant women are composed of people with different national or cultural backgrounds.

About one third of the projects and counselling institutions researched are not involved in politics and prefer political neutrality. Nearly half of the organisations in the sample seem to sympathise with feminist ideas or see themselves as part of an international women's movement. Among the rest of the organisations are also traditionally or religiously oriented groups and organisations. One reason for the political neutrality of the projects is that they want to attract girls and women who live in a context where there could be some reservations against feminist surroundings. There are also indications that women want to keep political and religious struggles with which they have to cope in every-day life within their ethnic communities outside the project. The term 'partisanship' which is used by the migrant's projects thus has to be understood in a feminist sense, which means to act from a perspective supporting women.

On a more theoretical level these intercultural and multinational counselling centres and meeting points of migrant and refugee women can be understood as transnational social spaces in which individual support is provided, important information is exchanged, political activities are planned, and political views are negotiated between diverse groups of women.

The following characteristics are therefore at the core of our working definition of the self-organisation of migrant women: The self-organisation of migrant women comprises all projects, groups, networks and organisations of migrants, racially discriminated and minority women which are aiming for social change with a certain continuity and with a variety of forms of action.[18]

---

18 Although the description of the self-organisation of migrant women fits certain characteristics of social movements such as organisational structures, continuity, political targets, supporters and participants, we prefer the term 'self-organisation of migrant women' as their diversity is as pronounced as their commonallities, and they overlap with the women's or antiracist movement.

As we already described some organisational characteristics of the self-organisation of migrant women, in the next paragraph we will focus on their struggles and the results.

5.3. Issues and Goals

We shall briefly present three issues which have been important for migrant women's initiatives in Germany during the last ten years: the struggle for an independent legal status of migrant spouses, the combating of trafficking in women, and antiracist activities.

An example for how migrant women's organisation in Germany influenced a regulation on the national level, is the *National Initiative for the Change of §19 of the Foreigners' Law*. The initiative is a coalition of several migrant women's organisations and counselling institutions. From 1993 until 1997 the initiative fought for an independent legal status for foreign spouses. At the end they succeeded in a moderate reform: now foreign spouses only need to be married to a German for two years instead of four to get an independent legal status. Furthermore a regulation was introduced that partners (mostly wifes) could stay in Germany after they divorced the person (mostly men) who subjected them to severe domestic violence. But still, many migrant women have problems with their right to stay in Germany in case they wish to separate from their (violent) husband, as the power of discretion and other tricky parts of the foreigners law hinder the women from achieving a better position (see Najafi & Schauen in this volume). Starting from the experiences which were made in the counselling centres for migrant women the campaign achieved two crucial changes: This issue was put on the political agenda, and a broad political advocacy network consisting mainly of women with different social and political backgrounds was organised. The campaign had some political impact as the different organisations of the initiative chose very diverse forms of actions on different levels. Signatures were collected, provocative street theatre was performed, and strategic lobbying activities were carried out simultaneously. Besides the activities of migrant women and feminist supporters, a broad party-independent coalition of women (mostly members of parliament, prominent women and academics) lobbied for the change of the law. Due to the existence of international networks, women's organisations from Asia and Latin America sent letters of support to the responsible German Minister of women's affairs. The activities were enhanced at symbolic days like the International Women's Day on March 8 or the International Day against Violence against Women on November 25. As a result a parliamentary majority could be mobilised in favour of some improvements. This example shows that the change of a national legislation was achieved through a combination of local experience, national network building, and international support and monitoring.

The issue of trafficking in women is another field in which many migrant women's organisations and counselling institutions are involved (see Najafi & Schauen in this volume). From their experience in counselling affected women, political goals were articulated which could change the legal practice. Until now, migrants who are victims of trafficking in women or forced prostitution, are asked to testify as witnesses, and after the trial they are deported to their country of origin. Many women, however, are traumatised by the violence of the traffickers and do not have the chance to get adequate treatment after returning to their home countries. Others simply want to stay in Germany and earn a living for themselves and their families. Migrant women's and counselling organisations therefore fight and lobby for a right of secondary charge (*Nebenklage*), witness protection, a secure legal status for the victims, financial compensation, job training and a work permit. For those women working in counselling institutions they demand a right to refuse to give evidence in court trials.

Feminist NGOs which fight against trafficking in women argue for a broadening of migrant's rights but they sometimes face specific ambivalences regarding the political support of politicians: German migration policy mostly tends towards restrictive or authoritarian legislation. Nevertheless the official approaches include the goal of combating trafficking in women. Thus it looks as if politicians and NGOs have the same goals. But the NGOs claim that the politicians do not argue from a political position which has the welfare of the affected women in mind. The NGOs also argue against the further victimisation of the women which is mostly a side-effect in criminal law policies the women face. This is often a difficult dilemma to handle and within the women's NGOs it is also reflected. As a result they stress their approach and political argumentation to broaden the rights of affected migrants.

At the beginning of the 1990s many groups of self-organised migrant women were fighting against racism and xenophobia in Germany, which rapidly increased after the German unification. The activities concerning the issue of racism illustrate that it is not only crucial to develop international linkages, but that it is vitally important to fight locally for non-discrimination and the right to physical integrity. Migrant women discussed their relation to (East) German women, the process of unification in general, organised demonstrations and coalitions against nationalism and racism, and developed strategies of self-defence against racist attacks. Some migrant women criticised German civil society and antiracist mass mobilisations for being relatively passive. They pleaded for more active forms of solidarity. Other migrant women were involved in broad coalitions with parts of German civil society, and still others concentrated more on collaboration with male dominated migrant organisations. A very controversial issue among migrant and German women was racism, also within the women's movement. Many hot debates took place in feminist publications and at special congresses. One of the results was a separation between many white

German feminists and migrant women, and some German feminists also accused themselves of being racist. A vivid and long-lasting academic debate about racism, anti-semitism and the conceptualisation of power relations between women and discrimination evolved since the mid 1980s.

6. Transnational Social Spaces and Activities

In this part we shall take up the multilevel approach by introducing the concept of transnational social spaces and providing some examples of transnational activities. In this context we would like to refer to the contributions of Amel Hamza and Yayori Matsui in this volume which are also important examples of transnational activities.

Transnational social spaces (Faist, 2000; Pries, 1999) are framed by a multilevel political and legal framework of migration regimes and policies: at the national level in the sending and receiving countries, and at the international level with bi- and multilateral agreements. The material infrastructure consists of modern communication technologies and the professional infrastructure, such as specialised legal assistance or the organisation of (illegal) passages. Moreover, a socio-cultural infrastructure, such as sport clubs, restaurants, child care facilities or music groups exists and is often based on cross-border social networks originating in family or ethnic relations. Migrants often locate themselves in the system of social structure in the country of origin as well as in the country of permanent or temporary stay. Gender relations are also negotiated in these systems of transition and power relations.

In migration studies this concept only emerged in the late 1980s (cf. Glick Schiller et al., 1992) as migration was considered for a long time as a one-way, permanent and unilateral movement, but the development of international migration is characterised by important changes. Complex and multi-directional migrations increased, which were often not permanent, but linked to certain stages of one's private or working life. These new forms of migration are based in cross-national and transnational living realities and networks. In these surrounding 'translocal subjectivities' (Gutiérrez Rodríguez, 1999) emerge, which are important for self-organised migrants. Especially in a post-colonial perspective and through the discussions about localities useful approaches have been developed to theorise living between spaces: Homi Bhabha (1990, 1993) introduced the concept of the 'third space' in post-colonial debates. The third space is somewhere between two geographical locations and combines experiences of several life realities and overcomes the dual logic of living here or there. Rosi Braidotti, on the contrary, emphasises the ongoing process of migrating between locations, but locations which cannot be combined with her concept of 'nomadic subjects' in transit. She clearly distinguishes between nomads and exiles, for whom the idea of a far away home is permanent. „The nomad does not stand for homelessness, or compulsive displacement; it is rather a figuration for the kind of subject who has relinquished all idea, desire, or nostalgia for fixity. This figuration expresses the desire for an identity made of transitions" (Braidotti, 1994, p. 22). Gayatri Chakravorty Spivak stresses the experience of exclusion, which she calls the geographic-political position, that often has a politicising effect. For her the question of political activism and responsibility is more important than the concrete space (Spivak, 1996). These various concepts of identity compositions and strategies of locating oneself cover the full range from neglecting categories of identity to strategic essentialisms. Strategic essentialisms could for example mean to talk strategically as 'women,' as 'Turkish migrant women in Germany', or as 'lesbian' with the goal to draw the attention to existing power relations. In new social movement theory these questions of subjectivity in migratory processes are to date not very well developed, neither on a theoretical nor analytical level, but we consider them useful to connect structural and subjective aspects in transnational social spaces concerning the self-organisation of migrant women, especially as different political strategies may be the result, e.g. the varying importance of homeland policies.

Some feminist migrant groups like *FeMigra* (abbreviation for: „Feminist Migrants") in Germany work explicitly with Spivak's ideas. Like Gayatri Spivak they stress the strong meaning of locality, but they are very critical about manifestations of national or cultural spaces as they promote the strategic and political identity 'migrant', understood as counter-identity situated to national hegemony. Their political strategy is to build up issue-specific coalitions with other social movements or political actors. Although groups like *FeMigra* have the limitations of such coalitions and universal discourses in mind, they refer to them. *FeMigra* mentions the criteria with which they measure policies and political fights: all their activities should aim at eradicating discrimination and exploitation (Yurtsever-Kneer, 1998, 2000; FeMigra, 1994; Gutiérrez Rodríguez, 1999). *FeMigras'* theoretical reflection of how to act politically as feminist migrants is strongly influenced by the reception of post-structuralist, black and post-colonialist authors like Gayatri Spivak, Nira Yuval-Davis, Adrienne Rich or Angela Davis. Migrant women like those active in *FeMigra* mostly have an academic background or work in the social sector. They are also involved in strong networking activities with other ethnic, migrant or Jewish women in Germany. Since the beginning of the 1990s regular conferences take place in which feminist migrant practicioners, artists, psychologists/therapists, intellectuals and other migrant women interlink with each other in order to develop political perspectives, to exchange experiences in different social sectors, and to create a supportive and powerful space. Besides these networking activities and political articulations of migrant women some other migrants' organisations and networks – mostly of younger migrants – exist which try to overcome the more traditional forms of homeland orientated migrant organisations. In the northern parts of Germany the journal and groups of *köXüz* which means „rootless", are quite active. Well known is also the initiative *Kanak Attak* which is active in some larger German towns. In 1998 they published a 'manifesto', which gained a lot of popularity among younger – and again predominantly those with higher education – migrants. „Our common position consists of an attack against the 'Kanakisation' of specific groups of people through racist ascriptions which denies people their social, legal and political rights. Kanak Attak is therefore anti-nationalist, and anti-racist, and rejects every single form of identity politics, as supported by ethnic absolutist thinking" (Kanak Attak, 1998). They criticise the approach of other migrant organisations: „Kanak Attak is therefore critical of the benefits possible from individual communities lobbying for their particularistic interests, and the non-confrontational mode of politics evident within contemporary democracies" (ibid.). The trademark of *Kanak Attak* is also the combination of politics and cultural events. „We sample, change and adapt different political and cultural drifts that all operate from oppositional positions. We go back to a mixture of theory, politics and cultural practice. This song is ours. Es geht ab. Kanak Attak!" (ibid.). Since the mid 1990s *Kanak Attak* received considerable media attention because of their cultural approach with provocative music and literary performances. But the activists evaluate their popularity quite critical: „Although Kanak Attak is predominantly a migrant movement it should not be seen as the 'cool voice' of the ghetto. That's how they would like it, the commercial vultures of the cultural industries, who are searching for 'authentic' and 'exotic' human experiences to be sold to those living in the grey mainstream of everyday German society" (ibid.).

These articulations of predominantly younger and well educated (feminist) migrants in Germany are mostly not those migrant organisations or individuals which engage in the negotiations about political regulations at any level. Rather, groups like *Kanak Attak* develop another approach in which they create political, cultural, theoretical and social spaces with a clearly articulated critique of German society. The point of reference is Germany, and their strategic political identity may be described as 'migrant in Germany'. In this regard these activities differ from transnational approaches and strategies of many other migrant organisations, which also shall be mentioned here.

Migrants and political refugees often internationalise supposedly national conflicts with a strategic purpose. By organising international solidarity and transnational cooperation, such as the mobilisation against military dictatorships in Latin America or the Kurdish question, such conflicts were brought to public attention. This kind of internationalisation requires the development of specific transnational activities in order to influence policy in all affected countries. The cross-national, synchronised and plurilocal protests depend on both the political and cultural context in the countries and on the existence of actors and social movement organisations interested in the issue. An important channel of mediation and communication are the migrants themselves, with their links to family members, friends and political comrades in the countries of origin and in other immigration countries as well. They constitute a semi-public network which is extended by more indirect means like modern communication technologies, mass media, institutional channels and contacts among social movement organisations. In addition to communication, the contents as well as the choice of strategy have to be negotiated transnationally. The relationship between the organisations in the different countries can contain some difficulties as the research of Eva Østergaard-Nielsen indicates: „Leaders of Kurdish oriented legal parties in Turkey are not always delighted with the efforts of the more radical Kurdish diaspora, and most certainly do not want to be identified as closely linked to them" (Østergaard-Nielsen, 2001, p. 20). These kind of frictions or discontents show that further problems can emerge in the context of transnational movements, especially if the flow of communication is uneven between the 'sending' and 'receiving' countries or if the choice of strategy is not congruent.

7. Conclusion

If we evaluate the political activities of migrants with instruments of policy analysis developed in political science we can state that the internationally orientated migrant's organisations and networks try to influence every step of the 'policy cycle' and that the question of success relates to several factors.

Most process models of policy analysis start with the agenda setting or the articulation or identification of a problem. Here migrants are partially successful, e.g. the global network against trafficking in women put it successfully on the international and national agendas, but in many cases within the hegemonic framework of the fight against organised crime and not with the aim of improving women's rights or eradicating the circumstances under which women and children are sold into prostitution and forced labour. Another issue that was brought successfully on the agenda is that of anti-discrimination and anti-racism, but as the experiences of election campaigns show there is always the danger of populist campaigns against foreigners.

The second step of an ideal typical policy cycle is the formulation of proposals and aims, followed by the decision making process. In this phase those activists with access to decision makers and media try to lobby and influence the direction of the proposals often with their 'alternative expertise' which they gained from grassroots' experiences. Especially since a number of feminists entered the decision making bodies of International Organisations or governments

– the so called femocrats – there could be made some improvements on regulations at least from a women's perspective which we illustrated earlier in this article.

A crucial point of the policy cycle is the implementation, e.g. of international regulations at the national level. NGOs take the function of monitoring in order to push their national governments to implement e.g. the Beijing Platform of Action. Therefore the implementation is accompanied by monitoring activities like the formulation of shadow reports or media coverage about the lacking implementation.

The policy cycle might go on with impact analysis, the revision of policies or the termination. But since the challenges of migration policy from a gender sensitive and human right's perspective will definitely not be met soon, the initiatives taken by feminists and migrants will continue.

An issue which kept us thinking was how far migrants can recover options in globalisation processes – in comparison with other marginalized groups – to fight for their political aims, although they start from a difficult situation which is in many cases characterized by limited formal citizenship rights and difficulties in accessing resources and public attention.

We found the existence of transnational social spaces to be crucial for these organisational processes. They are at the same time result of the activities of international migrants as they allow the negotiation and articulation of political opinions and networking. The conditions for these often highly politicised spaces grow e.g. with the emergence of global cities which become international and cosmopolitan. Migrants with their multilinguality and multicultural experiences are capable to name differences between societies and question the promise of equality, humanism and social welfare which is especially given in the industrialised countries. The combination of transnational experiences and often ethnic collectivism or solidarity with other migrants can lead – as the example of relatively new transnational (feminist) migrant's networks in Germany show – to transnational identities and political practices. But only a part of international migrants engage themselves politically. Regarding the growing number of highly qualified labour migrants who change their place of working and living quite frequently and who concentrate on professional capacities, the amount of migrants involved in politics is not growing automatically with the rise of transnational migration. The analysis of transnational agency thus has to concentrate on often contradictory and uneven developments. But if we do not start from deterministic concepts of globalisation, but rather from perceiving the *agency* of migrants, especially female migrants, and their networks, we can see how they start from a subordinate position with far less resources and power, but that they can open new perspectives and strategies on transnational processes, options and possible solutions.

References

Beauftragte der Bundesregierung für Ausländerfragen (1997). Bericht der Beauftragten der Bundesregierung für Ausländerfragen über die Lage der Ausländer in der Bundesrepublik Deutschland. Bonn.

Beauftragte der Bundesregierung für Ausländerfragen (2000). Bericht der Beauftragten der Bundesregierung für Ausländerfragen über die Lage der Ausländer in der Bundesrepublik Deutschland, Februar 2000. Berlin, Bonn.

Beauftragte der Bundesregierung für Ausländerfragen (2001). Migrationsbericht der Ausländerbeauftragten im Auftrag der Bundesregierung, November 2001. Berlin, Bonn.

Beauftragte der Bundesregierung für Ausländerfragen (2002). Daten und Fakten zur Ausländersituation. 20th edition, Februar 2002. Berlin, Bonn.

Bhabha, Homi (1990). The third space: Interview with Homi K. Bhabha. In J. Rutherford (Ed.), Changing Identities. London: Lawrence & Wishart.

Bhabha, Homi (1993). The location of culture. London, New York: Routledge.

BMFSFJ, Bundesministerium für Familie, Senioren, Frauen und Jugend (2000). Familien ausländischer Herkunft in Deutschland. Leistungen, Belastungen, Herausforderungen. Sechster Familienbericht. Berlin.

Braidotti, Rosi (1994). Nomadic subjects: embodiment and sexual difference in contemporary feminist theory. New York: Columbia University Press.

Castells, Manuel (2001). Das Informationszeitalter. Die Netzwerkgesellschaft. Opladen: Leske + Budrich.

Cohen, Robin (1997). Global Diasporas. An Introduction. London, Seattle: University of Washington Press.

European Commission (1996). Communication „Incorporating equal opportunities for women and men into all Community policies and activities", COM(96)67final. Internet: http://europa.eu.int/comm/employment_social/equ_opp/gms_en.html#def

Faist, Thomas (2000). The Volume and Dynamics of International Migration and Transnational Social Spaces. Oxford: Clarendon Press.

FeMigra (Feministische Migrantinnen, Frankfurt) (1994): Wir, die Seiltänzerinnen. Politische Strategien von Migrantinnen gegen Ethnisierung und Assimilation. In Cornelia Eichhorn, Sabine Grimm (Eds.): Gender Killer. Texte zu Feminismus und Politik. Berlin, Amsterdam: Edition ID-Archiv, pp. 49-63.

Filmer, Deon (1995). Estimating the World at Work. The World Bank, Policy Research Working Paper 1488.

Frerichs, Petra; Wiemert, Heike (2001). Ich gebe, damit Du gibst. Frauennetzwerke: strategisch, reziprok, exklusiv. Opladen: Leske + Budrich.

Giddens, Anthony (2001). Sociology. 4th Edition. Cambridge: Polity Press.

Glick Schiller, Nina; Basch, Linda & Blanc-Szanton, Christina (1992) (Eds.). Towards a Transnational Perspective on Migration: Race, Class, Ethnicity and Nationalism Reconsidered. New York: Annals of the New York Academy of Science: 645, pp. 1-24.

Gutiérrez Rodríguez, Encarnación (1999). Intellektuelle Migrantinnen – Subjektivitäten im Zeitalter von Globalisierung. Eine postkoloniale dekonstruktive Analyse von Biographien im Spannungsverhältnis von Ethnisierung und Vergeschlechtlichung. Opladen: Leske + Budrich.

Held, David (1999). Global transformations: politics, economics and culture. Cambridge: Polity Press.

International Labour Organisation (ILO) (1949). Convention No. 97, Migration for Employment Convention (Revised). Date of implementation: 22.01.1952. http://ilolex.ilo.ch:1567/scripts/convde.pl?C97

International Labour Organisation (ILO) (1975). C143 Migrant Workers (Supplementary Provisions) Convention. Geneva. http://ilolex.ilo.ch:1567/scripts/convde.pl?C143

Interparliamentary Union (IPU) (2002). Women in National Parliaments. Situation as of 1 March 2002. http://www.ipu.org/wmn-e/world.htm

Kanak Attak (1998). Manifesto: KANAK ATTAK UND BASTA! English version. http://www.kanak-attak.de/main.htm

Keck, Margaret E.; Sikkink, Kathryn (1998). Activists beyond borders: advocacy networks in international politics. Ithaca: Cornell University Press.

Klammer et al. (2000). FrauenDatenReport. Berlin: Sigma

Köxüz. Her türlu egemenlik iliskisiyle koklerimizi koparalim. Wurzellos: „Reißen wir uns von den Wurzeln los, die uns mit jeder Art von Herrschaftsform verbinden". http://www.comlink.de/cl-hh/koxuz/

Lenz, Ilse (1999). Politische Modernisierung und Frauenbewegungen in Japan und Deutschland. Zum Versuch einer vergleichenden Perspektive. In Pigulla, Andreas u.a. (Eds.). Ostasien verstehen. Peter Weber-Schäfer zu Ehren. Festschrift aus Anlaß seiner Emeritierung. BJOAS Bd. 23, München, pp. 217-231.

Lenz, Ilse (2000a). Globalisierung, Geschlecht, Gestaltung? In Lenz, Ilse; Müller, Ursula; Nickel, Hildegard; Riegraf, Birgit (Eds.) (2000), Geschlecht – Arbeit – Zukunft. Münster: Westfälisches Dampfboot, pp. 16-49.

Lenz, Ilse (2000b). What does the women´s movement do, when it moves? Subjektivität, Organisation und Kommunikation in der neuen japanischen Frauenbewegung. In Lenz, Ilse; Mae, Michiko; Klose, Karin (Eds.) (2000), Frauenbewegungen weltweit. Aufbrüche, Kontinuitäten, Veränderungen. Opladen: Leske + Budrich, pp. 95-133.

Lenz, Ilse (2001a). Globalisierung, Frauenbewegungen und internationale Regulierung. In Zeitschrift für Frauenforschung und Geschlechterstudien, 1&2, pp. 8-29.

Lenz, Ilse (2001b). Bewegungen und Veränderungen. Frauenforschung und Neue Frauenbewegungen in Deutschland. In: Hornung, Ursula; Gümen, Sedef; Weilandt, Sabine (Eds.) (2001), Zwischen Emanzipationsvisionen und Gesellschaftskritik: (Re)Konstruktionen der Geschlechterordnungen in Frauenforschung – Frauenbewegung – Frauenpolitik. Forum Frauenforschung Band 14. Münster: Westfälisches Dampfboot.

Lenz, Ilse (2002). Geschlechtsspezifische Auswirkungen der Globalisierung in den Bereichen Global Governance, Arbeitsmärkte und Ressourcen. Gutachten für die Enquete-Kommission „Globalisierung der Weltwirtschaft – Herausforderungen und Antworten" des Deutschen Bundestags.

Lenz, Ilse; Mae, Michiko (Ed.) (2000). Frauenbewegungen weltweit. Aufbrüche, Kontinuitäten, Veränderungen. Opladen: Leske + Budrich.

Lutz, Helma (2000). At your service Madame! Domestic Servants, Past and Present. Gender, Class, Ethnicity and Profession. A European Perspective. Unpublished Manuscript.

Mazur, Amy (Ed.) (2001). State Feminism, Women's Movements & Job Training. Making Democracies Work in a Global Economy. New York, London: Routledge.

McAdam, Doug; McCarthy, John D.; Zald, Mayer N. (1996). Introduction: Opportunities, mobilizing structures, and framing processes – toward a synthetic, comparative perspective on social movements. In D. McAdam; J. D. McCarthy & M. N. Zald (Eds.), Comparative Perspectives on Social Movements. Political Opportunities, Mobilizing Structures, and Cultural Framings. Cambridge: Cambridge University Press, pp. 1-20.

McCarthy, John D. & Zald, Mayer N. (1994). Resource Mobilization and Social Movements: A Partial Theory. In M. N. Zald; J. D. McCarthy (Eds.), Social Movements in an Organisational Society. Collected Essays. New Brunswick (USA), London, pp. 15-42.

Migrants' Rights International (2000): Achieving Dignity. Campaigner's Handbook for the Migrants' Rights Convention. Geneva. (Campaign Website: www.migrantsrights.org)

Østergaard-Nielsen, Eva K. (2001). The Politics of Migrants' Transnational Political Practices. Paper given at the Conference on Transnational Migration: Comparative Perspectives. Princeton University, 30 June – 1 July 2001. WPTC-01-22.

Pries, Ludger (2001). Internationale Migration. Bielefeld: Transcript.

Pries, Ludger (Ed.) (1999). Migration and transnational social spaces. Aldershot: Ashgate.

Raschke, Joachim (1987). Soziale Bewegungen. Ein historisch-systematischer Grundriß. Frankfurt, New York: Campus. (Original work published 1985)

Ritzer, G. (2000). The Macdonaldization of Society. 3rd edition. Pine Forge Press.

Robertson, Roland (1995). Glocalization: Time-Space and Homogeneity-Heterogeneity. In Featherstone, Michael et al (Eds.), Global Modernities. London: Sage.

Rupp, Leila (1997). Worlds of Women. International Women's Organisations 1888 – 1945. Princeton: Princeton University Press.

Schmidt, Verena (2001). Gender Mainstreaming als Leitbild für Geschlechtergerechtigkeit in Organisationsstrukturen. In Zeitschrift für Frauenforschung und Geschlechterstudien, 1+2, pp. 45-63.

Schmidt, Verena (2000). Zum Wechselverhältnis zwischen europäischer Frauenpolitik und europäischen Frauenorganisationen. In Lenz, Ilse; Mae, Michiko; Klose, Karin (Eds.), Frauenbewegungen weltweit. Opladen: Leske + Budrich, pp. 199-232.

Schwenken, Helen (2000). Frauen-Bewegungen in der Migration. Zur Selbstorganisierung von Migrantinnen in der Bundesrepublik Deutschland. In Lenz, Ilse, Mae, Michiko, Klose, Karin (Eds.): Frauenbewegungen weltweit. Opladen: Leske & Budrich, pp. 133-167.

Spivak, Gayatri Chakravorty (1996). The Spivak reader: selected works of Gayatri Chakravorty Spivak. Ed. by Donna Landry. New York: Routledge.

Statistisches Bundesamt Deutschland (2002). www.destatis.de/themen.

UNCTAD (2001). World Investment Report 2001. Promoting Linkages. Overview. New York, Geneva.

UNDP (1999). Human Development Report. New York.

UNDP (2000). Human Development Report. New York.

Unifem (2000). Progress of the World's Women. Unifem Biennial Report. UN, New York.

United Nations (1990). International Convention on the Protection of the Rights of all Migrant Workers and their Families. Adopted by General Assembly resolution 45/158 of 18 December 1990 (not in force). http://www.unhchr.ch/html/menu3/b/m_mwctoc.htm

United Nations (1995). Report on the Fourth World Conference on Women (Beijing, 4-15 September 1995). A/CONF.177/20.

United Nations (2000). The World's Women 2000. Trends and Statistics. New York.

Urry, John (2000). Mobile Sociology. In British Journal of Sociology, Vol. 51, 1, pp. 185-203.

Walby, Sylvia (2001). Analysing social inequality in the twenty-first century and modernity restructure inequality. Paper.

Wallerstein, Immanuel (Ed.) (1975). World inequality: origins and perspectives on the world system. Montreal: Black Rose Books.

Wichterich, Christa (2000). The globalised woman: Reports from a future of inequality. London: Zed Press.

Wichterich, Christa (2001). From Passion to Profession. Mehr Fragen als Antworten zu Akteurinnen, Interessen und Veränderungen politischer Handlungsbedingungen der neuen internationalen Frauenbewegung. In Zeitschrift für Frauenforschung und Geschlechterstudien, 1&2, pp. 128-138.

Woodward, Alison (2001). Die McDonaldisierung der internationalen Frauenbewegung: Negative Aspekte guter Praktiken. In Zeitschrift für Frauenforschung und Geschlechterstudien, 1&2, pp. 29-45.

World Bank (2000): Entering the 21st Century. World Development Report 1999/2000. New York: Oxford University Press.

Yurtsever-Kneer, Selçuk (1998). Strategien feministischer Migrantinnenpolitik. http://www.femigra.de/infos.html

Yurtsever-Kneer, Selçuk (2000). Transnationale Identität. Tagung zu Transnationaler Identität. Paulus-Akademie, Zürich, 9.9.2000. http://www.femigra.de/infos.html

Zald, Mayer N. (1992). Looking Backward to Look Forward: Reflections on the Past and Future of the Resource Mobilization Research Program. In A. D. Morris; C. McClurg Mueller (Eds.), Frontiers in Social Movement Theory. New Haven, London: Yale University Press, pp. 326-348.

Marina Calloni

International Women's Networks, Social Justice and Cross-Border Democracy

1. Introduction

The history of human and political rights clearly shows the presence of gender-based prejudices both at the national and transnational level. By contrast the history of women's movements testifies to the necessity to struggle against all forms of discrimination, reproducing traditional kinds of marginalisation and segregation of human beings. In the last few years, the 'globalisation' of gender issues and the increasing influence of international feminism have lead to a new approach, to the theory and praxis of human rights, social justice, and politics both in Western nation states and countries in development/transition.

Taking as a background these questions, my article is divided into two separate, but interconnected parts. In the theoretical framework I utilise a normative concept of social justice, and then take a pragmatic approach by reconstructing concrete initiatives, which I have helped to develop over the years as a co-ordinator of the *International Network for Research on Gender* (in the following: *Network*). The concept of network/networking connects these two parts. A network is a social structure based on interpersonal relationships and the shared values and interests of members in relation to a specific goal. Networking is a dynamic process, based on differentiated forms of interaction and knowledge and it is changing over time. In this sense, network and networking can refer both to research and political participation. From a gender perspective, networks/networking are aimed at developing a cross-border idea of inclusive democracy, starting from the concrete lives of women and marginalised/excluded social actors. Improving differentiated and overlapping networks, continuing to network, implementing cross-border research and promoting programmes of co-operation – also in countries in development/transition – are basic tasks for achieving a form of cosmopolitan democracy with more equal gender relations as a starting point.

2. National democracies, women's movements and cross-border research

The history of women's movements is closely connected to the creation and transformation of the nation state and the critique of a limited interpretation of citizenship. Yet since the eighteenth century human and political rights seemed to have ambivalent features and to be gendered. Namely, while human rights are universal and apply to all human beings, political rights are only accessible to members of a specific territorial/cultural community. Therefore, the concept of 'man' refers to a general definition including all human beings, while the term 'citizen' indicates a locally contextualised and culturally determined subject, which enjoys political rights. Until recently, man and citizen referred to a male individual in the history of human rights and citizenship. Citizenship is an 'unstable compound', implying the co-existence of both universal and political instances. This means that democracy includes the respect for the psychophysical dignity of all human beings on the one hand, and the self-government of citizens with the right to vote, the recognition of marginalised groups, and processes of inclusion of excluded social actors on the other. Nowadays the tension between human rights and citizenship lies at the basis of the controversy concerning migrants (Calloni & Lutz, 2000), refugees and asylum seekers, who are people applying for a new citizenship because of economic or political reasons. Indeed, boundaries are constitutive of politics. The challenge consists in how to 'transcend' them democratically. This is also one of the main problems in contemporary international women's movements and public discourses on gender and development.

Based on this consideration, this section will focus on a brief reconstruction of the main waves of theories and praxis of Western feminism, confronting them with the experiences of women coming from or living in countries in development/transition. I will use the transformation of the concept of human rights and citizenship as an example to illustrate my points.

Since the late nineteenth century, the history of women's movements showed the inherent limits of both human rights and political citizenship, as women have been excluded from the public domain for centuries. Women struggled for the recognition of human rights, obtaining full citizenship and contributing to transform the nation state into a welfare state based on socio-economic rights (Calloni, 2002b). Yet, women's movements have historically been based on the conviction that individual experiences connected to gender discrimination and prejudices can be generalised to the majority of women. However, over time women have become aware of the fact that specific experiences shaped by their sexual/gender diversity have a more general cultural and political meaning, and affect women belonging to the same territorial community as well as to other countries.

With the consolidation of industrial society and the recognition of political rights for women in the majority of Western countries after the Second World War, a new approach to women's questions was developed, taking the concrete lives of women as a starting point. It did not only include emancipation in the sense of the acquisition of rights, but also concerned the necessity to rethink the *human condition* of women from a deeper perspective, challenging methods from history, anthropology, psychoanalysis, philosophy, sociology and arts. Women became conscious of the fact that their destinies, considered as immutable until then, were historically constructed (de Beauvoir, 1949). New self-representations of women in their own voice and writing were promoted through autobiographies, novels, philosophical essays and political engagement. Biographies were seen as connected to history, society and individual lives. This new trend left space not only for an individual self-consciousness, but also for the development of both national movements and the initiation of differentiated forms of international co-operation among women, starting from common problems. For instance, in the early 1970s slogans like „the private is political" were aimed at showing the necessity to reconsider women's sexuality in the private/public life from the point of view of control by patriarchal rules (Pateman, 1988), as well as a sign of a possible liberation from familiar and social constraints. The liberty of women concerning their mind and body and the control over their fertility became crucial aspects in international feminism.

Women's movements grew over time within the limited space of a private room, a local community, or a nation state, but always had transcultural intentions and international aspirations. The history of Western contemporary feminism and women's movements can be broadly divided into three distinct waves:

1) First wave: from the eighteenth century onwards, women's movements struggled for the access to full citizenship. Emancipatory actions were intended to gain political rights and later socio-economic rights, such as equal access to education and all professions, protection of working mothers, and promotion of legislation/social policies against discrimination at the workplace. Socio-political initiatives were thus mainly aimed at achieving equality in employment and eradicating gender-based socio-economic inequalities.

2) Second wave: from the late 1960s onwards, the increasing importance of feminism as an autonomous movement, different from other social groups and political parties, opened up new controversies about specific gender-based issues in the public arena, in particular regarding sexuality and reproductive rights. These kinds of rights differ from universal ones because they cannot be applied to all human beings, but only to women. This is the case for contraception, abortion, in-vitro-fertilisation and reproductive technologies. Starting from the 1970s debates, demonstrations and protests for a legal recognition of sexual freedom, contraceptives and abortion were initi-

ated both in Europe and the United States of America. Abortion and the use
of certain contraceptives were considered a crime, which could be punished
by the penal law (Stetson, 2001). But commonalities as well as differences
between European and American women soon became evident, and national
legislation was quite divergent with regard to these questions. This was
partly due to the diverse models of welfare states, political representation,
and women's activism in different countries.

3) Third wave: a transnational approach to gender issues has developed in the
last two decades, in relation to globalisation, the end of a polarised world
order, and the transformation of the role of traditional nation states. In particular, a new connection between differentiated experiences of women's
movements, gender experts and supra-national institutions has produced basic transformations in the approach to gender questions. The United Nations
has in fact promoted world conferences and initiatives, based on platforms
for actions and pragmatic indications, like in the case of Beijing *Platform
for Action* (UN, 1996a). The European Commission has devoted specific
units, programs and directives to women's issues (Liebert, 2002). All democratic countries have ministries or committees devoted to equal opportunities. A new aspect has now emerged: the concerns of women living and
struggling in countries in development and in transition. They do not only
question the cultural and economic homogeneity imposed by Western societies and invoke bio-diversity and a different use of common resources
(Shiva, 2001, 2002), but also criticise prejudices and stereotypes reproduced
by Western feminism towards different communities, cultures and women.
Feminism has different voices and faces. Multiculturalism – which could be
„bad for women" (Okin in Cohen, 1999) – and the politics of identity have
thus become crucial aspects for re-conceptualising post-colonial feminism
(Butler & Scott, 1992) and the struggles for recognition (Fraser, 1999). Indeed, this dispute re-conceptualises an issue, which was already present in
the debate on black communities and feminism, started in the late '60s in the
USA. This was the case of Angela Davis, feminist scholar and leader of the
movement *Black Panther*.

The impact of women of colour and from countries in development/transition
has without doubt contributed to drawing attention to the crisis of the traditional
universalistic notions of subjectivity, rationality and human rights. A critique of
the Eurocentric perspective of Western feminism has stressed the complex realities
of women living in the 'third world' and the necessity to include their voices and
points of view for planning and applying fairer strategies for sustainable development. Gender must be connected to other social determinants, such as race, ethnicity, age, class, and culture. This means that feminism cannot be conceived as
a compact discourse and movement, but as multiple feminisms.

Yet, despite the critique of Eurocentrism and the observation of irreducible differences, it is important to investigate whether we can find claims for social and political justice in specific contexts of daily life that can be generalised. I think that although gender differences seem to be connected to cultural differences and daily life contexts, nevertheless women express common interests and engage in common struggles across regions, nations and continents, as has become clear in recent world conferences and cross-border initiatives.

Indeed, many commonalities can be found among women although they live in different socio-political-cultural contexts. General claims can be categorised into twelve critical areas of concern, as was done by the UN in the *Platform for Action*. It was signed in Beijing in 1995 by the representatives of national governments, participating in the fourth UN world conference devoted to the rights of women and girls. These areas are: 1) women and poverty, 2) education and training of women, 3) women and health, 4) violence against women, 5) women and armed conflict, 6) women and the economy, 7) women in power and decision-making, 8) institutional mechanisms for the advancement of women, 9) human rights of women, 10) women and the media, 11) women and the environment, 12) the girl-child (UN, 1996a).

Feminism no longer exists as a monolithic political macro-subject (if it ever existed). Experiences and policies in the last decades have in fact led to a more articulate public debate, which, until recently, was gender-blind. Moreover, gender studies have become a new academic discipline. Its insights are useful for research and epistemological considerations as well as for social policies against inequalities and for equal opportunities. Thanks to a broader social significance of science and a more adequate methodological structure of gender studies, a common search for social justice for individuals and vulnerable groups becomes possible. Yet the intent of achieving social justice needs an interactive assumption of normative and universal principles and a counter-factual idea based on the reciprocal respect among individuals and groups. Justice is strictly connected to the idea of rights and duties, a moral concept of equity for a fair socio-economic re-distribution of resources, respect for the dignity of the person, and the improvement of democratic institutions. In addition, women's experiences have been crucial for re-conceptualising rights and justice, making a purely formal definition of them impossible.

Indeed, justice is a matter of relations and feelings among human beings and is related to the construction of „love, desire, and care" (Nussbaum, 1999). Therefore, justice is not only a matter of distribution. It has to be applied in the concrete contexts of daily life, starting from the family. Indeed, family can be a 'school of justice', based on the respect among generations, women, men, children and the elderly. A sense of justice emerges always from concrete experiences of daily life, starting from the family and gender relations. Here the concept of equality acquires a more complex and concrete meaning. It does not mean sameness (women do not want to be like men), but tolerance and the respect of differences, without discrimination. We have to distinguish 'difference' based on the respect of diversity, and 'difference' in the sense of discrimination. For instance, while 'sexual difference' is a biological definition distinguishing men and women, 'gender difference' is a matter of relations between women and men, which have been socially constructed and therefore could indicate power dynamics and forms of suppression.

Gender becomes a crucial construct for approaching the issues of equality, diversity, commonalities and discrimination. As Susan Moller Okin argues,

> gender itself is an extremely important category of analysis, so that we ought not to allow feminist thinking about injustice to be paralysed by differences among women. So long as we are careful, and develop our judgements in the light of empirical evidence, it is possible to generalise about many aspects of inequality between the sexes. From place to place, from class to class, from race to race, and from culture to culture, we find similarities in the specifics of these inequalities, in their causes and effects, although often not in their extent or their severity (Okin, 1995, p. 294).

Gender and difference should therefore be analysed in a dialectic way. Indeed, they can indicate inequalities, but can also be used as a resource. As Iris Young argues, we have to understand „differences of culture, social perspective, or particularistic commitments as resources to draw on for reaching understanding in democratic discussion rather than as divisions that must be overcome" (Young, 1996, p. 39). Difference can be a resource (Young, 1997), improving human relations and building up social capital. Therefore it is important to talk about differences between women – both as a limitation and potential – in the age of globalisation, against a generic and unproductive ideological rhetoric of sisterhood. If it is true that we have already recognised our differences, nevertheless we have to learn how to 'translate' and use them as a new resource for theory and action and for enlarging existing potentials. Therefore, I would like to reframe the controversy about equality, difference, differences and social transformation (Barazzetti & Leccardi, 2001), affirming that factual injustice should not be confused with gender or cultural differences, which have to be respected, while injustice must be avoided. A normative approach to gender studies on the basis of cultural differences can be helpful in this regard.

My interest is to find 'normative' commonalities among women, while respecting various cultures. My research is thus aimed at developing a 'counter-factual' and cross-border approach to ethics, politics and justice, taking transitional – post-communist and post-colonial – societies as an example. Counterfactual and normative concepts refer to the moral dimension of the psychophysical respect of human beings, which cannot be disrespected (Margalit, 1996), and to the socio-political struggle against violence, poverty and discrimination. For instance, if we do not believe in a normative idea of equal respect between women and men, we cannot struggle against social/gender inequalities and violence. Normative issues can be employed for considering different dimensions of democracy in differentiated spheres and for considering at what extent social inequalities are affecting the private domain as well as the workplace and politics from the perspective of the individual.

These interconnected spheres concern:

- economy: equity/fairness (distribution);
- politics: political recognition of excluded human beings (full citizenship);
- law: democratic constitution and rules against violence and arbitrary acts (legal norms);
- morality: mutual respect of human beings and the development of human capabilities, starting from the family.

On the basis of this statement, my research aims at individuating the compatibility between the respect of cultures/bio-diversity and a reconsidered notion of 'concrete/differentiated universalism' related to human rights and social justice, starting from the daily experience and the 'transversal' political/research praxis of women. Indeed, „human rights and human development share a common vision and a common purpose – to secure freedom, well-being and dignity of all people everywhere" (UNDP, 2000, p. 1). Gender, rights, capabilities and development cannot be disassociated (Nussbaum, 2000).

3. Globalisation and development from a gendered point of view

Gender studies started as an interdisciplinary field, able to re-conceptualise the origins of social inequalities and cultural roles over centuries. Patriarchy, power, domination and the crisis of masculinity are considered key-points for rethinking the entire process of Western 'civilisation' and rationality. The natural and social sciences have been criticised for epistemological weakness and gender blindness. The notions of subjectivity and objectivity have been re-defined in a gendered and multicultural way (Harding, 1991, 1998). The socio-cultural feature of science – as gendered and ideological – has been clarified in different studies (Fox Keller, 1985). A gender perspective has thus been employed in different countries and fields since the 1990s as an interdisciplinary and mainstreaming approach for historical, epistemological and theoretical analysis, as well as for socio-political and pragmatic purposes. Thanks to this critique, science policies are recently changing through „mainstreaming gender equality" programmes (European Commission, 2000).

However, during the last years many changes in science, politics and culture have induced transformations in the epistemological status and methodological approaches of gender studies. Indeed, in the last decades research on gender – thanks to the critique of women of the South and East – has moved from a consideration of woman as a victim of patriarchy to a conceptualisation of woman as an active social actor, who can be discriminated against and subjected to others. Gender theory could therefore not be purely descriptive or narrative because it implies normative assumptions.

One of the crucial debates in women's studies concerned the controversy about the notion of equality/difference and sexual/gender difference (Irigaray, 1974, 1989; Scott, 1986, 2000; Diotima, 1987; Flax, 1990; Butler, 1990; Muraro, 1991; Benhabib et al., 1993; Braidotti, 1994; Moore, 1994; Klinger, 2001). This controversy contributed to open a new perspective for gender studies. In fact, even though a radical wing of feminist theorists were against an 'institutionalisation' of women's/gender studies at the academic level (and the design of Master's and PhD courses), nevertheless the 'internal' controversy on sex/gender difference started to have an impact in the universities, in politics and in society, augmenting the audience and publications devoted to experts in gender issues. Moreover, reflections on equality and differences have promoted trans-national projects on gender. This has contributed to the development of innovative forms of collaboration between Western societies and transitional countries, challenging the notion of globalisation as based exclusively on economic growth.

The aim of this section is the analysis of the third wave of feminism on the basis of the development of international networks and research, which redesign the traditional conceptualisation of social movements and the meaning of collective mobilisation. I propose to look at globalisation from a different angle. Globalisation – as in the case of the internationalisation of gender issues – can achieve unexpected goals in processes of democratisation and participation. Therefore I think that one of the most productive and innovative ways for approaching the issue of globalisation consists in re-framing the notion of development and international co-operation. The angle we have to introduce is a gendered cosmopolitan perspective for democracy from the pragmatic viewpoint of cross-border research networks, supported also by the use of new information technologies.

Yet how could we avoid the destructive effects of globalisation? The United Nations has defined globalisation as „a process whereby producers and investors increasingly behave as if the world economy consisted of a single market and production area with regional or national sub-sectors, rather than a set of national economies linked by trade and investment flows" (UN, 1996b). Three economic trends are then „commonly associated with the economic dimension of globalisation: (a) trade liberalisation and expansion; (b) the spread of production capacity around the world through foreign direct investment by multinational corporations; and (c) financial liberalisation and the increased international mobility of financial capital" (UN, 1999). This definition indicates that economic globalisation takes the priority over any political decision of democratic parliaments. Globalisation therefore refers in this context to the transformation of the world economy, and in particular to the change of the previous industrial forms of production/distribution and the increasing power of information systems (Held et al., 1999). It characterises post-Fordist societies and refers to the growth of the service sector. Private companies are able to regulate and control systems of production and distribution in a flexible way, overcoming the political control of parliaments and questioning labour regulation, traditionally guaranteed by trade unions. Therefore, productive activities are locally achieved but internationally directed by companies, aiming at controlling new global strategies of the capital market. For this reason, the process of economic globalisation has overcome the boundaries of the nation state. Indeed, „globalising processes have transferred powers away from nations and into depoliticised global space. [...] This space needs regulation, the introduction of rights and obligations" (Giddens, 1998, p. 141).

Indeed, many difficulties are at stake. Globalisation needs to be regulated, but its effects on women also need to be considered. The transformation of previous political and economic systems creates new differences and inequalities among populations, producing unemployment and new forms of subjugation of women, and even forms of slavery through the trafficking in human beings, which is becoming one of the biggest illegal business branches of the new millennium. In Western countries women are experiencing the effects of deficits in social protection due to the crisis of the welfare state and the enlargement of the European Union (many Nordic feminists voted against the EU). In post-socialist countries women are encountering neo-traditional forms of subjugation and the increase of domestic violence due to the inability of the state to enforce gender equality and guarantee work for women. In post-colonial countries different processes of development are exploiting and marginalising women both in Africa (with the destruction of bio-diversity and the persistence of civil wars) and Asia (with new economic exploitation without any social guarantees) (UNICEF, 1999; UN, 2000).

Globalisation has changed pre-existing labour relations and political dynamics (Sassen, 1998). Considering the mixed effects of globalisation, the *World Survey on the Role of Women in Development: Globalisation, Gender and Work* has tried to provide suggestions for developing gender-conscious policies at both the national and international levels. In particular, it has suggested: „1) Equal opportunity policies and programs aiming at reducing occupational segregation by sex. 2) Policies allowing women workers to consolidate the benefits of increased paid employment through access to basic workers rights. 3) Policies addressing the needs of women who form the bulk of the informal sector" (UN, 1999). Economic globalisation without incorporating a social and gender perspective can not be successful ("Gender and Development", 2000). For example, the political collapse in Eastern Europe and the economic crisis in East Asia have shown the limits of a global economy and capital market acting without legitimate democratic procedures and respect for human rights.

Globalisation produces many new problems as well as unexpected consequences, partly due to human mobility. Migration and human mobility have usually been understood as a complex and dialectical phenomenon, helping production in the host country as well as increasing well being for migrant workers, but there are new forms of discrimination emerging against foreign individuals and communities. Yet human mobility can help to establish new commonalities and new political perspectives for human society. It induces the mobilisation of resources, energies, social capital (Morrow, 2001) and knowledge, and throws new light on perspectives for a cosmopolitan democracy. This approach has already been employed by feminists for mobilising people, organising cross-border campaigns, fund raising, and creating new opportunities. Migration challenges the traditional and restrictive idea of political belonging by proposing a notion of 'social citizenship'. Democratic systems should, therefore, be reconsidered in relation to human mobility, globalisation, the establishment of supranational political institutions and the constitution of international juridical organisations. International relations can no longer be conceived as pure diplomatic relationships between sovereign nation states. On the contrary, international relations have become an overlapping composition of nations, international organisations, pressure groups and citizens.

Because of that, globalisation does not only have problematic economic effects (D'Andrea & Pulcini, 2001). New socio-cultural perspectives can be promoted, offering the possibility to bring countries and people in contact who for years have been rather distant. Furthermore, the mobility of human capital and the change of the previous world order based on the polarity between the Soviet Union and US have produced new kinds of 'transnational territories'. In addition to the constitution of the European Union, some tendencies for the construction of transregional and transcontinental citizenship are in fact emerging both in North-Eastern Europe as well as in Southern Europe. For example, the viewpoint of a 'Mediterranean citizenship' has been prospected because the Mediterranean Sea connects three different continents: Europe, Asia and Africa with countries in war. This kind of cross-continental citizenship would have the interest in establishing differentiated forms of collaboration and exchange among citizens belonging to the different Mediterranean countries and regions, which for centuries were connected by trade and common cultures. This main goal was indicated by the conference *Forum Civile EuroMed*, hold in Naples in 1997. The same transcontinental standpoint characterises the Arctic region, as for example in the *Circumpolar Coping Processes Project* supported by the UNESCO and promoted in eight different countries present in the Arctic zone. Both the

Mediterranean and the Arctic projects show that the present process of globalisation reconnects territories in new ways, which have already shared many commonalities in the past. However, the political borders of modern nation states divided them, worsened by the effects of the cold war. In all cases, women's engagement for gender issues is central in the context of global restructuring, in the analysis of the household, in redefining the labour division, and in maintaining/transforming local cultures/minorities, challenging traditional relationships between women, men and generations.

Concerning these 'trans-European' processes in progress, the European Union has indicated four 'frontier' areas: the *Barents Sea Region, the Baltic Sea Region*, the *Central-Euro Region* and the *Alps-Adria Region*, which have become centres of diversified exchanges of goods and mobility of people. In all these areas women activists and scholars have been engaged in developing cooperation and constructing new forms of collaboration and communication (Saarinen, 2000).

Comparative and cross-border research has thus become crucial for approaching issues on gender, migration and social justice from an inter-cultural perspective, linking international networking with the potentials offered by the information society. For instance, the internet can acquire a democratic meaning because potentially all people can have access to the same information and opportunities for increasing their knowledge. Yet we are aware that only a minority of literate people can use or buy a computer, so that the creation of new forms of social exclusion/inequalities is possible. Moreover, simply buying a computer does not mean to have access to information, or being able to use the internet for having more opportunities and possibilities to choose from. Technical knowledge does not always coincide with the capacity to use information and develop fruitful contacts and projects. However, this is precisely the challenge of the 'network society'. As Manuel Castells argues: „While networks are old forms of social organisation, they are now empowered by new information/communication technologies, so that they become able to cope at the same time with flexible decentralization, and with focussed decision-making" (Castells, 2000, p. 5).

The European Union is aware of the new cultural gap related to the gender digital divide. Therefore the EU is increasingly supporting women's networks and a new approach to technological means in European countries and abroad. Research and information systems become determinants of a sustainable development in an innovative way through the use of information technologies, as 'extra-territorial' communication means. Yet the use of information systems and networks can be instrumental in and addressed to strategic economic purposes, living out the contextualised interests of civil society. As Castells argues: „Global networks of instrumental exchanges selectively switch on and off individuals, groups, regions, and even countries, according to their relevance in fulfilling the goals processed in the network, in a relentless flow of strategic decisions. It follows a fundamental split between abstract instrumentalism, and historically rooted particularistic identities" (Castells, 1996, p. 3).

The meaning and use of information systems and global networks can thus be radically different according to their diverse or opposite goals. For instance, concrete experiences have shown that information networks and telematic forums can be helpful for social justice initiatives and international organisations. This is the case in the preparation process for *Beijing +5* by UNIFEM in 2000, aimed at considering the results of the platform for action decided in Beijing in 1995. Besides the official reports edited by interested national governments, most of the information received by UNIFEM came from the grassroots level. In fact, women and other groups from different, distant and remote countries exchanged messages. A comparison between different living conditions and world-wide institutions was carried out through simple communication means, which reproduced a sort of virtual arena of the debate and made a simultaneous communication possible and open to all interested participants. The results of these inter-continental investigations and cross-border debates have become a substantial part of the documentation on *Beijing +5*, which was discussed by the representatives of the member states during a UN plenary session, held in New York in July 2000.

Indeed, for years women's networks and NGOs have developed alternative and transversal forms of a 'global and extra-territorial bottom up democracy'. Indeed, considering the latest UN world conferences, we can notice that although official representatives of the nation-states took the final decisions, nevertheless gender issues were discussed by women's pressure groups and NGOs, and later presented to interested political organisations. Forms of deliberative democracy and global governance (Meyer & Prügl, 1999) have thus been experienced by women during the world conferences on human rights in Vienna (1993) and the rights of women in Beijing (1995). The recognition of gender-based violence as a crime against human rights can therefore be considered as a victory of the grassroots international women's movements. Globalisation can have 'another voice'.

4. Applying normative issues: The experiences of a research network

So far I have discussed new perspectives for approaching politics, international relations and gender issues. In particular, in the first part I have reconstructed the different waves of women's movements in relation to the transformation both of the nation state and of countries in development/transition. In the second part I have indicated how globalisation could be re-conceptualised and used as a resource by and for women and all human beings, developing alternative projects and networks. In this section I aim at developing a possible pragmatic application of gender research/studies using the individuation of normative aspects in concrete daily life contexts as well as counterfactual principles for avoiding social inequalities. Theory and praxis can thus find a new link, connecting social philosophy, politics and ethics with gender studies, empirical investigations and cross-border research. I use the experiences of a research network I have initiated and co-ordinated for years as a case study to illustrate my points.

Before presenting my argument, I want to remind readers of one of the main assumptions of feminism, which is also a crucial aspect in international networking: *I'm my body*. That means that we have to be very conscious of our culturally intrinsic limits as well as potentials while we are planning both local and transnational initiatives. Indeed, a constitutive interconnection between mind and body means that I am a concrete, gendered, situated self as a result of my experiences, environment, education, beliefs, and culture. Therefore, I am a Western woman, who is, however, able to 'transcend' her psycho-cultural boundaries. A concrete self, belonging to a specific culture, should always include decisions and actions that respect and value otherness in his/her life horizon (Habermas, 1996). He/she constantly includes others in his/her life, their presence and their points of view. Therefore, an individual should be capable of assuming an inter-cultural perspective in his/her daily experience, which refers to the vision of people coming from other cultures, their bio-diversity, and struggles for recognition. A democracy is based on legitimate political power, recognised as such by interested and equally represented citizens, who participate in public activities and are free to choose their candidates. However, as politics is based on territoriality and belonging, democracy remains elusive for minorities and other excluded human beings. These principles must always be implicit in deliberations taken by members of a specific political community (Benhabib, 1996). Civil society does not automatically coincide with political community – neither in numbers nor interests.

These questions have been at the basis of a research network on gender issues I have initiated in London in 1996. Before describing the main activities carried out by the *Network*, I would like to propose a definition of network and networking.

Castells (1996) associates the concept of network, conceived as a social structure, with the notion of network as produced by information systems. In this way, social relations and information technology become linked. In regards to my case study, I do not want to simply apply Castells' approach, or to employ a network analysis to gender issues (Piselli, 2000). My interests concern the challenge of constructing and using a network for producing research, improving individual/collective capabilities, emphasising commonalities, connecting people, and creating possibilities for social policies. Indeed, a network – as I conceive it – is an overlapping constellation of resources and people, who, based on common values and interests, can be flexibly associated in order to achieve common goals. Therefore, on the one hand a network or a system of overlapping networks (constituting bigger or smaller groups, according to the programme at stake) refers to already existing social capital, capacities, knowledge, expertise, and personal links. On the other hand, a complex network is interested in reinforcing capabilities, potentials, resources, opportunities, and well-being in the planning of projects, institutions, connections, and so on. In particular, a research network is based on the assumption of the presence of specific scientific expertise, reciprocal esteem, loyalty and reliability among the participants, the capacity to work together, and a common interest for social justice. Yet a productive disagreement is considered as a communicative resource for improving plans. In addition to these aspects, a pragmatic perspective is also necessary for planning projects, research and creative actions, which are aiming at studying and raising awareness of the causes of unfair conditions in life. Therefore, the borders of a network are flexible in terms of participants, disciplines, cultural belonging, professions and geo-political confines. Individual biographies become communicatively and professionally interconnected with more general issues and goals. Networking is an assiduous process of contacts and planning, which makes knowledge and research dynamic, and an interactive and cross-border process.

On the basis of these assumptions, the example of the *Network* I have initiated can be useful for understanding in theory and praxis the value of normative and cross-border assumptions for social justice in different cultures and various countries. The applicability of gender theory to societal issues, public ethics, politics and the social sciences can thus be proved.

The *European Network* was established in 1996 at the Gender Institute of the London School of Economics and Political Science (LSE) in London. It was connected to the activities of the *European Gender Research Laboratory*, a project financed by the European Commission. In 1999 the *European Network* was renamed *International Network for Research on Gender* because of the development of new initiatives exceeding the limits of the European Union.[1]

The aim of the *Network* is to develop international research agendas in gender studies, with a particular interest in institution/capacity building, global gov-

---

1   Thanks to the support of the director of the Gender Institute, Henrietta Moore, and the
     help of colleagues, I became the co-ordinator and responsible for the improvement of the
     Network (Report of the activities 1996-2000: http://www.lse.ac.uk/Depts/GENDER/Marina/
     inrghome.htm). In 2001 the *Network* was transferred to the interdisciplinary centre Ate-
     neo Bicocca Coordinamento Donne" (ABCD), based at the Faculty of Sociology of the
     „Università degli Studi di Milano-Bicocca" in Milan, where I moved and taught social
     and political philosophy/philosophy of social sciences.

ernance and civil society. In particular, the main areas for initiatives concern public ethics; social justice and cosmopolitan democracy; European citizenship and human mobility; women and science; reproductive rights and the struggle against violence; and perspectives for social policies. The *Network* has developed collaboration with scholars, researchers, activists, feminists, NGOs, the media, entrepreneurs, decision-makers and politicians. This framework has required the establishment of contacts with several international institutions, universities, research centres, the European Commission and the United Nations.

The establishment of the *Network* was quite complex and occurred in different phases. After having prepared the theoretical framework and goals of the *Network*, information collection and databases, which had to be managed as well, were soon organised. Moreover, it was necessary to gather bibliographies, identify areas of expertise and names of researchers working on topics of interest for the *Network* and interested in a possible collaboration, and to collect information about research centres, NGOs, conferences and projects for applications. The unifying aspect joining the participants in the networks was a cross-cultural interest for social justice and gender, as evidenced by the sample of projects I will mention below. When a project or proposal was initiated, members of the *Network* with related expertise were approached regarding a possible participation.

The activities of the *Network* therefore covered different areas: 1) technical organisation of information, databases, contacts with interested groups, application forms, etc.; 2) initiatives, like seminars and national/international conferences, aimed at discussing theoretical frameworks, and meetings, aimed at planning projects and discussing common issues; 3) participation in various projects, programmes and networks linked to the main areas of interest of the *Network; 4)* consulting mainly in countries in development/transition and institution building; 5) publication of reports, papers and drafting of documents; 6) circulation and dissemination of information through papers and web pages.

The *Network* was and still is a work in progress. At the beginning the *Network* did not have a model to imitate, so that the challenge was to connect social/natural science, knowledge, principles of social justice, biographical experiences and political engagement in an innovative way. Therefore, the use of our own biography, profession, networks of researchers, activists, and so on, became the basis for interactively developing our own individual and collective capabilities, competencies and potentials. However, networking requires linguistic proficiency, professional competencies and the capacity to apply interdisciplinary methodologies. It requires a specific inter-cultural sensitivity and awareness, communication skills and comprehension of body language, which is basic for understanding cultures, people, and their points of view when their idiom is not familiar to us.

Yet normative frameworks were the core of the Network. For instance, a re-conceptualisation of the notions of gender and social justice has been made possible by a seminar on Social Justice, Gender and Cultures, which for four years was organised weekly at LSE. A large number of colleagues and visitors (from various countries and disciplines) gave lectures and contributed to intensive intellectual discussion forums and the assessment of current debates in the social sciences, philosophy, politics and public discourse. Empirical analyses were interconnected with a reflection about the basis for a theory of deliberative democracy in a trans-cultural way.

This weekly seminar was also very successful because it was used as a discussion space, where it was possible to elaborate topics which were later addressed in comparative projects (Beck et al., 2001). In this framework, European research acquires an innovative character because it is conceived in the form of European thematic networks (Athena, 2000, 2001) (directed by Rosi Braidotti) and discussed at national and international conferences.

This was the case with the *conference The Changing Welfare State: Citizenship, Gender, and the Family. Experiences of Northern and Southern Europe*, organised at LSE in 1997, with the participation of politicians, scholars and researchers coming from Italy, Spain, Greece, France, Finland, Sweden, Norway, Denmark, and the UK. At this occasion, we had the opportunity to conduct a comparative analysis about similarities and differences in Europe concerning gender relations and the state. In particular, we were interested in investigating whether the different models of welfare states and social provisions in Northern and Southern Europe were actually based on a different structure of gender relations and of the family. In fact, while in Northern Europe gender relations are based on individualistic assumptions, in Southern Europe gender relations are based on the centrality of the woman as a mother within the family (Calloni, forthcoming). National welfare states and social policies have been designed according to these different models of gender relations and structures of the family.

Indeed, the attempt to connect research, institutions and social policies in processes of democratisation was one of the goals of the Network. European citizenship and mobility, the creation of a social Europe, the transformation of unfair gender relations and a different approach to science were in fact the main topics, and the basis for several initiatives. For instance, the collaboration with the unit Women and Science of the European Commission (previously based at the Direction General XII and now situated at DG Research), directed by Nicole Dewandre, became crucial starting with the draft of the *Declaration of Networks Active in Europe* (see appendix).

The perspective of an enlargement of the European Union to include the Eastern European countries and the dramatic geo-political changes in the former Soviet Union and the Balkan region induced the *Network* to widen its research interests, and become truly international. In particular, one of the more urgent questions, which emerged from the international scenario, concerned the dramatic escalation of private as well as public violence in post-communist countries. The previous socio-political order based on the formal recognition of equality between women and men was replaced by a widening gender gap in terms of social inequalities and economic prosperity as well as an increase in illegal business, trafficking of human beings, and forced prostitution.

In these countries women tried to face this new dramatic situation by building up networks and crisis centres to help people deprived of public assistance and the welfare system. International feminism was immediately mobilised in order to co-operate with Eastern European women. Northern as well as Southern European scholars and activists planned projects financed by national institutions and ministries in order to contribute to cushion the perverse effects of neoliberal economic policies. New research strategies and models of co-operation were developed by women. Collaboration among NGOs, networks and researchers became widespread. Out of necessity the *Network* also started collaborating with some projects in post-communist countries.

I now want to briefly describe three case studies concerning gender-based violence in post-communist countries (Russia, Albania and China) as success stories to illustrate this new trend in feminist co-operation and research.

The first project was called *A Network for Crisis Centres in the Russian Barents Region* and was directed by Aino Saarinen from the University of Oulu in Finland (http://wwwedu.oulu.fi/ktl/NCRB/). The *Network* was asked to provide consulting services concerning theoretical frameworks, normative issues (from social justice to reproductive rights) and experiences in the constitution of networks. The project was focused on the Barents region, a remote Arctic area of North–West Russia, which is now experiencing a dramatic economic transformation. It is due both to the fall of the Soviet Union and the collapse of the military sector and production characterising this area. Domestic violence is increasing as a result of the subversion of the previous socio-economic and political order. Women are loosing their economic autonomy and experiencing the return of traditional forms of patriarchal power in the household as well as in the workplace. In this situation, grassroot movements have established crisis centres, developed as a social response of the civil society to solve conflicts and overcome the disorientation and the psychological breakdown of people. Yet experts and new professionals (e.g. social workers) are required. Women's networks, which already existed in the Soviet time for exchanging goods and favours (Ledeneva, 1998), have now been reorganised in the form of self-organised NGOs, as centres for psychological help, acquiring a specific civic and political meaning in new processes of democratisation. In this way a transnational research collaboration acquires a socio-political local meaning for gathering information, financing local researchers, giving the possibility to establish new crisis centres, providing advise for the development of new professions, establishing international co-operation, and sharing knowledge. This experience has been crucial not only for the *Network*, but also for my personal biography. I have learned a lot both in the professional and personal arena from the interaction with Russian/Nordic colleagues and activists, in sharing my knowledge and experiences and giving advice about constituting networks and building institutions. This was the case of the *School of Politics 'Alexandra Kollontai,* created at the Pomor State University in Arkhangelsk (Calloni & Saarinen, 2002).

Another project in Eastern Europe, which interested the Network, was initiated in Albania. I was approached by Valli Corbanese, head of the programme in Albania, and asked to participate in the project *Promotion of Social and Economic Status of Women in Albania* (http://www.al.undp.org/projects/gender. htm). It was financed by the United Nations Development Program/United Nations Office for Project Services (UNDP/UNOPS), and the Italian Ministry for Foreign Affairs in collaboration with the Soros Foundation. I was asked to consider the possibility of establishing a Gender Institute at the University of Tirana. In particular, I was appointed to draft a statute for the Gender Institute, to organise a training course for teachers in gender studies, and to design a related master's degree. The project was divided into three main phases: meetings with representatives of Albanian society (scholars, politicians, NGOs, activists, professionals, religious, and various pressure groups); collection of data and information (such as historical, anthropological and socio-economic studies, statistics and legal documents); and getting advice from local and international experts on legal and political questions, Albanian gender issues, and projects for co-operation. After this first stage, which revealed the socio-cultural need and institutional possibility to establish a Gender Institute, the statute could be drafted. Suggestions for supporting the advancement of women were made. Moreover, the *Albanian Gender Institute* had to be designed as a sustainable organisation, eventually becoming independent from donors. The *Albanian Gender Institute* opened in 2000 and has become a permanent institution, belonging to the University of Tirana, and based at the Faculty of Social Sciences. It is a research, training and professional centre also accessible for NGOs and civil servants (Calloni, 2002a). This project, meant as an example of institution/capacity building in gender issues, had the aim to reconnect political institutions and the university with civil society, individual expertise, new professions, and the private domain. In fact, during communist time Albanian women lived in a schizophrenic situation: employment was guaranteed by the party, and a formal right to equality was recognised. Yet in the household traditional forms of division of labour and patriarchal behaviours persisted. Private questions related to fairer gender relations in the family did not matter for social policies and the State. After the fall of communism, the reality of poverty and gender-based violence became evident. Moreover, kidnapping and trafficking in women and girls for prostitution abroad have become the most profitable illegal business. As a reaction to this tragic situation, Albanian women have very quickly found new forms of organisation and mobilisation. Thanks to projects financed through international co-operation and the collaboration of feminist Western NGOs that worked on awareness campaigns both in cities and in rural areas, Albanian women were supported in their activities. As this example shows, the connection between grassroots experiences, cross-border research, international mobilisation and transversal co-operation can become pivotal for improving democratic institutions and developing human capabilities, starting with fairer gender relations.

The last example of an international research co-operation I want to describe, takes place in China, where the population is experiencing a new problematic mix of political roles still controlled by the power of the Communist Party, and free economic initiatives, strategically implemented with the support of a global capital market. Gender issues have become relevant in the ambivalent transformation of Chinese society. The increasing power of a free economy, the transformation of the traditional family, the radical change of ways of life, the urban environment and the structure of villages, has created far-reaching modifications in gender relations as well. In particular, the question of gender-based violence and women's human rights has become crucial. In fact, since the Vienna conference on Human Rights 1993 and the UN Women's Conference 1995, gender-based violence is considered a crime against humanity. As the Chinese government signed the platform for action, a bill had to be promoted. Therefore, the government appointed a commission of experts, drafting a proposal for a law against domestic violence to be submitted to the parliament. This issue has opened a strong debate in China about women's human rights, which resulted – among others – in the creation of a hot line against violence, managed by a NGO, independent from the *Women's Federation* affiliated with the Communist Party. Moreover, national/international organisations are financing projects for helping local women to deal with the new effects of globalisation as well. In particular, a British delegation of scholars and experts in the field of gender, the media, domestic violence and networking, was invited to take part in meetings and discussions in Beijing and Guangzhou, within the initiatives supported by the Cultural and Educational Section of the British Embassy in China. The participation of the *Network* was required to support this initiative and discuss questions about domestic violence, communication and the transformation of gender issues put forward by journalists, lawyers, sociologists and interested people (Radio Guangdong – Cultural and Educational Section of the British Consulate-General, 2000). Lectures were given at the *Centre for Women's Studies* of the University of Beijing, with the participation of students and colleagues interested in developing gender studies. Discussions and exchange of ideas with the participants were very intense, fruitful and productive. Two seminars and various meetings were also organised both with the Chinese commission working on gender-based violence, and members of *Radio Guangzhou*, working for the program *Women's hour*. In fact, a radio programme was devoted to problems concerning family and the daily lives of women, due to the increase in conflicts caused mainly by the socio-economic development of Chinese society. The audience also raised new questions: divorce, property, employment, and child custody. Indeed, new psychological/social problems are affecting Chinese women because of the difficulty to find a balance between family and career. Women are more mobile than in the past, live far from their villages of origin and are in many cases better educated and more successful than men are. This new situation challenges the traditional equilibrium among genders, generations, traditions and society. Chinese women are now encountering problems, which Western women have faced for decades. A stronger connection between Western and Asian women has become more urgent. Common problems among women are becoming more and more evident. The experience in China was thus very successful in terms of an exchange of information and an improvement of cross-border networks concerning specific common gender problems.

The researchers, activities and personal experiences I mentioned above intended to emphasise the necessity to conceive the scientific work as strongly linked to normative assumptions, social critique and claims of validity about democracy and justice, moving from the bottom up. They are brought to life by different groups of the civil society, as the dramatic emergence of gender questions in countries in development/transition has shown.

5. Research planning, institution building and human capabilities

Planning research, organising meetings, writing papers, drafting documents and continuing to networking, I always kept in mind the compatibility between scientific work, normative assumptions and political goals, which forms the basis of cross-border forms of social justice. Mutual respect among human beings, fair distribution of resources, political recognition and application of legitimate laws are thus connected to the attempt to project programmes, aimed at obtaining sustainable development.

Normative concepts became a constitutive basis in planning research, which is illustrated by the following aspects:

a) *Functioning and empowerment of human capabilities*. The notion of basic human functional capabilities, theorised by Amartya Sen (Nussbaum & Sen, 1993) can be summarised in a decalogue, as done by Martha Nussbaum: 1: *Life*: „Being able to live to the end of a human life of normal length." 2: *Bodily health*: „Being able to have good health." 3: *Bodily Integrity*: „Being able to avoid unnecessary and non-beneficial pain." 4: *Senses, Imagination and Thought*: „Being able to use the senses." 5: *Emotion*: „Being able to have attachments to things and persons outside ourselves." 6: *Practical Rea-*

son: „Being able to form a conception of the good and to engage in critical reflection about the planning of one's own life." 7: *Affiliation*: „Being able to live for and to others, to recognise and show concern for human beings, to engage in various forms of social interaction." 8: *Other Species*: „Being able to live with concern for and in relation to animals, plants, and the world of nature." 9: *Play*: „Being able to laugh, to play, to enjoy recreational activities." 10: *Control over one's environment, political and material*: „Being able to live one's own life and nobody else's." (Nussbaum, 1995, pp. 83-85). This means that a social critique or social policies cannot be promoted when the functioning of these human capabilities is neglected.

b) The building of legitimate institutions is crucial for reinforcing democratic systems, because of the necessity to connect the claims of validity of pressure groups and excluded social actors with the political power freely chosen by citizens belonging to a specific community or nation state but interrelated with 'foreign' individuals. Different multifaceted groups of the civil society can remain disconnected from the representatives in parliament and government.

c) The implementation of equal opportunities for all citizens is basic for the implementation of human and citizenship rights, starting from the educational and communication system. The conception of scientific projects should thus have the aim of providing access to disadvantaged individuals, starting from women/children mainly in countries in development/transition and creating new social opportunities for vulnerable groups. Science and development must be conceived as a common process of knowledge and action for obtaining freedom for all (Sen, 1999).

d) The improvement of the social quality of daily life is also a fundamental task for research, gender studies, and the strengthening of a democratic society. This implies the acquisition of a fair distribution of wealth, income, social protection and the empowerment of human resources and social capital.

These frameworks can be applied in Western as well as in post-colonial/post socialist countries. These matters offer the possibility to reinterpret a formal universalism in a concrete/differentiated way. Indeed, the normative principles I mentioned above can be applied or verified in culturally differentiated contexts of daily life in case they are neglected.

As researchers, or better as „research workers" (Calloni, 1998), we have the privilege to give consistency to ideas and projects, contributing to strengthen our capabilities and the talents of other people. Networks and networking are based on the capability to connect human resources, knowledge, experiences, exchange of information and opportunities in a productive way. But women are traditionally better at networking than men. Why don't we use this potential for contributing to develop forms of cosmopolitan democracy, overcoming the borders of nation states and fighting against injustices, starting from gender relations in different countries?

These are the experiences of networks/networking, the meaning of social justice and the vision of the role of research I wanted to share with you. But I do not want to sound too optimistic. Responding to a possible critique in this regard, I want to conclude by quoting a sentence of a well-known Italian intellectual and politician, Antonio Gramsci, who died in 1937, a few days after his release from a fascist jail: „We must have the pessimism of reason and the optimism of the will." Let us continue to network and be creative in our projects, comparative analyses, and perspectives for social justice, maintaining a constant vision for a better future, remembering those who have been violated or continued to be persecuted and humiliated. Hope can be concrete.

References

Athena – Advanced Thematic Network in Activities in Women's Studies in Europe (2000 and 2001). The Making of European Women's Studies. Eds. R. Braidotti & E. Vonk. Utrecht: Utrecht University.

Barazzetti, Donatella & Leccardi, Carmen (2001). Genere e mutamento sociale. Le donne tra soggettività, politica e istituzioni. Soneria Mannelli: Rubbettino.

Barry, Brian (2001). Culture and Equality. An Egalitarian Critique of Multiculturalism. Oxford: Polity Press.

Beck, Wolfgang; van der Maesen, Laurent; Thomése, Fleur & Walker, Alan (eds.) (2001). Social Quality: A Vision for Europe. Boston: Kluwer Law International.

Benhabib, Seyla (ed.) (1996). Democracy and Difference. Contesting the Boundaries of the Political. Princeton: Princeton University Press.

Benhabib, Seyla (2001). Dismantling the Leviathan: Citizen and State in a Global World. In: The Responsive Community, vol. 11, 2, pp. 1-10.

Benhabib, Seyla; Butler, Judith; Cornell, Drucylla & Fraser Nancy (1993). Der Streit um Differenz. Feminismus und Postmoderne in der Gegenwart. Frankfurt a.M.: Fischer.

Braidotti, Rosi (1994). Nomadic subjects: Embodiment and Sexual difference in Contemporary Feminist Theory. New York: Columbia University Press.

Butler, Judith & Scott, Joan W. (eds.) (1992). Feminists Theorize the Political. New York, London: Routledge.

Butler, Judith (1990). Gender Trouble. New York, London: Routledge.

Calloni, Marina (1998). Neopopulism and Corruption. Toward a New Critique of the Élite. In: Constellations, 1, pp. 96-109.

Calloni, Marina (2002a). Albanian Women after Socialism and the Balkan War. In: Athena, The Making of European Women's Studies. Eds. R. Braidotti; I. Lazaroms & E. Vonk, Vol. III. Utrecht: University of Utrecht, pp. 49-60.

Calloni, Marina (2002b). Women's Human Rights, Equal Opportunities and Bio-politics in Europe. In: R. Braidotti & G. Griffin (eds.). Thinking differently: A European Women's Studies Reader, London: Zed Books, pp. 95-120.

Calloni, Marina (ed.) (forthcoming). Lo Stato sociale in cambiamento: cittadinanza, genere e famiglia. Esperienze del Nord e del Sud Europa. In: Inchiesta, special issue.

Calloni, Marina & Lutz, Helma (2000). Gender, Migration and Social Inequalities: The Dilemmas of European Citizenship. In: S. Duncan & B. Pfau-Effinger (eds.), Gender, Economy and Culture in the European Union. London, New York: Routledge, pp. 143-170.

Calloni, Marina & Saarinen, Aino (eds.) (2002). Gender, Research and Networks across Boundaries. A different approach to globalisation. Copenhagen: Nordic Council of Ministers.

Castells, Manuel (1996). The Information Age: Economy, Society and Culture, Vol. 1: The Rise of the Network Society. Oxford: Blackwell Publishers.

Castells, Manuel (2000). Materials for an explanatory theory of the network society. In British Journal of Sociology, Vol. 51, 1, pp. 5-24.

Cohen Joshua, M. Howard M., E M. Nussbaum (1999). Is multiculturalism bad for women? Susan Moller Okin with respondents. Princeton: Princeton University Press.

D'Andrea, Dimitri & Pulcini, Elena (eds.) (2001). Filosofie della globalizzazione. Pisa: Edizioni ETS.

de Beauvoir, Simone (1949). Le deuxième sexe. Paris: Gallimard.

Diotima (1987). Il pensiero della differenza sessuale. Milano: La Tartaruga.

European Commission – Research Directorate-General (2000). Science policies in the European Union. Promoting Excellence Through Mainstreaming Gender Equality. Brussels: European Commission.

Flax, Jane (1990). Thinking Fragments: Psychoanalysis, Feminism and Postmodernism in the Contemporary West. Berkeley: California University Press.

Fox Keller, Evelyn (1985). Reflections on Gender and Science. New Haven, London: Yale University Press.

Fraser, Nancy (1999). Social Justice in the Age of Identity Politics: Redistribution, Recognition, and Participation. Unpublished paper.

Gender and Development (2000). Gender and Globalisation. Special issue, Vol. 8, 1.

Giddens, Anthony (1998). The Third Way. The Renewal of Social Democracy. Oxford: Polity Press.

Habermas, Jürgen (1996). Die Einbeziehung des Anderen. Frankfurt a.M.: Suhrkamp.

Harding, Sandra (1991). Whose Science? Whose Knowledge? Thinking from Women's Lives. Ithaca, New York: Cornell University Press.

Harding, Sandra (1998). Is Science Multicultural? Postcolonialism, Feminisms, and Epistemologies. Bloomington and Indianapolis: Indiana University Press.

Held, David; McGrew, Antony; Goldblatt, David & Perraton, Jonathan (1999). Global Transformations. Politics, Economics and Culture. Cambridge: Polity Press.

Irigaray, Luce (1974). Speculum: de l'autre femme. Paris: Minuit.

Irigaray, Luce (1989). Le Temps de la différence: pour une révolution pacifique. Paris: LFG.

Klinger, Cornelia (2001). Gleichheit und Differenz. Von alten Sackgassen zu neuen Wegen. In: Transit, 21, pp. 186-207.

Ledeneva, Alena (1998). Russia's economy of favour: blat, networking, and informal exchanges. New York: Cambridge University Press.

Liebert, Ulrike (ed.) (2002). Europeisation, governance of gender (in)equalities, and public discourses in EU-member states. New York: Peter Lang.

Margalit, Avishai (1996). The Decent Society. Cambridge: Harvard University Press.

Meyer, Mary K. & Prügl, Elisabeth (eds.) (1999). Gender, Politics in Global Governance. New York: Littlefield Pub..

Moore, Henrietta L. (1994). A Passion for Difference. Oxford: Polity Press.

Morrow, Ginny (ed.) (2001). An appropriate capitalisation? Questioning social capital. Research in progress series, 1. London: LSE Gender Institute.

Muraro, Luisa (1991). L'ordine simbolico della madre. Roma: Editori Riuniti.

Nussbaum, Martha C. (1995). Human Capabilities, Female Human Beings. In: M. C. Nussbaum & J. Glover (eds.). Women, Culture, and Development. A Study of Human Capabilities. Oxford: Clarendon Press, pp. 62-104.

Nussbaum, Martha C. (1999). Sex and Social Justice. Oxford: Oxford University Press.

Nussbaum, Martha C. (2000). Women and Human Development. The Capabilities Approach. Cambridge, New York: Cambridge University Press.

Nussbaum Martha C. & Sen, Amartya (eds.) (1993). The Quality of Life. Oxford: Clarendon Press.

Okin Moller, Susan (1995). Inequalities Between the Sexes in Different Cultural Contexts. In: M. C. Nussbaum & J. Glover (eds.), Women, Culture, and Development. A Study of Human Capabilities. Oxford: Clarendon Press, pp. 274-297.

Pateman, Carol (1988). The Sexual Contract. Cambridge: Cambridge University Press.

Piselli, Fortunata (2000). La Network Analysis negli Studi di Genere. Unpublished paper.

Radio Guangdong – Cultural and Educational Section of the British Consulate-General (2000). Media, Community and Women Seminar. Guangzhou.

Saarinen, Aino (2000). An Umbrella Project on Democratisation in the European Frontier Regions and Collaboration against Gender Violence. University of Oulu.

Sassen, Saskia (1998). Globalization and its discontents. New York: New Press.

Scott, Joan (1986). Gender. A Useful Category of Historical Analysis. In: American Historical Review, vol. 91, pp. 1053-1975.

Scott, Joan (2000). Fictitious Unities. »Gender«, »East«, and »West«. Paper presented at the 4th European Feminist Research Conference, Bologna.

Sen, Amartya (1999). Development as Freedom. Oxford: Oxford University Press.

Shiva, Vandana (2001). Tomorrow's Biodiversity (Prospects for Tomorrow). London: Thames & Hudson.

Shiva, Vandana (2002). Buy Water Wars: Privatization, Pollution and Profit. London: South End Press.

Soysal, Yasmine N. (1994). The Limits of Citizenship: Migrants and Post-national Membership in Europe. Chicago: Chicago University Press.

Stetson, Dorothy (ed.) (2001). Abortion politics, women's movements, and the democratic state. Oxford: Oxford University Press.

UNIFEM. http://www.undp.org/unifem

United Nations (UN) (1996a). Platform for Action and Beijing Declaration. New York: UN Department of Public Information.

United Nations (UN) (1996b). Globalisation and Liberalisation: Development in the face of two powerful currents. Report of the Secretary General to the ninth session of the UN Conference on Trade and Development. New York, Geneva: United Nations.

United Nations (UN) (1999). World Survey on The Role of Women in Development: Globalisation, Gender and Work. New York: UN Department of Public Information.

United Nations (UN) (2000). The World's Women 2000. Trends and Statistics. New York: United Nations.

United Nations Children's Fund (UNICEF) (1999). Women in Transition. Regional Monitoring Reports, 6. UNICEF: Florence.

United Nations Development Programme (2000). Human Development Report 2000. New York, Oxford: Oxford University Press.

Women's Human Rights. http//www.hrw.org/hrw/worldreport99/women

Women Watch. http://www.un.org/womenwatch

Young, Iris. M. (1996). Communication and the Other: Beyond Deliberative Democracy. In: S. Benhabib (1996), pp. 130-135.

Young, Iris M. (1997). Difference as a Resource for Democratic Communication. In: J. Bohman & W. Rehg (eds.), Deliberative Democracy. Essays on reason and politics. Cambridge MA: MIT Press, pp. 383-406.

Appendix

Women and Science: Networking the Networks
Declaration of Networks Active in Europe (Brussels, 8-9 – July 1999),
supported by a resolution of the European Parliament in February 2000

We,
the representatives of networks of women scientists and organisations committed to the improvement of the gender balance in research policy;
present at a meeting in Brussels on July 8 and 9, 1999;
Welcome the initiatives being taken on women and science by DGXII.

State that:
The gender balance in research policy is to be perceived from three different perspectives: research by, for and about women. Progress has to be made in these three perspectives, i.e. (i) promote women's participation in research activities, (ii) ensure that women's needs and interests are taken into consideration when setting research agendas, (iii) promote the understanding and the inclusion of the gender issue.

– The under-representation of women in science and decision making bodies is both wasteful of human resources and a serious obstacle for the development of the sciences and for European society as a whole.
– Scientific development leads to new frontiers for human responsibility and implies increasingly fundamental ethical choices. This also calls for the need for an improved gender balance in the field of research.
– Networking among women scientists is essential to empower women scientists in their respective fields.

Recognise that:
The *rationale* for the networking of women scientists is:

– To support, enhance and empower members in their careers;
– To inform, encourage and motivate girls and young women to choose scientific subjects; to campaign to make scientific careers more attractive;
– To provide a database of role models and mentors for individuals and organisations that require them;
– To take part in decision-making processes to contribute to the shaping of scientific institutions and their culture;
– To encourage employers of scientists to ensure that women have access to, can return to and progress in scientific careers; to campaign for family-friendly measures to be incorporated into fellowships and mobility scholarships and for special projects in each Member State to facilitate women's return to scientific careers;

–   To lobby and take part in policy processes in order to improve the gender
    balance in research and research policy as well as the position of women in
    science and science policy.

The networks and organisations committed to the improvement of the gender
balance in research policy use *different tools* for communicating, informing and
lobbying. They recognise, however, the importance of Internet-based tools and
new technologies in that they make the networking of networks easier and
cheaper and facilitate the achievement of networks' objectives. Databases,
newsletters and other conventional means are useful tools especially at the local
and national levels. Tools for public outreach and regular and permanent contacts with journalists are also relevant. Networks should consider themselves resources for the media. It is important to develop benchmarking systems as well
as auditing systems on gender balance in the various institutions.

To improve the gender balance in research, the reasons for the actual imbalance must be researched and analysed. *Gender research* on all aspects of science (the contents, the methods and the processes) is crucial to produce change.
The exchange of knowledge between the different networks of gender research
specialists, women scientists, and equal opportunities policy makers is important
to identify efficient ways of solving the main problems in the area of women,
gender and science. It is also important for networks of women scientists to establish links and partnerships with the main networks of scientists in the same
field.

The European *added value* is linked to all aspects of the rationale for networking. It provides »value to the members« by bringing more women scientists
into the Fifth Framework Programme thus not only enriching the research but
also giving visibility to the research done by women scientists. In addition,
women scientists will benefit from the European scale in their research activities. On the policy side, the European added value is three-fold: (i) it strengthens
each network by allowing an exchange of experiences and good practice; (ii) it
facilitates co-operation and consultation across sciences, between women scientists and networks, which will allow for a greater participation in the European
Union policy process and public debate; (iii) it encourages the development of
European evaluation tools in order to monitor the impact of current policies at
both national and European level on women in science.

Recommend
The development of tools by the networks:

–   Awareness and educational tools: EU and Member States should support the
    development of expert databases of women scientists and commission re-
    search on the databases held by networks on women in science.
–   Communication tools: EU and Member States should support, fund and
    provide training – if needed- for the development and use of the Internet and

new technologies for the dissemination of information and communication with and between networks as well as improve the use of traditional means of disseminating information and communication.

– Lobbying and advocacy: Information kits on FP5 and the importance of women in science should be provided by the Commission and each network could add its material too. These kits would be disseminated to local and national political representatives. A mechanism that would encourage local visits by women scientists to their political representatives should also be developed. This could be done at the national and European level.

– Measurement tools: EU and Member States should provide and facilitate the benchmarking of network organisations.

– Tools to better network the networks: EU and Member States, which use networks on a professional basis for advice, expertise and dissemination of information, should recognise and formally support the networks, as well as the establishment of national nodes of existing networks.

The promotion of the link between gender research and the „women and science" issue

– The networks should promote discussion on the definitions of science and scientific quality.

– The need for expert knowledge on questions of women, gender and science should be inventoried;

– The issues which are raised in the inventory should be implemented in the next framework and, where possible, in the remaining part of FP5 ; this means that there should be a dual approach to gender research: mainstreaming and specific attention to gender research programs;

– Journals of women scientists and gender research should be inventoried in order to provide a common platform; the scientific journals among these should be recognised as such.

The creation of a European network of networks on women and science:

– The European network of networks on women and science should regroup existing networks of women scientists and organisations committed to the improvement of the gender balance in research policy from the European Union and from Eastern and Central Europe.

– Such a network would exchange information in particular on European and national legislation and programmes and would also give visibility to the opinions of women scientists on all areas related to women in science. It would also exchange experiences and strategies on a regular basis. The creation of this network should be facilitated by the existing networks themselves by including a European dimension in their work and consultation.

–   The creation and maintenance of such a network should be supported on a long-term basis by the European Union, in particular through enabling women scientists to meet on a regular basis and allocating resources for the maintenance of such a network.

Finally,

–   The European Commission should commission a project, which documents best practice in supporting women in science in the Member States (drawing on the networks).
–   Institutions employing scientists should produce annual statistics on gender monitoring.

The next European Commission and the new European Parliament should continue to support the serious commitments that have been made to gender and sciences in the Fifth Framework Programme, and help facilitate the creation, maintenance and strengthening of a European network of women scientists.

Amel Hamza

Women Living Under Muslim Laws (WLUML):

A Women's Movement in the Islamic/Muslim World between Struggles, Strength, Challenges and Empowerment[1]

1. Introduction

This article discusses the issue of women's empowerment using the network of „Women Living under Muslim Laws" (WLUML) as a case study.[2] It tries to link the historical manifestations of religion to women's situation living under Muslim laws and discusses resistance from the women's movement. I do not want to suggest here that the low status of women in Muslim communities has resulted from misinterpretations of Islam alone. On the contrary, I explore some other factors influencing women's status as well. The factors that influence women's lives can be summarised as a rigid interpretation of Islam, the structure of the society, national identity vis-à-vis culture, the economic crisis, state policies and, finally, the dominant patriarchal ideology. Scholars of Islam have shown that history has influenced the situation of women on two levels: One level is the level of Islam and its historical context, while the other one deals with the socio-economic and political conditions of Muslim communities.

Islam has developed in specific socio-political and economic contexts. While this should have led to place-specific ways of thinking, a rigid form and misinterpretation of Islam has developed widely. This was a result of conservative thinking led by conservative groups, whether at the level of politics or at the level of religion. Research shows that Islam depends in its thought on four discourses. These discourses are the *Quran, Sunna, Figh* and *Ijthad.* The first one is the holy book from which all the *Ibadat* (meditation) and rule of law (*Sharia*) are derived. The second is the *Sunna*, the Prophet's teachings and practices. The third one deals with juridical thinking, and the fourth one is meant to create spaces to understand the holy text. Within all these processes of understanding the text and applying it to reality, misuse in a practical sense has been the case

---

1 An earlier version of this paper with the title "International Women's Solidarity: Case Study WLUML" was presented at the *ifu*, Project Area Migration, in Hanover, Germany on the 4th of August, 2000.

2 For further information, publications or current statements of WLUML please visit the website www.wluml.org.

throughout the history of Islam. Furthermore, the Islamisation of so-called Muslim communities has been the main and continuous effort of Muslim scholars and Muslim nations. In this regard, another dimension has interfered, namely the dimension of culture, belief and the practice of Islam in different communities, meaning that with thorough examination of what happened during the time of the Prophet and after, huge gaps and different uses of Islam were found.

These factors are the language in which the *Quran* was revealed, the reason for using certain verses, and the socio-political context, among others. As was shown for example by Leila Ahmed, Abdullahi An Na'im, Fatima Mernissi and Sharabiit it is not advisable to take a verse from the *Quran* and generalise without taking the whole essence of Islam into account. This means that for instance the verses that deal with women's issues cannot be considered without considering the messages about justice and equality that are also part of Islam. If we consider them in isolation, we tend to make Islam look like a religion of injustice, not fair to women, and in fact oppressing women's rights.

2. Islam/Muslim Discourse

2.1. Differentiation between Islam and Muslim thinking/laws

It is imperative to take other issues into account in analysing women's issues from an Islamic perspective. In this regard, Farida Shaheed's work is important because it differentiates between Islam and Muslim. She analyses the existing Islamic structures by distinguishing between how Islam influences the way Muslims think, and how Muslims perceive Islam and make use of it. Viewed this way it becomes clear why some Muslim organisations developed into intolerant organisations that seek to rule using Islam for their own benefit. In addition, the international power situation, South-North relationship, economic crisis and the issue of nationalism vis-à-vis identity have created spaces for religious revivalism. One should acknowledge the importance of these factors, but due to the limitations of this paper no reference will be made to illustrate the different interpretation of verses that deal with women, verses that control women's lives, bodies and integrity. In this regard, it is essential to concentrate on discussing the sociological location in which these verses were revealed and how they can be interpreted differently. The different interpretation does not just mean taking the verse and trying to look at it from a different angle. Rather, the difference becomes clear when we look at the message of Islam in a holistic way, in addition to examining the sociological aspect, the language and the contemporary situation, where women have occupied different positions and status levels.

2.2 Sociological factors and women's struggles

Believing in sociological factors and the impact of history on women's lives today, the history of Muslim communities with special reference to Muslim and
non-Muslim women living under Muslim laws must be considered. The position
of women in Muslim communities is characterised by low educational attain-
ment, little political involvement, limited access to economic occupations and
social integration. In this way the focus is on the historical picture of women's
organisations and their achievements. This was meant to break up the whole notion of women as the victim of traditions, culture and religion. This is not to
suggest that these factors are not of significance in control over women, but to
emphasise the fact that women have been struggling throughout history for their
survival and rights, whether this is at the level of their roles as mothers, wives or
other social actors. However, it is worth mentioning that research on Muslim
women should aim at giving women another human dimension, meaning the
well being of women as human beings without being associated with any social
function.

2.3. Women's situation in relation to their rights

Another important element is to discuss women's situation in relation to their
rights. In this regard, the situation of women's personal matters in the form of
Muslim Personal Law and its impact on women's empowerment has to been
taken into consideration when analysing and supporting Muslim women. The research „Muslim Women and Civil Rights: A Comparative Study between Cape
Town and Omdurman, Sudan," 2002[3], showed that Muslim Personal Law in Sudan and South Africa are based on *Sharia* Law, and that there are certain similarities and differences between the existing law in the Sudan and the suggested
proposal for Cape Town.[4] However, both of them somehow attempt to follow
other Muslim countries in applying *Sharia* Law for personal matters. While
some Muslim countries have a progressive *Sharia* Law, most of the Muslim Personal Law in Muslim countries and communities is oppressive for women. Sudan's case clearly shows the difficult situation of women that results from an
oppressive legal system, rigid fundamentalist government and a conservative society. The South African draft proposal for Muslim marriages shows signs of
more equality. However, as was discussed in the same study, certain measures
have to be added to the draft proposal for Muslim marriages. This mainly con-

---

3   This research was published under the Women and Law: Sudan Project (Women and
     Law in the Sudan, 1999a, b, c).
4   The Muslim population in Cape Town is numerous and holds considerable economic
     power.

cerns completion of the law and the issues of polygamy, child custody, maintenance, inheritance and other issues that might be brought up by Muslim scholars. In other words, Muslim women's organisations, in co-operation with the
South African legal system, have to prepare themselves in case proposals regarding Muslim scholars and their view of the Muslim Personal Law.

Furthermore, the case of Sudan case reveals that there are other mechanisms
that the Muslim State has put into place to control women's behaviour, mobility
and personal freedom. The so-called 'Public Order Act' of 1996 was established
to regulate socially unacceptable behaviours. A television programme called
Wajah lwe Wajah (face to face), broadcast every week, shows the misuse of
power by the public police who are assigned by the Public Order Act to control
the streets. The debate, which took place on July 19, 2000 on the occasion of
current changes that have occurred in the Sudanese political system, brought
evidence of the misuse of power. It is high time to discuss issues that have never
been discussed before in public. The purpose of the programme was to gain
support for the Opposition Parties, who argue for the lifting of the Public Order
Act, to show that the issue has been discussed publicly, and to engage public
opinion. Despite the purposes of the programme, it was very clear that the whole
system, in enforcing the Public Order Act, spent lots of government money to
create a special police force to control people and their ways of life, this of
course with special reference to women. Moreover, the programme discussed
the issue of Public Order from another dimension, a dimension that has to differentiate between controlling the society and rehabilitation of the society. The
latter should be dealt with from the educational and socialisation points of view
as has been recommended. The first one has something to do with the law, *Hud-
dud,* criminality, etc. A differentiation between control and rehabilitation has to
be made in order to reach a healthy society, as one of the invitees concluded.
One hopes that with the recent political changes in Sudan, legal reform will take
place. Anyway, it is as if the current changes are trying to differentiate between
what Rania Hassan El Amin (1996) called 'established Islam' and 'cultural Islam' in her study entitled „Sudanese Women – Why the Silence". Sudanese
people have been Muslim for centuries without having complications in their
private lives. These complications occurred when 'established' Islam, in the
form of political bodies, came to power.

2.4 Women's personal empowerment

Legal changes and reforms have to go hand in hand with women's personal
empowerment. As research showed, women have internalised their oppressive
situation to the extent that changing it is the first priority. This is not to generalise the situation, as the paper will illustrate as well the efforts made by some

women to change their situation, but the fact remains that women need to be educated, organised and empowered for their own sake, not for being a hand of the government as the Sudanese government's policies suggested in the National Comprehensive Strategy. The low literacy rate among women, ignorance of the law, social pressures and the poor economic situation which make them dependent, have contributed to their low status and inability to change. Therefore, to change the situation requires a strong political system that believes in women's issues, a progressive educational system in which women's issues are addressed and, finally, gradual social changes towards bringing values that enhance women in Sudanese society rather than dismissing them.

Control over women's lives is built up from different points: One is the issue of nationalism and identity vis-à-vis culture and religious revival. The second major reason could be the fear of women as competitive agency. The two reasons are interlinked, and their manifestations are clearly shown in policies towards women, whether at the private or public level.

3. The emergence of WLUML

Drawing from the previous analysis of the situation of women in Muslim communities, many organisations have been established to counter the force of Islamist and other oppressive systems. There is, however, a general tendency to associate women's rights, resistance and fighting for equality with western ideology. Because of the hammering on nationalism, identity has limited women in general to associate with their sisters in the West or elsewhere. Moreover, women's rights in so-called third world communities are always seen as a being based on radical feminism, which the 'South' does not want to acknowledge.

> The concept of feminism has been the cause of much confusion in Third World countries. It has variously been alleged by the traditionalist, political conservatives and even certain leftists that feminism is a product of 'decadent' western capitalism; that it is based on a foreign culture of no relevance to women in the third world; that (it is the) ideology of women of the local bourgeois; and that it alienates or diverts women from their culture, religion and family responsibilities on the one hand, and from the revolutionary struggles for national liberation and socialism on the other hand (Jayawardena, 1986, p. 2).

Still in many countries the women's movement's struggles for women's liberation have been controversial. On the one hand there is a general tendency to deny feminism and its existence in the so called 'Third World' countries, while on the other hand many writers suggest that women all over the world suffer from a rigid and oppressive traditional value system which has changed due to current cultural exposure to the West (ElWathig et al. 1982, p. 5). In 1979, for instance, western feminists attempted to launch effective and poignant campaigns in defending Iranian women who were 'condemned' to wear the veil in order to protect them against the 'Fanatical Islamic Movement'. Throughout history, women have resisted oppressive (tyrannical) systems whether in terms of norms, culture or religion fanaticism. The historical connection between national liberation and women's liberation proved that feminism and women's liberation were not imposed on 'Third World' countries by the West where women participated actively in these struggles and were not merely pawns for men. However it is important to acknowledge the concept of sisterhood and solidarity without borders.

The emphasis on local women's movements actually comes from the attitudes of contemporary Muslim rightists (fundamentalists) towards women's ability to change their position, which is usually very limited. Fundamentalists see women's struggle in Muslim communities as a Western conspiracy. Their policies tend to ensure women's dependency and subordination to men or to the system at large. It seems to me that the basis for understanding the potential for women's social emancipation is an analysis of women's subordination, for instance the external and internal construction in a society which determines women's access to education, decision making and social reforms constrained by patriarchal structures. To address women's needs and interests, a number of related social, cultural, religious and political factors and the way of women's mobilisation within certain political organisations has tended to minimise, devalue and degrade the aspiration for women's liberation. Despite all this, and irrespective of the different cultures and religions, the women's movement in Islamic/Muslim countries tends to be critical towards the existing system.

WLUML is a network that works to overcome oppressive situations like that of the situation of women living under Muslim laws irrespective of whether they are Muslim or non-Muslim women. It is crucial to mention that Islam as a religion of faith is not oppressive or constrains women's status as many think, but those who introduce and enforce Islamic/Muslim laws have formed and produced such an oppressive legal system. To ensure fairness when dealing with this matter it is important to differentiate between Islam and Muslim laws.

3.1 The Establishment of WLUML

The legal situation of women living in Muslim countries and communities has been deteriorated over the past two decades through the process of Islamisation, i.e. the creation of 'Islamic States.' A certain version of Islam (known in the media as fundamentalism) is being promoted and is expanding, mainly to the detriment of women (Hélie-Lucas, 1986, p. 2).

The International Solidarity of Women Living under Muslim Laws emerged in response to:

- The struggle of Muslim and non-Muslim women within Muslim communities.
- Problems of Muslim women migrants and the issues of child custody, child marriage, forced (arranged) marriages etc.
- The rise of fundamentalism and its oppressive ideology regarding women
- The general assumption of a unified Muslim ideology and law

Other activities emerged as the network developed, and there was growing need to develop different programmes and different strategies.

For many years women from Muslim countries and communities have lived under oppression and attempted to counter it in total isolation within their national context. As a result of this isolation we „Muslim Women"[5] tended to analyse our own situations exclusively in the framework of the internal policies of each country. Moreover, psychologically this isolation gave us the feeling of loneliness and guilt. Increasingly, however, the deteriorating situation of Muslim women has become known. The reports of the situation might be seen as anti-Islam in general or as a conspiracy from the West, but in both cases Muslims women themselves felt the need to change their situation and to criticise any attributed aspect referred to under the name of religion, culture or national identity. Thus women from ten Muslim countries came together in 1986 in one of the international women's meetings in Amsterdam to discuss such problems and the situation of women in Muslim communities or living under Muslim Laws or States. These women felt that there was an urgent need to develop an organisation to counter the Islamic forces for the sake of women's liberation. The participants came from Algeria, Tunisia, Morocco, Egypt, Sudan, India, Pakistan, Bangladesh, Sri Lanka and Iran.

The first plan of action to be undertaken by WLUML was in April 1986. The core discourse of the network was aimed at filling the gap of information and knowledge that exists between women. The women agreed that there is a lack of information on Islam, the sources of Islam, historical manifestations of Islamic culture etc. They felt the need to fill the gap, interact with other women and disseminate their ideas. With the exception of a few countries these women have enough information and can engage in a debate when talking about Islamic concepts. Needless to say, the plan of action tried to discover the best means and ways of bringing Muslim women together to share their experiences, exchange information, explore the various realities of Muslim women in different Muslim communities and obtain enough and adequate information to challenge the existing structure. Accordingly the success of the first campaign for urgent cases encouraged the women participants to formulate a permanent structure and set

---

5   I am aware of the heterogeneity of Muslim women, but in this paper I would like to homogenise them to show their solidarity.

up a network. However, it was very clear that the concept of networking is very old and thus new ideas and innovations were needed to revitalise it.

3.2 Projects

Initially, the network felt that the need to break the isolation of Muslim women was a primary concern. Building ideas, strategies and means of communication was required (between 1986 and 1988). Eight out of the ten founding members organised an exchange programme to bring women from different Muslim communities, states and Muslim minorities together. The exchange programme took place between August and December 1988. The basic idea was to foster cultural insights that would enable women to distinguish between religion, culture and politics in their own set-up, as these three elements are closely intertwined and become easier to separate if one looks at them from different points of views.

One of the objectives of the WLUML is that Muslim women understand the realities by themselves without the intervention of any feminist or women's organisations etc. Building on women's struggle within Muslim communities should be the top priority for change. Under these objectives the exchange programme was divided into three topic areas: an orientation session, an exchange visit and a synthesising session. The preparation, collection of information, selection of participants' resource persons, and national women's organisations etc., were organised by two women, one from Sri Lanka and the other from Nigeria, with the help of ISIS International Women's Centre in Geneva.

Participants were mostly activists from Muslim countries and communities working at the grass roots level, organisers, and lawyers or academic women involved in research. The main focus was on those who have not been exposed to a foreign environment. The educational level, age and family status of the women varied. The twenty-four participants came from Algeria, Bangladesh, Egypt, India, Indonesia, Iran, Malaysia, Nigeria, Pakistan, the Philippines, Somalia, Sudan, Sri Lanka, Tanzania and Tunisia. The feedback from the participants piloted extensive effort and extensive responsibilities for the network to carry out further research, disseminate information, create supportive means for solidarity etc. For instance, some of the Pakistani women who visited Somalia reflected on the following commonalities.

> Legally there are some similarities, the man is the head of the family, religion (Islam) is the most sensitive issue, women if not married are considered a social deed [...] not understandable this social deed, wife beating, ill-treatment of wives who are sterile or produce female children, preference given to male children etc. Customary laws have a strong influence on the lives of women, preference of early marriages, polygamy, believing that female genital mutilation is Islamic (Kamala, 1989, p. 9).

When comparing the situation of the Malaysian women with Sudanese women the participants stated:

> The women in Malaysia seem to be more enlightened on women's issues. They are also more involved in activities concerning women. The legal situation is much better as there are women lawyers who are fighting to change some of the laws (Late & Kamala, 1989, pp. 9-10).

In comparison to the Sudanese women (as indicated by participants from India, Indonesia and Malaysia who visited Sudan)

> Muslim women in Sudan are really isolated within their own country as well as from the rest of the world. Since there are no voluntary groups to form a link between urban and rural women both tend to get isolated in their own context. As a result, their position and opinions are ambiguous in relation to important issues or questions (ibid., p. 10).

Taking these reflections into consideration, when the participants came back for the synthesising period, they suggested two strategies and collective projects to be undertaken by the network. The two strategies showed dichotomies within women's movements: some believe that change has to take place within the theological framework, while others believe in a completely secular discourse. Out of these two discourses, the network undertook two collective projects: One was the progressive interpretation of the *Quran* and the other was a project „Women and Law."

Subsequently, the *Quranic* Interpretation by Women took place in July 1990. The meetings brought together thirty women activists and resource persons from ten different countries to read for themselves the verses of the *Quran* related to women. This meeting focused on three main elements, a) the issue of the socio-economic and political history of Islam, b) the linguistic dimension (translation via interpretation) and c) the sources of Muslim legal system. Two publications[6] came out as a result of this meeting, which have been translated into French, Arabic, Urdu and English. I believe that there are still many people who take this issue and follow up e.g. Prof. Rafat Hassan.

While the *Quranic* interpretation meeting allowed women to develop an alternative interpretation, the „Women and Law Project" explored and analysed the laws and their application in the broader socio-political cultural domains. Despite its secular nature, the women and law project had to focus on all kinds of laws, varying from customary law to civil to *Sharia* law. It involved twenty-three Muslim countries, communities and Muslim minorities.

The main objectives were:

1. To deconstruct the myth of a homogenous world of Islam where only one definition of womanhood is possible.

---

6   The publication are (1) Les Femmes Dans Le Coran, kit information, Karachi 8 – 13 July 1990 (in French), (2) Information kit "Women in the *Quran: Quranic* Interpretation by Women", July 8 – 13 1990 (in English).

2. To make clear that there is a difference between Islam as a *DEAN*, which literally means faith, and Islam as a practise (Muslim practise, Muslim interpretation, Muslim way of life etc)

3. To demystify the sources of laws and customs that try to immobilise women in different ways.

4. To provide women with an information pool on the multiple strategies developed by women to counter patriarchal norms, laws and systems so that each woman and group can distill inspirations from one another and develop strategies and positions most suitable to their needs and contexts.

The information collected has built the WLUML documentation unit and has been used for networking, dissemination, and in building different strategies, mobilising women to change their situation etc.

The network initiated the „Feminist Institute" in response to Muslim scholars. The transformation of knowledge by Muslim women and for Muslim women was the core objectives of the institute. Moreover, the capacity building of Muslim women has been the main focus of the two summer institutes that took place in Turkey and Nigeria.

Importantly, the network has committed itself to support women affected by Muslim states or even general oppressive systems. The commitment is directed towards the struggle of women in their daily lives, which is achieved by several means like alerts of action, the publication of dossiers (in different languages), the establishment of a documentation centre and last but not least by networking activities with international and national women's organisations, universities etc.

4. Strengths of WLUML

The network has developed and expanded tremendously since its start. This expansion showed the strength of the network to accommodate different interests and needs of Muslim women. The following points show the strength of the network. The network developed in many ways – for instance in terms of outreach programmes, developing a structure to be an effective advocate for women, and devising different strategies to meet the need of Muslim women etc.

a) The network has developed tremendously from 1985 to the present day as the demand has increased. The growth of the network (an extensive women's movement) was inspired by many other local women's organisations.[7]

---

7   Twenty-six countries from Asia, Africa and the Middle East have participated in the Women and Law Project. They covered quite a range of areas, information and out-reach programmes at the grass roots level. Publications to compare the situation in nineteen countries have been translated into different languages. "Alert of Action" is sent every

b) In terms of the structure of the network and the methods of working, there are two ways of information flow and solidarity, which is the heart of the WLUML. In order to develop structurally in a satisfactory way the WLUML managed to make connections to and use of the following committees:

   – The co-ordination office, which used to be in France, has moved to London in order to have a wider impact. The office is run through bottom-up approaches, meaning the co-ordination office is in direct contact with regional co-ordination offices (Asia, Africa and the Middle East). The core group consists of a flexible number of women who at any given time are involved in co-ordinating specific activities of the network and take responsibilities for implementing them at international, regional and local levels.

   – The network itself consists of women and women's groups who work together in a non- hierarchical structure. Each group/individual is fully autonomous in analysing their own situation and developing strategies according to their own subjective conditions and circumstances. However, the essence of the network's work is the feeling of inspiration, which comes from solidarity and sisterhood between Muslim women working with the network. This feeling of sisterhood is also strengthened by sharing common objectives, which are reflected in their activities carried out locally.

   – National working groups are responsible for implementing the network's plan of action, disseminating information and feeding the network documentation unit.

c) The demystification of Islam as a homogenous religion with homogenous believers provided new inputs for the activists and scholars and created spaces to challenge the existing situation. The knowledge of one Muslim identity, one practice was challenged and changed through the study and research by the network. The diversity gives space for manoeuvring, thus catering to different projects according to the need and the interest of women.

d) The WLUML has adopted the concept of flexibility and accommodation of different interests. Fixed activities are based on the daily struggle of Muslim women and non-Muslim women living under Muslim communities or laws. The network launches regular alerts for action, newsletters and dossiers. The information is collected through the alert of action, newsletters and through other means support and documented in the documentation unit. The documentation unit works hand and hand with all the other members of the networks, national working groups, individuals, libraries etc. The main objec-

---

day to thousands of people, while the mailing list is increasing given the fact that the Alert of Action and the Dossiers are emailed to the people in the WLUML mailing list. Many local organisations have participated, involved and carried out activities of the WLUMLs.

tive of the documentation unit is to broaden Muslim women's mind in relation to acquiring information and knowledge and in terms of solidarity and helping each other through the exchange program, progressive interpretation of the *Quran*, the project „Women and Law," and finally the aspect of women and armed conflict and the issue of sexuality in the Muslim world (Imam, 1997).

e) The role of the documentation unit of the WLUML is to provide information, disseminate and analyse it. Moreover, one of the plans of action of WLUML is to transform knowledge. This has been done through the implementation of the Muslim Feminist Institute.

f) The network has drawn its spirit from the diversity of the Muslim women and the continuation of the struggle, which determine its priorities and future strategies. Given the diversity of the situation of Muslim women, the network felt that no priorities could be planned as long-term activities. The priorities are distilled according to the needs of women in any given situation. Solidarity and collectivism are the soul of the network spirit, as are adopting different strategies to cope with the changing and evolving Muslim situation.

g) Limitation and future plans of the network: The current challenges of the network to cope, communicate and work with the existing women's movement in Muslim communities and countries – which apparently has been existing for a long time – that we have to deal with are: a.) the national focus, b) the secular type referred to as a radical one, and finally c) the Islamist women's movement with some kind of reservation. However, there are also various methods utilised and employed by WLUML in order to achieve its goal as an international network: adopting different approaches, openness and transparency, and interacting with international/national women's organisations, human rights activists, commitments and competence in addition to the collective efforts by all those who believe in women's solidarity.

5. Conclusion

The conclusion will focus on two main issues that brought some changes in women's lives and were adopted by the WLUML. These are the issues of education and women organising for change. Education does not only refer to a certain stage in life. On the contrary, feminist education, which was suggested in this research as a top priority for changing women's lives, sees writing and reading as a form of power. Acquiring knowledge in the beginning means one should have access to literature, books and other means of information. Charlotte Bunch emphasises the political element of literacy in her essay entitled 'Feminism and Education' in which she states that:

Revolutionary movements have almost always seen developing a general literacy as one of the most important tasks. Yet in this country, where we assume that most of us can read and write, it is often overlooked. Reading and writing are valuable in and of themselves, and women should have access to their pleasure. Beyond that, they are vital to change for several reasons. First, they provide a means of conveying ideas and information that may not be readily available in the popular media. For example, the idea of women's liberation first spread through mimeographed articles. Second, reading and writing help develop an individual's imagination and ability to think. Third, an individual's access, through reading a variety of interpretations of reality, increases that person's capacity to think for herself, to go against the norms of the culture, and to conceive of alternatives for society – all of which are fundamental to acting politically. Fourth, reading and writing aid each woman's individual survival and success in the world, by increasing her ability to function in her chosen endeavours. And finally the written word is still the cheapest and most accessible form of mass communication. When we recall why literacy is important to movements, it becomes clear that we should neither assume that women are already literate, nor ignore the value of teaching women to read, write, and think as part of feminist education (Bunch, 1990, p. 32).

In reference to WLUML's priority, specific recommendations could be given to women's organisations working on legal issues, that is the issues of law reform and structural reform. In this approach to change, the law is the target of change. In general, laws are put forth and the needs of women have to fit the law – whereas the opposite is necessary. The actual needs of women differ from the perceived needs, thus to accommodate the needs certain laws need to be reformed to provide for women's rights. Strong political leaders who are gender sensitive and sympathise with women's needs could work towards reforming the law. Women's groups can organise and lobby for law reform through political outlets that have such power.

Research can be conducted to study the problems of women and their varying needs to support and encourage law reform. This approach, of course, strictly relies on changing laws to suit women's needs. Approaches to change may vary, as the case may be, where law reform may not be the answer. Rather a social approach is more appropriate. Law reform can be a very slow process and in itself may not change a social practice. For example, law reform may be difficult to implement in the case of inheritance because of the parties who are to benefit. In the process of law reform it may be difficult to get the woman's support because of her mixed feelings about the possibility of her losses and also difficulties of getting a man's support due to his mixed feelings of loss of power over the female members of his house.

The difficulty is getting government support despite contradictions within official policy: support arising from the general policy for equality of women and opposition because of the long-standing party and government policy to support and maintain traditional culture and customs. Regarding the structural reform, this approach to change refers to a client's representation in the courts and litigation. It is more often than not the case that women are not given sufficient representation in the legal system for them to defend themselves. Courts and legal system structures marginalize the need of the woman's proper and equal representation for the preparation of the defence. In this light it is necessary for legal administrators that women have proper and sometimes more than equal representation in court. Also, the litigation procedures are worked out with them in order to satisfy court requirements. Law enforcement agencies must be gender sensitive realising that women may have a great lack of awareness of procedures and administrative tasks regarding the legal system. Proper and sound counselling should be given with emphasis on listening to the women's problems and needs, and how they can be solved and satisfied.

Looking at all issues and recommendations, one assumes that a feminist ideology would safeguard women's issues and improve their situation. A number of foundations have to be established to develop a comprehensive approach to empowering women's organisations for the sake of women's empowerment. As was stated by bell hooks „to develop political solidarity between women, feminist activists cannot bond on the terms set by the dominant ideology of the culture. We must define our own terms" (hooks, 1984, p. 47). This is one of the factors that can empower feminist organisation. Another factor is to discuss our differences openly and without prejudice and build solidarity from there.

References

Bunch, Charlotte (1990). Women's Rights as Human Rights: Towards a Re-Vision of Human Rights. In *Human Rights Quarterly*, Vol. 12, 4, November 1990.(Reprinted in several other publications in English and published in Spanish in La Mujer Ausente: Derechos Humanos En El Mundo, Santiago, Chile: ISIS International, 1991; also translated and published in Chinese, Dutch, French, Portuguese, Russian, Sinhala, and Tamil.)

El Amin, Rania Hassan (1996). *Sudanese Women – Why the Silence.* In partial fulfilment of the requirements for obtaining the degree of Master degree in Women and Development, Institute of Social Studies, the Hague, unpublished research.

ElWathig et al. (1982). *The State of Women's Studies in Sudan.* DSRC, Khartoum University, Sudan.

Hélie-Lucas, Marie-Aimeé (1986). *Dossier of WLUML*, No. 1. www.wluml.org/english/publications/engdossiers.htm

hooks, bell (1984). *Feminist Theory: From Margin to Center.* Boston, MA: South End Press, USA.

Imam, Ayesha M. (1997). *The Muslim Religious Right ("Fundamentalists) and Sexuality.* Dossier 17. Grabels, France: Women Living Under Muslim Laws publications. http://www.wluml.org/english/publications/dossiers/dossier17/religrightandsexuality.htm

Jayawardena, Kumari (1986). *Feminism and Nationalism in the Third World.* London: Zed Publiction.

Kamala, Sultana (1989). The Exchange Programme. In *Isis*, No. 21–22, pp. 23ff.

Shaaban, Bouthaina (1995). The Muted Voices of Women Interpreters. In Afkhami, Mahnaz (Ed.) (1995): *Faith and Freedom.* London, New York: I.B.Tauris Publishers, pp. 68ff.

Shaheed, Farida (1994). Controlled or Autonomous: Identity and the Experience of the Network of Women Living Under Muslims Laws. In *Signs: Journal of Women in Culture and Society*, Summer 1994, Vol. 19, No. 4.

Warg Report (1997). *Aspects of Culture and Society: Muslim Women in India.* Published by Women's Research and Action Group, Vakala, India.

WLUML, Women Living Under Muslim Laws (1990). *Women in the Quran. Information Kit. Prepared for Women Living Under Muslim Laws: International Working Meeting in Quranic Interpretation by Women, July 8-13, 1990.* Karachi, Pakistan.

Women and Law in the Sudan (1999a). *'Women's Image, Laws and Islamisation'.* Published by the Women and Law Group „GroW". Cape Town, South Africa.

Women and Law in the Sudan (1999b). *Customary Laws and Indigenous groups and Islamisation.* Published by the Women and Law Group 'GroW'. Cape Town, South Africa.

Women and Law in the Sudan (1999c). *Women's Seclusion in Private and Public Life.* Published by the Women and Law Group 'GroW'. Cape Town, South Africa

Jae-Soon Joo-Schauen, Behshid Najafi

Support, Lobbying and Networking in the Context of Trafficking in Women

1. Introducing „agisra", the „Working Group against International Sexual and Racial Exploitation"

First, we would like to introduce our organization, „agisra". „Agisra" is the abbreviation for „Working group against international sexual and racial exploitation" in Germany. Agisra is a counselling and information centre for female migrants, refugees, black and Jewish women. The aim of our organization is to provide practical support and assistance for our clients, as well as advocate and campaign for migrant women's rights and women's rights in legislation and social policy. To be specific, we counsel migrants and refugee women who experience problems with state authorities. We support victims of trafficking in women and sexual and racial discrimination, women who have been coerced into prostitution or marriage, and we advise women in asylum matters. We provide psychological therapy to women who have lived through conflict and violence in their relationships or who have experienced prison and torture. We accompany our clients to the offices of state authorities if necessary, and support women testifying as victims or witnesses in criminal investigations and in court. We find space (room) in women's shelters for those who are in danger. We also offer seminars about migration-issues, racism and sexism.

Our team is very inter- or cross cultural. Most of our staff members are themselves migrant and refugee women. We speak many languages, such as Persian, French, German, Korean, English, Portuguese, Spanish and Turkish. This means that in many cases our clients can get counselling in their own mother tongue. In other cases we engage an interpreter. „Agisra" was founded in Frankfurt/Main in 1983 when the women's movement was still strong, and sex tourism and trafficking in women were increasing. Ten years later another office opened in Cologne, where the authors of this article work.

2. The Feminisation of Migration

Women migrate because of political, economic, social, and individual reasons. According to the International Labour Organization (ILO), globally almost half of all labour migrants are women. Furthermore, 80 to 90 percent of all refugees worldwide are women and children. The gendered nature of the labour market forces most women to work only in certain jobs: Many have to sell their bodies or their reproductive capacities. These jobs are rarely recognized as a profession, are poorly paid and are not socially valued. Examples include work in the informal and unregulated sectors of prostitution, domestic work, the entertainment industry, and 'marriage.' Paragraph 41 in the final report of the Beijing+5-Conference of the United Nations in New York in June 2000 states:

> „The patterns of migratory flows of labour are changing. Women and girls are increasingly involved in internal, regional and international labour migration to pursue many occupations mainly in farm labor, domestic work and some forms of entertainment work. While this situation increases their earning opportunities and self-reliance, it also exposes them, particularly the poor, uneducated, unskilled and/or undocumented migrants to inadequate working conditions, increased health risk, the risk of trafficking, economic and sexual exploitation, racism, racial discrimination and xenophobia, and other forms of abuse, which impair their enjoyment of their human rights, and in some cases, constitute violations of human rights." (United Nations, 2000, p. 27)

Women who decide to migrate are courageous, strong, powerful and willing to take the initiative. They decide to migrate in order to change their lives for the better. These women do not fit the stereotypical picture of the 'poor woman.' Despite the active roles women take, they frequently lack information regarding living conditions, social conditions, laws, etc. in the country of destination and need support. It is difficult for migrant women to make a life for themselves or work independently because of the laws and social conditions. One example is §19 of the German Foreigner Law (Ausländerrecht) which regulates the residence status of migrating spouses. According to this law for an independent residence permit at least two years of marriage are required.

2.1 Working in Prostitution

Prostitution is still regarded as a taboo among women's movements and migrant advocacy groups. Apart from a prostitute's movement, our network and a small part of the feminist women's movement have been involved in trying to improve this situation. In Germany, prostitution is not illegal, but it is not fully recognized as a profession. The German legislation has recently changed and now recognizes prostitution as a profession, allows prostitutes to join a trade union, and makes them eligible for employment insurance. However, it is not yet clear if this law is going to improve women migrants' situation with regard to prostitution.

Every day almost one million men in Germany visit prostitutes. There are 300,000 to 400,000 prostitutes in Germany who work under difficult conditions. In the big cities over 50 percent of them are migrants. But there is a difference between German prostitutes and migrant prostitutes: Migrant women who do not have a residence permit, which would give them unconditional access to the labour market, are not allowed to work as a prostitute and run the risk of deportation or imprisonment. Most migrant women entered the country on tourist visas which means that they cannot legally pursue employment. It is very hard work, and they can at the most earn fifty percent of what the clients pay. High costs for rent, fees for lawyers and traffickers etc. reduce the earnings. For example, a single room in a Cologne brothel can cost up to 150 Euro per day, while earnings are between 15 and 25 Euro per client. Their undocumented status, combined with lack of information and the language barrier, promotes such exploitation. In Cologne's public health centre migrant women prostitutes can obtain a free medical examination. This is not at all common. For example in other towns, migrant prostitutes without papers are not eligible for a medical examination. The authorities ask for documents such as a passport or an ID before granting permission for the examination.

2.2 Migrant Women Employed in Domestic Work

Many migrant women are employed as domestic workers in Germany. This is often the only way to earn money for them. They work full-time in different households with low pay and sometimes under nearly feudal working conditions. They work very hard without the protection of a trade union and without any type of insurance, and frequently without a residence or work permit. It is very difficult for these women to go to the police if they have been raped or beaten. In addition, it is a problem for them to claim their salary from the employer because of their undocumented status. In comparison to male migrants, who usually work in groups (mostly in the construction business or as seasonal workers), the female migrant is isolated because of her individualized work.

2.3 Marriages and Migratory Processes

It is our goal to support the implementation of migrant women's human rights in regard to marriage. In this era of mass media women regularly use newspapers and the internet to find a wealthy, handsome, and loyal partner in another country. Comparable movements occurred frequently in the past: In the 1950s and

1960s European women migrated to the United States in order to get married. But from the point of view of gender justice, the social and legal situation with which migrant women are confronted in Germany is highly problematic. Women who arrive in Germany married to a German, or with the intention of getting married, are seldom informed about the social and legal conditions in which they will be living. According to the German Foreigner Law, their residence permit is dependent on their marriage for a period of two years. In this period these women are forced to obey their husbands in order to keep their residence permit. This results in an unequal relationship. To overcome these inequalities, „agisra" demands an independent residence permit for migrant women immediately after marriage.

3. Trafficking in Women in Germany

3.1 The Definition

Trafficking in women is violence against women in the migration process. Many different definitions have been used by international organizations, such as the International Labour Organization (ILO), the International Organization for Migration (IOM), the United Nations (UN), the European Parliament, the German Criminal Code and counselling centres for women. For example, the 1997 Hague Ministerial Declaration on European Guidelines for Effective Measures to Prevent and Combat Trafficking in Women for the Purpose of Sexual Exploitation" defines the term trafficking as follows:

> Trafficking in women relates to any behavior which facilitates the legal or illegal entry into, transit through, residence in, or exit from the territory of a country, of women for the purpose of gainful sexual exploitation by the use of coercion, in particular violence or threats, of deceit, abuse or authority or other pressure which is such that the person has no real and acceptable choice but to submit to the pressure or abuse involved (European Union, 1997).

This definition is limited to the purpose of sexual exploitation and does not consider the situation of women who are forced to marry and to work in the informal sector.

The German Criminal Code 180b and 181 (Strafgesetzbuch, 2000) uses the term trafficking in persons in cases where a perpetrator has forced someone into gainful prostitution by exploiting her vulnerability as a foreigner. The perpetrator recruits the person by deceiving her into coming to a foreign country and then abuses her for the purpose of commercial prostitution. This definition is also limited to prostitution. Domestic workers and spouses who are pressured or threatened are not mentioned in this definition.

"Agisra" and other independent counselling centres thus advocate a broad definition of trafficking in women such as that put forward by the „Global Alliance Against Trafficking in Women" (GAATW):

> All acts or attempted acts involving the use of force or threat of force or abuse of authority or debt bondage, deception, or other forms of coercion connected with the recruitment and transportation of a person for purposes of employment or services, regardless of whether or not national boundaries are crossed (GAATW 1999).

The important point here is that not only sexual exploitation and forced prostitution are considered trafficking. This definition considers the type of work for which the person is recruited, and the circumstances and the use of coercion are the most important criteria. Accordingly, victims of trafficking in women include domestic workers, migrants who enter the country for the purposes of marriage, au-pair girls, etc.

3.2 How Can a Woman Become a Victim of Trafficking?

There are two types of traffickers: well organized international organizations as well as private persons. Both types of perpetrators use the same methods to recruit mostly young women. Recruitment is usually done by a mediator who offers them a job in a Western European country. The mediators also place announcements in newspapers. Some mediators organize the trip and obtain all necessary documents. Usually women have to pay large sums of money for this service and agree to pay back the debts from their income. When the woman arrives at her destination and later realizes that she does not work in the job promised by the mediator, she often has no chance to leave the pimps. Usually she is told that if she is caught in a police raid, she will be deported directly or put in prison, and no one would believe her and help her. She is told not to say anything about the pimps and the mediator or else terrible things will happen to her family. Through such methods women are intimidated and scared. However, an additional problem is that it all happens in a foreign country. The women cannot speak the language, do not know the social system, and do not have friends or relatives, so that they cannot get any help.

Despite all these facts, we don't like the commonly used term „trafficking in women", because it reduces those women to merchandise to be trafficked. But, they are active individuals, they take risks to change and improve their situation and they are not afraid to migrate. Without taking risks there is no improvement. Despite the dangers, women in a bad economic situation generally think that nothing will happen to them.

4. Support for the Victims of Trafficking in Women

We will now describe the experiences of three of our clients who were victims of trafficking in women.

4.1 Prostitution

In Germany, almost fifty percent of women working in the sex industry are migrants. Among them are women who decide to work in prostitution of their own free will, but many others are forced into this profession. For all migrant prostitutes, obtaining a work permit is difficult. In addition, the women – no matter whether they entered the profession out of their free will or were forced into it – are not familiar with the language, and know little about the social structures. Furthermore they do not have family or friends to rely on. Therefore they can easily become victims of exploitation.

Mary[1] worked as a prostitute in Romania for a few years. Because her family's financial situation got worse, she decided to take up an offer to go to Hungary. However, she did not know that the man who offered to take her there was working for an internationally organized mafia. He took her to Italy and then to Germany where she began to work in a brothel under his strict control. She could not speak German and could not send any money to her family. She was caught in a police raid two weeks later and was very afraid of deportation, especially of the deportation prison. Although she was very frightened of reprisals, she provided useful information about the traffickers, because the police threatened that she would be put into prison. At that time her fear of being imprisoned was much greater than that of reprisals by the traffickers. And she wanted also to punish the criminals. After she received counselling from us, she was relieved to realize that she would not be imprisoned, independent on the fact whether she is ready to testify in a court as a victim of trafficking in women or not. With this information her attention was quickly changed. She was very concerned about the situation of her family, especially about her father who was sick and needed medical treatment, but he did not have any income. The biggest problem the family was facing was to be thrown out of their flat, because they could not pay the rent.

However, she realized how urgently her family was waiting for her money and for her return. She did not want to think how dangerous the traffickers could be although they knew her home address. But it did not matter to her, she just wanted to return home and hoped that the traffickers would think she had been

---

1   All the names have been changed.

caught by the police and deported to Romania. She also hoped that maybe they would observe her but not harm her. We do not know how Mary is doing now.

4.2 Domestic Work Instead of University Study

Fatma, a young woman from Tunisia, decided to study in Europe, but could not raise the money to go abroad. One day one of her cousins told her she could study in Germany. She was very happy. A few months later she arrived in Germany. This cousin told her that she had to take care of his children for a short time and that she would start her studies later, as the university and other schools were on holiday. So she took care of his children at first. Later she had to cook and clean the house as well. Fatma realized she was supposed to take care of the whole household and not only of the children. Due to the fact that her tourist visa had already expired, she had become illegal. Every time she asked her cousin when she would begin to study he told her in one month.

Seven or eight months passed by. In this time she figured out what type of business the cousin and his family were engaged in. They earned money by running brothels and dealing with drugs. She realized that she would never be able to study as long as she stayed in this family. The cousins threatened to kill her and her family if she told her own family or the police about their business. She got in touch with another female cousin in a similar situation. This cousin had come to Germany one year earlier than Fatma. She was very intimidated and scared. Fatma tried to help her, but she did not know how. Finally Fatma met a young German man who encouraged her to go to the police and promised to help her.

One day she went to the police and asked for help as she did not want to stay with the family any more and could not return home because of the cousins. The police promised her that she could stay in Germany and demanded her to tell them everything about the family, because this family were well-known drug dealers and pimps. She told them everything she knew and emphasized that she could not testify in court against this family as she was too afraid. She knew her cousins were not lying. The police tried to persuade her to testify in court. When she came to our office, her whole body was trembling. She could not drink and eat anything. She thought she would be deported soon and then she and her family would be killed. With our counselling and support she applied for asylum, based on her life being in danger in her country of origin. In the meantime her boyfriend asked her to marry him and she agreed. Her application for asylum was denied, but she obtained the right to stay in the country through her marriage.

4.3 Consequences of a Convenience Marriage

A young Ukrainian mother named Natasha met a fifty-year old German man travelling in her country. He was very nice and gentle to her. Later he invited her to visit him in Germany. At that point, she was unhappy with her life as she had a little child, was separated from her husband, and did not have a job. She thought that the man, who was 30 years older than her, would not be demanding and it would not be difficult for her to take care of him and to make him content with her. She would not need to find other work and could stay at home with her child. So she decided to marry him.

At first she came to Germany without her child. Her mother took care of her child during the visit. The man impressed her with his way of life. Two months later this man tried to persuade her to go into prostitution. He was unemployed for a long time and told her that he had financial problems now and that she could help him. At the same time he told her that she could not get any other job because of the work permit and put her under a lot of pressure. A few weeks later she decided to go into prostitution because she needed money to send to her mother as she did not have any. Natasha thought she could do it for short time, but at that time she did not know that her partner was an experienced pimp. He organized parties she had to go to and provide sexual services for men. A little later he started to take money from clients, but did not pay her for her work. When she asked him for the money, he gave her a little to send her mother. She was very lonely. Her partner prohibited her to get in touch with her neighbours, but she still tried to see the positive side of her friend and believed him for a long time, despite the many warning signs. She was already emotionally dependent on him and ignored the warning signs and finally got all the papers from Ukraine for the marriage. She married him, although she already had experienced violence from him, and upon her marriage received a work permit. One year after the wedding she made up her mind not to work as prostitute any longer. But her husband forced her to continue. When she refused to work or protested against his commands, he beat her. The neighbours knew him well and wanted to help her. She was glad to be able to talk with the neighbours from whom she got a lot of information about her husband. But Natasha wanted to try to solve the problem on her own. She was convinced that he would be afraid of her because she knew so many things about him and could blackmail him with what she knew. She told herself many times that she had nothing to lose except her own life but was not really aware of his criminal energy. As the beatings became more frequent, a neighbour got in touch with „agisra".

Natasha brought a criminal charge of bodily injury against her husband. She was a very strong woman. While the criminal investigation against her husband was going on, it was not clear if her husband would be kept in custody. She was not safe, so we advised her to move. She had not considered that she might have to change her home – the batterer should have been ordered to stay away from the flat. She was in the right, but German authorities are still a long way from realizing that women need to be protected from their husbands during this type of proceeding. She was lucky that her husband was kept in custody for a long time. The long criminal investigation and her testimony revealed that this man had brought many women from Poland, Ukraine and Russia to Germany and had forced them into prostitution and exploited them for a long time. Finally he was sentenced to four years and nine months of prison.

As Natasha was married to a German during the investigation, she did not have any problems with the residence permit. However, after the sentencing, she was required to apply for an extension of her residence permit. At that time according to §19 of the Foreigners Law she was required to live with her husband for at least three years in Germany to qualify for a residence permit independent of her marital status. However, she had only lived with her husband for one year and a few months. But the investigation and trial took more than one year, so as she applied for the extension, she had lived more than two years in Germany as the spouse of a German. In June 2000, the law was changed and the amount of time which women are required to live with their husbands in order for them to be eligible for a residence permit independent of the marital status was reduced from three or four to two years. Natasha was lucky that she applied for an extension of her permit just as the law changed, so that she finally got her independent residence permit.

Generally women who are victims of trafficking do not have a residence permit. If the attorney and state authority for foreigners are convinced that a woman is a victim, she can obtain a temporary residence permit. According to the regulation on victims of trafficking in persons (*Verwaltungsvorschrift zum Ausländergesetz*), regardless if s/he testifies or not, the victim is eligible for a four-week residence permit. Women who are prepared to give testimony are eligible for a temporary residence permit for the length of the trial. Usually women do not want to say that they were forced into the work because of fears of reprisal. The traffickers do not want to ruin their business, therefore they often try to put pressure on the witnesses if they know where they are staying. Some victims are traumatized because they were detained by force, raped and transported to unknown destinations, and because of their living conditions like lack of light, heating and regular food. Although such women need psychological therapy for a long time, social welfare does not provide it.

On average, trials regarding organized crime take one and a half year. During the criminal investigation the witness/victim may stay in Germany. Until recently witnesses were not allowed to work or be trained in a different profession. Many of them had traumatic experiences and they need to distance themselves from their past, and need psychological support. Working or learning something can help them psychologically.

Finally the trial is closed and the perpetrators are sentenced to terms in prison. The witnesses are required to leave Germany, unless there is evidence that a return to their home country would present a danger to their lives. This requirement is very unfair, because women who have testified against the perpetrators risk their own and their families' lives. We therefore advocate permanent residency for these women, and demand that they receive opportunities to learn some skills.

5. Our Networking Activities

5.1 Round Table at a Local Level

The „Round Table against Trafficking in Women" in Cologne was co-initiated by „agisra" in 1996. The aim of the Round Table is on the one hand to sensitise local authorities to the issue and on the other hand to intensify the coordination of support for victims of trafficking in women. Participants of the Round Table include the local Office for Women's Affairs, women's shelters, the Office for Intercultural Affairs, the police, the office of the Public Attorney, the Health Office and the Office for Foreigners' Affairs (in other countries this would be the Immigration Office). The Round Table meets three to four times a year. There are similar Round Tables in other towns as well as on different levels such as on the local, regional and federal level.

5.2 Regional Networking Efforts

There are nine special counselling centres for victims of trafficking in women in the state of North Rhine-Westphalia (NRW). NRW is one of the largest federal states with a large population. It is the only state with this number of counselling centres. Apart from having a Round Table in North Rhine-Westphalia which has existed since 1994, these centres meet four times a year in order to exchange information and experiences, and coordinate political demands. One of the issues is that some cities do not make use of the laws for victims of trafficking in women. In NRW there have been a few legal provisions for victims of trafficking in women since 1994. The most important of these states that if a victim of trafficking is prepared to testify in court, she is eligible for a temporary resident permit for the length of time the criminal proceedings require her to remain in Germany as a victim/witness. Those who are not able to testify in court, but have enough evidence that they are victims of trafficking, are also eligible for a temporary resident permit of four weeks. Many cities argue that despite indications of trafficking, the women do not want to give testimony and just want to return home as quickly as possible. They might be put in deportation prison without having made contact with an independent counselling centre.

5.3 Lobbying at a National and International Level: The „KOK"

The „Federal association against trafficking in women and violence against women in the migration process" (KOK) represents the political and social interests of more than 35 women's projects and counselling centres. The KOK was founded in 1987. At that time womens NGOs saw the necessity of a joint network to combine and strengthen the forces and networking efforts on a national level. Due to the social and political changes, as well as the growing responsibilities, a coordinating office was set up in Potsdam in 1999. Our main goals are the improvement of the legal and social situation of all female migrants in Germany, the promotion of political and legal measures against trafficking in women in national and international human rights documents, and the granting of a residence permit for victims of trafficking in women, as well as an independent residence status for foreign spouses. The KOK works in the field of public relations as well as in the organization of campaigns and political actions against violence against women in the migration process. It lobbies on a national and international level in order to have input in the political process and promote its political demands concerning legislative and political decision-making.

Since 1993 we have carried out a campaign to abolish the restrictive and discriminatory rule of §19 of the Foreigner Law. This law regulates residence permit according to marital status and links the residence title of the migrant spouse for a period of four years to an ongoing marriage. The result is that even the happiest relationship gets into a situation of unjust dependency. The rule was finally changed in June 2000, but we are not satisfied: the required period of four years was changed to two years, but the discriminatory structures remain the same. The KOK is still fighting to abolish the required period for an independent residence permit for migrant women.

The network is also dedicated to developing women's human rights through the use of existing international instruments such as ICERD (International Convention on the Elimination of All Forms of Racial Discrimination) and CEDAW (Convention on the Elimination of All Forms of Discrimination Against Women) and making the German government accountable for these conventions. One example for this effort is the shadow report (KOK 2000; KOK 2001) which we have submitted along with the Federal Report of Germany to the committee members at the UN CEDAW Committee in January 2000 in New York. Our report provides data about and an analysis of the situation of migrant women and violence against them in the migration process especially in the fields of marriage, domestic work and prostitution. In their evaluation of the situation in Germany, the committee expressed its concern on the subject of trafficking in women, and demanded the German government to improve the social and legal situation of prostitutes.

Apart from using existing legal instruments, the KOK was also active in the design of new UN documents such as the Beijing+5 document which was discussed in June 2000 in New York, and the documents of the World Conference Against Racism (WCAR) in Durban South Africa which took place in September 2001. We were involved in both processes, nationally and internationally, in lobbying, networking and monitoring. In Beijing+5 and Durban we helped influence the formulation of the provisions in the outcome documents on prevention of trafficking in women and protection of victims. In the Durban process we successfully promoted recognition of trafficking in women in the broader context of gender specific racism (DAW, OHCHR, UNIFEM 2000). Even if the final outcome documents are just declarations, and are not legally binding, the formulation of these documents can be useful for the political arguments of the NGOs.

6. Conclusion

Migrant women's projects and counselling centres in Germany have been actively working against trafficking in women and violence against women in the migration process for the last twenty years. During this time trafficking in women has been successfully put on the political agenda, resulting in some improvements: Public awareness of the problem has increased, and there is more support available for the victims. However the victims have still no guarantee for governmental protection and respect of their human rights. To offer economic, social and work opportunities for women in the countries of origin and legal migration opportunities to the destination countries still require our continued effort. We demand the implementation of human rights standards for migrant women.

References

European Union (1997). The Hague Ministerial Declaration on European Guidelines for Effective Measures to Prevent and Combat Trafficking in Women for the Purpose of Sexual Exploitation. Ministerial Conference under the Dutch Presidency of the European Union, 24-26 April 1997, The Hague.
Global Alliance Against Traffic in Women (GAATW) (1999). Human Rights Standards for the Treatment of Trafficked Persons, http://www.inet.co.th/org/gaatw/

KOK (2000). Schattenbericht unter Art. 6 CEDAW (Frauenhandel) zum Staatenbericht der Deutschen Bundesregierung, Januar 2000. Potsdam.

KOK (2001). Trafficking in women in Germany. A Documentation. 140 pages. Available in German and English. Potsdam, Internet: www.kok-potsdam.de (Copies can be ordered at kok.potsdam@t-online.de).

Strafgesetzbuch der Bundesrepublik Deutschland (2000). Strafgesetzbuch (StGB). Vom 15. Mai 1871 (RGBl. S.127) in der Fassung der Bekanntmachung vom 13. November 1998 (BGBl. I, S.3322), zuletzt geändert durch Artikel 3 des Strafverfahrensänderungsgesetzes 1999 (StVÄG 1999) vom 2. August 2000 (BGBl. I. S.1253). Internet: http://www.datenschutz-berlin.de/recht/de/rv/szprecht/stgb/allg1-2.htm

United Nations (2000). Report of the Ad Hoc Committee of the Whole of the twenty-third special session of the General Assembly. A/S-23/10Rev.1. New York, Internet: http://www.un.org/womenwatch/confer/beijing5/

United Nations Division for the Advancement of Women (DAW), Office of the High Commissioner for Human Rights (OHCHR), United Nations Development Fund for Women (UNIFEM) (2000). Gender and racial discrimination. Report of the Expert Group Meeting. 21-24 November 2000, Zagreb, Croatia, Internet: http://www.un.org/womenwatch/daw/csw/genrac/report.htm

Yayori Matsui

Overcoming the Culture of Impunity for Wartime Sexual Violence –

The Historical Significance of the Women's International War Crimes Tribunal 2000[1]

> *"Haunting Mirrors"*[2]
> Haunting mirrors
> show
> reflections of girls
> not fully formed
> show
> thieves of innocence their blood-drenched deeds
> no hiding place
> no escape from echoes of desperate cries
>
> ... ...
> Their punishment is our redemption --- our liberation
> impunity is the last comfort station
> shake it
> rattle it
> tear it down
> *(Jaribu Hill)*

Sixty-four survivors from eight countries and 5,000 participants

On the last day of the Women's International War Crimes Tribunal in Tokyo in December 2000, the judges read the Summary of Findings, which found the Emperor Hirohito guilty of crimes against humanity, and determined that the

---

1   The article has been published in an earlier version in Kanagawa University Review, No. 39, July 1, 2001.
2   The above is an excerpt from „Haunting Mirrors" by Jaribu Hill, African-American poet and Civil and Human Rights Attorney who was the Tribunal's Artist in Residence. Jaribu Hill performed this poem on the Asian Culture Night after the third day of hearings, December 10, 2000.

government of Japan had incurred state responsibility. It was a historic moment. The hall filled with cheers as the aged survivors sitting in the front row, weeping with joy, one after another climbed onto stage to express their gratitude to the judges, and the country prosecutors opposite them embraced one another.

The initial motivation for the Women's Tribunal came from a picture entitled *Punish the Perpetrators!* painted by Korean former 'comfort woman' Kang Duk Kyung before her death in 1997. At the 1998 Asian Solidarity Conference on 'Comfort Women' Issues in Seoul, the Violence Against Women in War Network, Japan (VAWW-NET Japan) proposed that a tribunal should be held as a means of responding to her call. After difficult two and a half years of preparations, the Tribunal was finally held in December 8-12, 2000.

On each of the first three days, more than 1,000 participants (about 500 from abroad, including 200 from Korea; 600 from within Japan, and more than 300 representatives from the international and national media) gathered in Kudan Hall in Tokyo to hear the proceedings and to watch over the sixty-four survivors from eight countries. On the 12th, the last day, the venue moved to Nihon-Seinenkan, where 1,300 participants listened for two hours and a half as the four judges read the Summary of Findings. Thus, during the four days of the Tribunal, the number of participants reached a total of about 5,000.

Judgement handed down by internationally renowned legal experts

Chief Justice Gabrielle McDonald (former President of the „International Criminal Tribunal for the former Yugoslavia", African-American) and the four judges, Ms. Christine Chinkin (Professor of International Law, University of London), Ms. Carmen Mari Argibay (Argentine judge and former President of the International Women's Association of Judges; recently chosen to serve on the International Criminal Tribunal for the former Yugoslavia), and Mr. Willie Mutunga (President of the Kenya Commission on Human Rights and Professor of Kenya University), lined the stage in their black judges' robes.

Chief Prosecutors Patricia Viseur-Sellers (Legal Advisor for Gender-Related Crimes for the International Criminal Tribunals for the former Yugoslavia and Rwanda; African-American) and Ustina Dolgopol (Senior Lecturer in International Law at Flinders University, Australia), seated at the center stage, wore similar attire. Prosecutors from ten countries (North and South Korea, China, Taiwan, the Philippines, Indonesia, Malaysia, East Timor, the Netherlands, and Japan) arose one by one to present their arguments.

Survivors' testimonies and documentary evidence were projected onto large screens on either side of the stage, while backstage a team of simultaneous interpreters translated English, the Tribunal's official language, into Japanese, Korean, Chinese, and other languages.

The Tribunal was sponsored by the International Organizing Committee (IOC), composed of women from the perpetrating country Japan, six of the victimized countries, and activists specializing in armed conflict from throughout the world who joined to form an International Advisory Committee. The IOC cooperated with teams of prosecutors from each country to draft the Charter of the Tribunal, on which the hearings were based.

Ten years have passed since survivors of the 'comfort woman' system began to speak out, and now the aging survivors are dying one by one. No longer able to deny its involvement, the Japanese government finally admitted to moral responsibility for wartime sexual slavery in 1993, but on the grounds that the issue of reparation was resolved by the San Francisco Peace Treaty and bilateral reparation agreements, it continues to deny its legal responsibility. Furthermore, since the fiftieth anniversary of the end of World War II in 1995, nationalistic rightwing forces such as the so-called 'liberal historical view group,' which affirms Japan's pre-war ideology, and denies responsibility for both wartime and colonial aggression, have suddenly gained new strength. These rightwing advocates repeatedly insult former 'comfort women' by declaring that there is no evidence that they were kidnapped and forced into service, that they were professional prostitutes, or that they volunteered their services in order to make money.

Restoring the honor of the survivors by punishing those responsible

The survivors ask, „Why must we end our lives in pain while the perpetrators go unpunished and unrepentant?" They know that if their honor is to be restored, sexual slavery must be recognized as the crime it is. The international community is in agreement concerning war crimes and crimes against humanity: the three essential points are investigation into the facts, reparation for the victims, and punishment of the perpetrators. With reference to the 'comfort women' issue, great efforts have been and are being made to uncover the facts, and eight civil suits have been instigated to demand the Japanese government reparation for former 'comfort women.' Six of these, however, have ended in rejection of the plaintiffs' claims, and in denial of state responsibility on the part of the Japanese government. Although a movement to enact a new compensation law has been initiated, but with the current political situation in Japan there is little hope of its success.

In addition, punishment of the perpetrators is a taboo in Japanese post-war society. The Japanese government has never prosecuted a single war criminal, either for the 'comfort women' system, or for any other war crime. Even activists have been lukewarm on the issue of punishment. In 1994, when the Tokyo District Court refused to accept a letter of indictment presented by survivors and members of „The Korean Council for Women Drafted for Military Sexual Slavery by Japan", even the movement on the issue of 'comfort women' didn't support the Korean demand for prosecution.

How, then, were we to deal with the problem of punishment? In Japanese courts, which refuse to recognize even the claims of civil lawsuits, the prospects for criminal prosecution are dim indeed. Setting up an international tribunal would also have been difficult. Since prosecution by the state was impossible, we would have to resort to judgement by the people. And so, taking the Russell Tribunal – which found the United States guilty of war crimes during the Vietnam War in the 1960s – as our model, we decided to set up a Peoples' Tribunal.

This Tribunal has two major purposes. The first is to clarify the criminality of Japan's military sexual slavery, and to force the Japanese government to take legal responsibility for it. The second is to end the cycle of impunity for wartime sexual violence, and to prevent its reoccurrence, thus addressing a universal women's human rights issue. The judges, who met in The Hague in October, 2000, agreed that the three major characteristics of the Tribunal were to be: 1) that it be a trial based on people's sovereignty, and not on state sovereignty, 2) that it be an appendix of the Tokyo Trial 1949, [3] which failed to prosecute Japan for military sexual slavery and other wartime sexual violence, and 3) that its principal aim be the restoration of the dignity and honor of the survivors.

Survivors' testimony: „Give me back my life!"

The three days of hearings began with the two Chief Prosecutors reading their common indictment, which stated that Japan's military sexual slavery was a crime against humanity, and indicted the Emperor Hirohito and ten top military and government officials, including Tojo Hideki, Matsui Iwane, and Yamashita Tomoyuki. The indictment inquired into the criminal responsibility of these individuals, as well as the state responsibility of the Japanese government. There is a photograph of four Korean 'comfort women,' one of whom is in an ad-

---

3   The International Military Tribunal for the Far East (Tokyo Tribunal, 1946-48) was established to judge Japanese war criminals in the army, the government, the bureaucracy and the economy; it extended to the planners and the persons responsible for the war. But the sexual violence against and forced prostitution for the army was not covered (editor's note).

vanced stage of pregnancy, taken by the American military which captured them on the Burmese border after the defeat of Japanese forces. The pregnant woman in this photograph is Pak Yong-Sim, who came from North Korea to participate in the Tribunal. Ha Sang-Suk, who was taken from Korea to a 'comfort station' in Wuhan, China, and is still living there, unable to return home, wept as she testified in court that she was raped so many times it was too painful to walk.

Wan Ai-Hua, from Xiansi Province in China, was a 14-year-old anti-Japanese guerilla when she was kidnapped and repeatedly raped. When she was caught after trying to escape, she was hung from a tree and severely beaten, then stripped naked and thrown into a freezing river. As she gave her testimony, she rose to show the court her scarred, shortened body – the most striking evidence of the brutal treatment she had received – but overwhelmed by anger, she fainted and had to be carried from the hall on a stretcher. One survivor of the Rape of Nanking dissolved in tears as she told how Japanese soldiers barged into her home to first murder her father and then rape and murder her mother. She herself, a child of nine at the time, was then raped, and left as an orphan to beg and sleep in the streets.

Teng-Kao Pao-Chu, one of three witnesses from Taiwan, was deceived and taken to Burma. „I want the younger generation to know what their parents did to us," she declared. Lu Man Mei, also from Taiwan, was taken to Hainan Island, where she became pregnant. Her child died 38 days after it was born. She ended her testimony with a poignant request: „My youth was stolen from me. I want it back." Lin Sen Chung, an aborigine from Taiwan, told of how the Japanese police took her from her village to work at the nearby garrison of the Japanese army. She was imprisoned in a pitch-black cave where Japanese soldiers came to rape her every day; her life was a series of pregnancies and abortions. She married after the war without knowing she got pregnant again; when her husband learned that she had been a 'comfort woman,' he brutally beat and divorced her. She had to divorce three times; she made numerous attempts to commit suicide. Wiping away her tears, she said, „The Japanese government ruined my life. I want them to apologize."

From the Philippines, a former 'comfort woman' and a survivor of the mass rape of Mapanique Village came to testify. The former, Tomasa Dioso Salinog, from Panai Island, told how Japanese soldiers came to her house when she was thirteen. After watching them cut her father's head off, she was kidnapped and forced to be a 'comfort woman.' „"I never married. I have been alone since the war. What I want is justice," she said. Maxima Regala de la Cruz, from Mapanique Village, was raped nightly together with her mother although she had not yet begun to menstruate. „I escaped with my mother, but we were so ashamed that we dug a deep hole and buried our memories in it," she said through her tears.

Voices from the Netherlands and East Timor

Ms. Suhana, from Bandung, Indonesia, told her story. „I was playing outside my house when Japanese soldiers drove up in a jeep. They dragged me in by the hair, and took me to a 'comfort station.' I tried to fight back, but they asked me if I wanted to live or die. I wanted to live, so I gave up." She returned home three years later to find that her father had been cut down in the street by Japanese soldiers, and her mother had become sick with grief and died as well.""I am old now, and I can't wait much longer for an apology and compensation." Ms. Mardiyem was thirteen when she was taken with forty-seven other girls from Yokyakarta to a 'comfort station' in Borneo, where she was given the Japanese name Momoe, and was raped repeatedly every day. When she became pregnant, the child was aborted. She also expressed her hopes that the Japanese government would apologize and provide her with compensation, as well as telling the younger generation of these crimes.

The Tribunal provided an opportunity for former 'comfort women' from East Timor to speak out for the first time. This was an important achievement. Three women legal experts from East Timor were sent by the UN to participate in the prosecutors' meeting, held in Taipei in September, 2000. When they informed the meeting that they knew some East Timorese former 'comfort women,' they were immediately asked to arrange for their participation in the Tribunal and writing indictment. Esmeralda Boe, in traditional East Timorese dress, told of how Japanese soldiers had threatened to kill her entire family. Only then did her parents reluctantly relinquish their daughter. She was forced to work in the fields during the day, and was raped every night. There were tears in Marta Abu Bore's eyes as she said, „On the first day I was raped by ten soldiers. Blood was pouring out of my vagina, and I couldn't walk. I was so sad. They treated me like an animal." But the tears turned to anger as she finished her testimony. „We didn't come here to see Japan. We came to tell the truth!"

Two Dutch women also participated in the Tribunal. One came directly from The Netherlands, while the other, Jan Ruff O'Herne, now lives in Australia. Both women were living in the Dutch colony of Indonesia, where they were put into prison camps after the Japanese invasion, and then recruited as 'comfort women.' „I prayed to God but the Japanese officer threatened me with a Japanese sword, and I couldn't escape," recalled O'Herne. „I cut all my hair off so that I would look ugly, but still the soldiers lined up outside my bedroom to take turns raping me every night. After the war I got married, but I still have bad dreams, and although I love my husband, I have never been able to enjoy sex with him." Holding a copy of her book *Fifty Years of Silence*, O'Herne said angrily, „I gave testimony here in Tokyo eight years ago, but the Japanese government has done nothing."

Afraid to come to Japan to give public testimony, a survivor from Malaysia told her story on videotape. She is now over eighty, living alone, was separated from her two children and taken to a comfort station. „I was given a Japanese name, and forced to have sex with between ten and twenty Japanese soldiers every day. I got pregnant, and had a baby. With the three children, I suffered every imaginable hardship after the war."

Testimony of Japanese veterans and testimony about Japanese 'comfort women'

Fujime Yuki, assistant professor at Kyoto University of Foreign Studies, appeared as an expert witness to give testimony about Japanese 'comfort women.' Because many Japanese survivors had worked in the sex industry before the war, very few have spoken out. There were over 130 comfort stations in Okinawa. Almost all of the 1,000 Korean women brought to work in them died, but in addition, about 500 Okinawan *juri* (courtesans) were brought from the licensed quarter in Naha city to serve in comfort stations. Survivors have published accounts of their experiences in book form. „The legalized prostitution system of those days in Japan was itself extremely militaristic, and extremely violent," Fujime declared, asserting that women engaged in prostitution before the war are also victims of Japan's military sexual slavery.

The testimony, including that on videotape, of survivors from nine countries was shocking, both to Japanese participants and to those from abroad. Their stories made it clear that the 'comfort women' system was practiced on an extremely broad scale, from Harbin, near the Siberian border in the north, to the southernmost islands of the Pacific, and that it resulted in very young girls being deceived, kidnapped, threatened, imprisoned, beaten, and gang-raped. Under Japan's military sexual slavery, women and young girls were subjected to forced labor, and endured unwanted pregnancies and forced abortions. They were sometimes murdered and abandoned in the jungle. Those who survived were either unable to return home, or were rejected by their families. Today, more than half a century after the war, they continue to suffer from poverty, loneliness, and trauma.

The hall was silent as two Japanese veterans confessed that they had raped women in China, and helped to transport 'comfort women.' Their testimony showed that soldiers were taught to regard the Chinese with utter contempt, and that rape in the field was an everyday affair, not alleviated in the slightest by the presence of 'comfort stations.' Although these former soldiers had assumed at first that the 'comfort women' were volunteers, they realized that this was not true on hearing that the women had been deceived by an advertisement offering positions as nurses. Thus, their testimony corroborated that of the survivors.

Expert witnesses clarify the Emperor's role

Some of the voluminous evidence collected by the teams of prosecutors of participating countries was projected onto two large screens on either side of the
stage to back up the survivors' testimony. In addition, expert witnesses clarified
the structure behind the violent, inhuman system of military sexual slavery. The
issue of the Emperor's criminal responsibility was particularly crucial. At first,
the Western members of the International Advisory Committee, who did not
fully understand the Emperor system, felt that it would be difficult to link the
'comfort women' system to the Emperor, and feared that this might obscure the
essential nature of wartime sexual violence.

The majority of members from the victimized countries, however, strongly
believed that unless it addressed the issue of the Emperor's war responsibility,
the Women's International War Crimes Tribunal would be meaningless. Accordingly, VAWW-NET Japan organized a special „H (Emperor) Team" of
historians and legal experts, and submitted the documentary evidence they compiled, along with the written statement they drafted, to the Chief Prosecutors.
Relieving the Emperor of all responsibility for the war was an important political objective of the US Occupation Forces stationed in Japan during the post-
war period. The task of judging the Emperor, left untouched by the Tokyo Trial,
was therefore perfectly suited to a people's tribunal, free of all political vested
interests. The Chief Prosecutors expressed a serious interest in addressing this
issue.

After the war, in order to protect the Emperor, the US Occupation Forces
intentionally created and circulated the myth of his total ignorance of the war. At
the Tribunal, Yamada Akira, assistant professor at Meiji University, delivered
testimony that destroyed this myth. His research shows that as Supreme Commander, the Emperor not only received detailed reports on the situation of the
Japanese military, but also gave orders concerning military operations. The testimony of Professor Hayashi Hirofumi (Kanto Gakuin University) on the organizational structure of the Japanese military, and of Professor Yoshimi Yoshi-
aki (Chuo University) on the 'comfort women' system, also showed that responsibility for the establishment of 'comfort stations' ultimately lies with the Emperor, who was the Supreme Commander.

Other expert witnesses included Professor Frits Kalshoven (Leiden University), who addressed the issue of state responsibility, pointing out that since
there is no statute of limitations for war crimes, the Japanese government is ob-
ligated to pay reparation in cases where international law has been violated. In
addition, Serbian feminist Lepa Mladjenovic, Director of the Autonomous
Women's Center Against Sexual Violence in Belgrade, emphasized that punishment of the perpetrators is a necessary condition for the realization of justice,
which helps to ease the survivors' trauma.

In her closing statement, Chief Prosecutor Dolgopol stated, „What went on in the comfort stations was rape, and sexual slavery is a crime against humanity. What the survivors need is justice, and this Tribunal hopes that justice will be done." Chief Prosecutor Sellers added, „As we listened to the testimony of the survivors, we also heard the muted voices of those who did not survive. Let us all put ourselves in the place of these survivors, at the age when they experienced this horror, and experience vicariously the possibility of being raped tonight ourselves." She concluded, „How could those in command not be responsible? The Emperor Hirohito had the greatest power: the power to know, to investigate, to control, to command. How could he not be responsible?"

The Summary of Findings in Tokyo and the judgement rendered in The Hague

The Summary of Findings was read aloud on the 12th of December, the final day of the Tribunal[4]. It begins with a section entitled „Breaking the History of Silence," which praises the courage of the survivors, and includes direct quotations from their testimonies. It clearly states that this Tribunal was set up by global civil society, and that its authority comes not from a state but from the peoples of the world. The Tribunal judges Japan's military sexual slavery, which was not prosecuted at the Tokyo Trial, according to the laws of the time; they found state responsibility of the government of Japan, and Emperor Hirohito criminally guilty.

It was one year after the Tribunal in Tokyo that the final judgement was rendered in The Hague on December 4, 2001. It is a book of 245 pages with 1,066 paragraphs and, in addition to Emperor Hirohito, nine highest level leaders of the Japanese government and military during the war were found guilty for crimes against humanity. Besides, the judgement argues against the potential arguments of the accused and the Japanese government, including lack of jurisdiction, denial of due process or violation of double jeopardy, and also statute of limitation, no individual standing to claim reparations and individual claims settled by peace treaties. It also elaborates the history, characteristics and continuing harm to victims of the Military Sexual Slavery.

It is useful for further action after the Tribunal that the judgement includes detailed recommendations: twelve to the Japanese government, three to former allied nations and two to the UN and all its members states. We should not lose

---

4   The Summary of Findings of Women's International War Crimes Tribunal 2000 for the Trial of Japanese Military Sexual Slavery from 12 December 2000 can be found at VAWW-net Japan at http://www1.jca.apc.org/vaww-net-japan/e_new/judgement.html.

time to mobilize international solidarity action to force the Japanese government to implement these recommendations before aged survivors pass away.

Following in the wake of the International Criminal Tribunals for the former Yugoslavia and Rwanda, it represents one more step toward ending the cycle of impunity for wartime sexual violence.

The survivors' joy at the restoration of justice

The first significant aspect of the Tribunal is that it heeded the voices of the survivors who had broken their silence, and responded to their cries that justice, dignity and human rights be restored. Their testimonies formed the basis of the Tribunal, and as they spoke of the suffering they had endured, the judges responded with words of comfort and gratitude for their courage.

The success of the Tribunal can perhaps best be measured by the joy in the survivor's faces as they listened to the verdict. One witness, Tomasa Solinag from the Philippines, says that she will now be able to hold her head high. „After ten hard years of seeking justice, I have finally found it at the Women's International War Crimes Tribunal. This is the first trial to truly listen to us, to help us in our search for the truth, and to restore our dignity." She had brought her case before the Tokyo District Court; in 1998, on hearing the judge read the decision in which he dismissed her claim in a mere thirty seconds, she wept, saying, „I can't go home this way." This bitter experience made the Tribunal all the more meaningful for her.

When the final judgement was read by four judges in The Hague, survivors looked deeply moved to hear its last paragraph which said,

> The judges would like to dedicate this decision to all the survivors. Their testimony of their traumatic experiences in front of hundreds of spectators demonstrated their fortitude and dignity. The crimes committed against these survivors remains one of the greatest unresolved injustices of the Second World War. There are no museums, no graves of the unknown 'comfort woman,' no Oscar-winning movies, and most importantly, no judgement days for the victims. Many of the women who have come forward to fight for justice have died unsung heroes. While the names inscribed in history's page are often those of the men that commit the crimes, rather than the women that suffer them, this judgement bears the names of the survivors that took the stage to tell their stories, and thereby, for four days at least, put wrong on the scaffold and truth on the throne.

Ten survivors who traveled all the way to The Hague were handed the thick judgement by four judges; some of them put them up over head and other embraced them with joy.

The role of a People's Tribunal: Transcending the Tokyo Trial

The second important point concerning the Tribunal is its positive meaning as a People's Tribunal; in other words, a tribunal whose judgement was based on people's sovereignty, rather than on state sovereignty. Many Japanese lawyers either completely ignored the Tribunal or dismissed it as a mere „mock trial" with no binding power to enforce its verdict. Yet we should remember that it was the political agenda of a particular state to absolve the Emperor of guilt for war crimes at the Tokyo Trial, and that the „Women's International War Crimes Tribunal", precisely because it was free of such political interests, succeeded in judging Hirohito and finding him, as well as other top military and government officials, criminally responsible for Japan's military sexual slavery. In addition, whereas Japanese courts have failed to acknowledge the plaintiffs' claims in civil suits brought by former 'comfort women,' denying state responsibility time after time, the Women's Tribunal handed down a judgement based on international law that recognized the state's obligation to provide compensation for survivors not only for violations of international law that occurred during the war, but also for continuing violations since the war's end.

Judge Christine Chinkin, who has reexamined international law from the point of view of gender, comments, „A People's Tribunal makes law the tool of civil society, rather than an arm of the government; it therefore operates on the premise that when the state fails to fulfill its obligation to realize justice, the people must step in." At a UN press conference on March 8, 2000, Presiding Justice Gabrielle Kirk McDonald stated that the authority of the Women's Tribunal depends on the people. She went on to say that the Tribunal's credibility is substantiated by the mountain of evidence assembled through the efforts of the people and survivors' testimonies, and by the decision it handed down, based on this evidence, and on meticulous application of international law as it existed at the time. It can be said that whether this decision, and the recommendations of the Tribunal are „enforced" or not depends on the people with whom the Tribunal originated – on the power of the people across national borders.

Still mired in the old way of thinking which interprets international law as a conventional agreement between one state and another, Japanese courts have fallen behind the current global trend to regard it as a tool not of states, but of the people themselves. The Women's Tribunal presented a challenge to Japan's outdated, state-centered judicature.

Women's reexamination of International Law from the standpoint of gender

Thirdly, by consistently maintaining the viewpoint of gender justice, the Tribunal made an important contribution toward further extending the current reexamination of international law from the standpoint of gender. Testimonies of 'comfort women' in the early 1990s, along with news of mass rape in the former Yugoslavia and Rwanda, culminated in the UN World Conference on Human Rights in Vienna in 1993. This in turn instigated a movement to put an end to the history of impunity for wartime sexual violence, which has become one of the central themes of the international women's movement. As a result, wartime sexual violence was prosecuted for the first time at the International Criminal Tribunals for the former Yugoslavia and Rwanda. Furthermore, in the Charter of the International Criminal Court (1998), sexual violence in armed conflicts is clearly stated to be a war crime and a crime against humanity. There is now an increasing desire throughout the world to see the perpetrators of rape and sexual slavery on the battlefield prosecuted and punished. This is because in the armed conflicts that are currently breaking out all over the globe, sexual violence against women is an extremely serious problem.

One day of the Tribunal was devoted to a Public Hearing on Crimes Against Women During Recent Wars and Conflicts, organized by the Women's Caucus for Gender Justice for the International Criminal Court, at which more than ten survivors testified. The intention was to link the 'comfort women' system of over fifty years ago to the sexual violence women are still suffering in armed conflicts, in order to change the culture of impunity.

The Tribunal's Summary of Findings also mentions the prejudice against women under patriarchal society that led soldiers to treat women like animals, as well as forcing the women themselves to remain silent about what they had endured. This fundamental prejudice against women, when linked to militarism, becomes the root cause of the sexual violence that routinely takes place around military bases and in the aftermath of armed conflicts.

The Summary of Findings also points out that the Peace Treaty and Bilateral Reparation Agreements[5] used by Japanese courts as justification for denying

---

5   The Peace Treaty of San Francisco 1951 included Japan, the US and 47 other nations; in the parallel US-Japan Security treaty a close military cooperation and stationing of US troops in Japan was established. The issues of reparation of Japan towards most Asian countries were not conclusively worked out and were later agreed in separate Bilateral Reparation Agreements (Birma 1954; the Philippines 1056; Indonesia 1958; South Vietnam 1959). The People's Republic of China and Soviet Russia did not agree to the San Francisco Peace Treaty; Moscow and Tokyo negotiated the end of war and diplomatic relations in 1965; the People's Republic of China and Japan normalized relationships in 1972 (editor's note).

survivors' claims for compensation are gender-biased, having been drafted and negotiated only by men, who ignored the question of sexual violence. This also reflects the current global trend toward encouraging the participation of women in peace negotiations and other efforts to solve armed conflicts. The Women's Tribunal, supported by the international women's movement, was clearly conducted from a position of gender sensitivity.

A counter-attack on nationalism, which denies the existence of the 'comfort women' system

The Tribunal's guilty verdict, handed down to Emperor Hirohito fifty-five years after the war's end, had immeasurable historical significance for Japan. It challenged the greatest taboo of post-war Japan, which not only has failed to prosecute a single war criminal, to say nothing of the Emperor, but also continues to deify war criminals as 'heroic spirits' in Yasukuni Shrine when they die, and to pay enormous amounts to their surviving family members in the form of military pensions. Accordingly, while the foreign media gave the guilty verdict for Hirohito extensive coverage, it was largely ignored by Japanese media which is afraid of touching the taboo of the Emperor's war responsibility.

Rightwing forces, which had initially dismissed the Tribunal as „a bunch of silly women playing at having a trial," began to viciously attack it as soon as it was over. The Educational Channel of NHK TV, the only visual Japanese media which planned to produce a documentary program on the Tribunal, gave in to violent demands that the broadcast should be cancelled. The program that NHK did air on January 30, 2001, entitled „Wartime Sexual Violence Questioned," was sabotaged, its content bearing no resemblance to the program originally planned. Scenes of the Tribunal were heavily cut, and there was no mention of the organizers, of verdict, or of keywords such as „the Japanese military," „sexual slavery," or „punishment." Important images of and information about the Tribunal were replaced with commentary that was harshly critical of it. The effect was strange indeed, and this strangeness speaks volumes about how great a taboo the Emperor's war responsibility still is to the Japanese media.

This history of failing to prosecute war crimes has given free rein to the rightwing „liberal historical view group" and to nationalistic forces which deny Japan's wartime and postwar responsibility. These views have now begun to creep into the media. They are making headway in the field of education as well, as is evidenced by the fact that the junior high school history and civics textbooks written by the Society for Textbook Reform passed the Ministry of Education's screening, despite their distorted view of history and blatant bias against women. Authors of this textbook have publicly stated their reasons for not mentioning the 'comfort women' system as, „That would be like writing the history of the structure of toilets." To Japanese nationalists today, the issues of the 'comfort women' and the Rape of Nanking are the greatest targets to be attacked; they are devoting all their energy to erasing the 'comfort women' from history. The Women's Tribunal was therefore a counter-attack on this strengthening nationalistic trend.

Leaving a record for the future, we continue the fight for justice

My final point concerns the important role the Tribunal played in uncovering the facts, and in recording them for future generations. The mountain of documentary evidence compiled by Japan and the victimized countries in order to draft the country indictments, which was then submitted to the Tribunal (the documents submitted to the judges for use in drafting the final decision weighed eighty kilograms) was assessed highly by both judges and prosecutors. This evidence included survivors' testimonies, video recordings, documents concerning the both Japanese military and the Allied Forces, particularly the US, as well as the written statements of expert witnesses; all this material will help future generations to understand the true situation of Japan's military sexual slavery, as well as the underlying structure that created it. In addition, visual records of the Tribunal itself have been produced in various countries, including a sixty-eight-minute documentary video entitled *Breaking the History of Silence* (English edition) in Japan.

This evidence, and these records, are in themselves the most effective weapon against forces that seek to erase the 'comfort women' system from history. And until the Japanese government fulfills its responsibility to apologize to the survivors and provide them with state reparation, the record left by the Tribunal will no doubt prove useful to survivors, and after their deaths, to their descendents who are determined to carry on their struggle for justice.

The Women's International War Crimes Tribunal can be said to be the fruit of the women's movement and global civil society, seeking to counter the conflicts and violence now being produced by the globalization of the market economy with a globalization of women's solidarity to fight for justice and human rights. The question now is whether we can honestly face up to our war responsibility in the past, in order to use our power to prevent war and violence in the future.

Authors and Editors

Aneela Babar (born 1971) has received her Master's degree in Gender and Development Studies from the Asian Institute of Technology, Thailand and a second M.A. in Defense and Strategic Studies from the Quaid-i-Azam University, Islamabad, Pakistan. Currently, she is pursuing her PhD at the Institute of Cultural Research, University of Western Sydney, Australia looking at how different media forms in diverse societies – both Islamic and non-Islamic – represent wars involving Islamic societies. She has published among others: „Texts of War: the Religio-Military Nexus and construction of Gender Identity in Pakistan and India" In *Gender, Technology and Development*, 4(3), 2000, pp. 441-464.

Ayşegül Baykan received her M.A. in Philosophy and her Ph.D. in Sociology from the University of Pittsburgh where she studied with Gayatri Spivak and consequently became interested in Postcolonial Theory. After teaching in Istanbul for seven years, she is currently an Off-site Research Associate of the Center for West European Studies and European Union Center of the University of Pittsburgh. Baykan's latest publication on Turkey is with Roland Robertson, „Spatializing Turkey"(in Eliezer Ben-Rafael, ed., *Identity, Culture and Globalization.* Leiden: International Institute of Sociology and Brill Academic Press, 2001.) She is also the author of a forthcoming chapter in another *ifu* Publication, „Urban Geography and Women in the Periphery's Metropolis: The Example of Istanbul, Turkey" (Ulla Terlinden, ed., *The intercultural discourse on gender, urbanism and architecture*).

Marina Calloni is professor of Social and Political Philosophy and Philosophy of Social Sciences at the State University of Milano-Bicocca, and director of the „International Network for Research in Gender." She received a Ph.D. in Philosophy at the University of Pavia, and a Ph.D. in Social and Political Science at the European University Institute in Florence. She was a research fellow at the University of Frankfurt and senior researcher at the Gender Institute of the London School of Economics and Political Science in London. Here she also initiated and directed the «International Network for Research on Gender». Moreover, she was a visiting professor at the Universities of Pisa, Bremen, Vienna, Lugano, Tirana and Beijng. She is rapporteur for the DG Research Unit

„Women and Science of the European Commission," and of the „Expert Group to report on the situation of women scientists in the Eastern and Central European countries and the Baltic States." She participated in various international projects and developed research projects in post-socialist countries. Her main topics include social and political philosophy; theories of ethics, politics and justice; democracy and cultural conflicts; European citizenship and mobility; and international research networks. She is member of the editorial board of several journals. Her most recent publications are: M. Calloni & A. Saarinen (eds.), *Gender, Research and Networks across Boundaries. A different approach to globalisation,* Copenhagen: Nordic Council of Ministries, 2002; M. Calloni, A. Ferrara & S. Petrucciani (eds.), *Pensare la società. L'idea di una filosofia sociale,* Rome: Carocci, 2000; M. Calloni, B. Dausien & M. Friese (eds.), *Migrationsgeschichten von Frauen. Beiträge und Perspektiven aus der Biographieforschung,* Bremen: IBL – Universität Bremen Verlag, 2000.

Malathi de Alwis is a Senior Research Fellow at the International Centre for Ethnic Studies, Colombo, Sri Lanka and presently a Visiting Assistant Professor of Anthropology at the New School for Social Research, New York. She received her PhD in Socio-Cultural Anthropology from the University of Chicago and is the Co-editor, with Kumari Jayawardena, of *Embodied Violence: Communalising Women's Sexuality in South Asia* (Delhi: Kali for Women/London: Zed Press, 1996), as well as Co-author with Kumari Jayawardena of *Casting Pearls: The Women's Franchise Movement in Sri Lanka* (Colombo: Social Scientists' Association, 2001). Many of her articles which focus on feminist and peace movements in South Asia, as well as on issues of gender, nationalism, militarism and humanitarianism have been published internationally both in English and in translations. She is a founder-member of the National Women's NGO Forum and the Women's Coalition for Peace, Sri Lanka and a regular contributor to „Cat's Eye" – a feminist column on contemporary issues – in the Island Newspaper. She is also a member of the Women in Conflict Zones Network, an international body of feminist scholars, activists and policy makers.

Amel Hamza is engaged in the international network Women Living Under Muslim Laws (WLUML), especially in the Women and Law Group. She received her PhD for her research on *Muslim Woman and Civil Rights: A Comparative Study of Muslim Women in Khartoum, (Sudan) and The Cape Town Metropolitan Area, (South Africa).* She currently works at the Ahfad University for Women in Omdurman, Sudan at the Women's Studies Unit. She is member of the editorial board of the bi-lingual journal *Africa Development /Afrique et Développement,* issued by the Council for the Development of Social Science Research in Africa.

Jae-Soon Joo-Schauen studied Pedagogy and was trained in Systemic Therapy. She came to Germany as a migrant worker as a nurse. Since the 1980s, she has been active in different women's and migrant's organisations such as the *Korean Women's Group*, the *International Women's Group* and ELISA (Migrants, Refugees and Black Women against Racism) in Cologne. Currently, she works at *agisra* (Information and Counseling Centre for Female Migrants and Refugees) in Cologne.

Late *Neela Ashok Karnik* had been officially invited as an *ifu* lecturer in the project area „Migration." She had submitted her paper but unfortunately her health condition made it impossible for her to take part in *ifu*. Neela Ashok Karnik died in January 2001. To honour her and her scientific work we include her planned contribution to the *ifu* curriculum in this book. We thank Mr Karnik for his kind support in editing her paper.

Neela Karnik received her PhD from the University of Pune in 1993. Her dissertation on „Transpositions from Fiction to Film: A Semiotic Approach" explored the application of semiotic theories developed by Pierce, Eco and Deleuze to the study of narrative in fiction and films. With a Rockefeller Post Doctoral award she worked at the University of Chicago in 1992 focussing on expressions of nationalism in Indian cinema and on cultural reception of cinema. Among her numerous publications are „Space, Gender and Nation/Body in *Mirch Masala* and *Home and the World*" in *Monograph on Culture and Consciousness in South Asia,* „The Sphinx and the Mirror: Female Spectators of Early Cinema" in *Monograph: Seminar on 100 Years of Cinema in India* „Displaying Histories: Museums and the Politics of Culture" in *State Intervention and Popular Response: Western India in the Nineteenth Century*, ed. Mariam Dossal, pub. Popular Prakashan, Mumbai, 1998 and „Museumising the Tribal: Why Tribe Things Make me Cry" in *Translatings: Images from India's Half Century,* Journal of South Asian Studies Vol.xxi, no.1, June 1998. Most recently Neela Karnik worked as a professor at the Department of English, Ferguson College, University of Pune.

Ilse Lenz studied Sociology, Political Science, History and Japanese Studies at Munich University and Free University of Berlin. Her main fields of research are gender and work, gender and globalisation, women's movements, gender and ethnicity, and feminist theory between structural and post-modern approaches. She examines these issues from a comparative perspective (mainly Germany and Japan). She is a professor at the Faculty of Social Science of the Ruhr-University Bochum and adjunct faculty of the Department of East Asian Studies. She is the coordinator of the Marie-Jahoda Visiting Professorship for International Gender Studies, Ruhr-University Bochum. Together with Prof. Michiko Mae she is the coordinator of the yearly workshop on gender studies on

Japan. She also was the speaker of the women's section of the German Sociological Association (1995-1999) and is coeditor of the series: *Geschlecht und
Gesellschaft* (Leske+Budrich publisher). Extensive field research and study in
East Asia (Japan, South Korea, Indonesia, Malaysia). Among her last publications are: Lenz, Ilse; Mae, Michiko; Klose, Karin: *Frauenbewegungen weltweit.*
Opladen 2000; Lenz, Ilse; Nickel, Hildegard; Riegraf, Birgit: *Geschlecht – Arbeit – Zukunft.* Münster 2000; Lenz, Ilse; Schwenken, Helen Hg. The-
menschwerpunkt: Lokal, national, global? Frauenbewegungen, Geschlechterpolitik und Globalisierung. *Zeitschrift für Frauenforschung & Geschlechterstudien* 1+2, 2001. Living with her partner and her son.

Helma Lutz is a reader in Education and Social Sciences at the University of
Münster, Germany. Her research interests are in the area of female migrants in
20th century Europe, in particular issues of gender, migration, ethnicity, multiculturalism, nationalism and racism. She has conducted and co-ordinated various international research projects about „Immigrant women in Europe," and is
also the organisor of many international conferences and research networks on
the topic of female migration; gender, ethnicity and difference; and nationalism,
racism and gender in Europe. Among her publications in English are: Women in
Transit: Between Tradition and Transformation. Special issue of the *European
Journal of Women's Studies* (7) 3, 2000 (co-editor with Kathy Davis); *The New
Migration in Europe. Social Constructions and Social Realities.* (co-editor with
Khalid Koser, London: MacMillan, 1998); *Crossfires. Nationalism, Racism and
Gender in Europe.* (co-editor with Ann Phoenix and Nira Yuval-Davis, London:
Pluto Press,1995). In German: *Unterschiedlich Verschieden. Differenz in der
Erziehungswissenschaft.* (co-editor with Norbert Wenning, Opladen: Leske und
Budrich, 2000).

Yayori Matsui is one of Japan's leading journalists and feminists. She worked
for over thirty years on the renowned newspaper *Asahi Shimbun* (also on the
editorial board); with others she started the Asian Women's Association (Tokyo) in the early 1970s, is a founder of the Asia-Japan Women's Resource
Center and is editor of its journal, *Women's 21st Century.* She has engaged in
feminist international networking, especially in East Asia, for more than thirty
years and worked for transnational feminist cooperation and trust; she also has
promoted networking of social movements. She is chairperson of the VAWW-
NET Japan (Women against Women in War Network) and a driving force for
the Women's International War Crimes Tribunal 2000. Books in English are:
*Women's Asia.*1990. London, New York: Zed Press. *Women in the New Asia.
From Pain to Power.* 199. London, New York: Zed Press

Mirjana Morokvasic-Müller, sociologist, is a research director at the Centre National de la Recherche Scientifique, Paris and professor at the Université Paris X. She was Marie Jahoda professor in Gender Studies at the Ruhr Universität Bochum in 1999-2000 and visiting professor at the Ochanomizu University, Tokyo, in 2001. She was a dean of the International Women's University *(ifu)* Hannover in Germany 2000. Sociology of migration, gender studies and inter-ethnic relations are her areas of research and extensive publications in French, English and German. She is currently involved in several projects which explore the relationship between transnationalism, migration and gender.

Behshid Najafi studied Political Science and Education. Since the late 1970s she has been active in different movements against oppression in Iran and Germany, especially in women's and migrants' movements. Since 1993 she works at *agisra* (Information and Counselling Centre for Female Migrants and Refugees) in Cologne. She publishes regularly on the issue of women migration and trafficking in women, e.g. Paragraph 19: Das 'Rückgaberecht' im Ausländergesetz. In: *Beiträge zur feministischen Theorie und Praxis,* 42, 1996, pp. 29-32; Frauenhandel im Kontext frauenspezifischer Migration. In: Dominik, Katja et al. (1999), *Angeworben – eingewandert – abgeschoben. Ein anderer Blick auf die Einwanderungsgesellschaft Bundesrepublik Deutschland.* Münster: Westfälisches Dampfboot, pp. 150-170.

Ann Phoenix is a Senior Lecturer in Psychology at the Open University, UK. She was member of the editing collective of *Feminist Review* for more than 10 years. She was Ribbius Peletier Professor at the University of Humanist Studies,Utrecht, The Netherlands (1997-98). Her main publications include: *Young Mothers?* Cambridge: Polity Press 1991; *Black, White or Mixed Race? Race and Racism in the Lives of Young People of Mixed Parentage.* (co-author with Barbara Tizard) London: Routledge 1993; *Shifting Identities, Shifting Racisms* (co-editor with Kum-Kum Bhavnani) London: Sage 1994; *Crossfires. Nationalism, Racism and Gender in Europe.* (co-editor with Helma Lutz and Nira Yuval-Davis, London: Pluto Press, 1995); *Young Masculinities* (co-author with Stephen Frosh and Rob Pattman) London: Palgrave, 2001.

Saskia Sassen is Professor of Sociology at the University of Chicago and Centennial Visiting Professor at the London School of Economics. Her most recent books are *Guests and Aliens* (New York: New Press 1999) and *Globalization and its Discontents* (New York: New Press 1998). Her books are translated into ten languages. She directs the project „Cities and their Crossborder Networks" sponsored by the United Nations University and continues work on her project „Governance and Accountability in a Global Economy." She has started a student-oriented program on Transnationalism at the University of Chicago. Her most recent books are *Guests and Aliens*. New York: New Press 1999; *Global Networks/Linked Cities*. New York, Routledge 2002; *The Global City. New York, London, Tokyo*. Princeton: Princeton UP 2001 .

Claudia Schöning-Kalender, Cultural Anthropologist, studied in Hanover, Tübingen and Istanbul, and wrote her dissertation about internal migration and aspects of material culture in Turkey. She conducted a DFG-funded research project on dress politics and the symbolic transformation of the Turkish Republic, was a member of the curriculum working group and academic coordinator of the project area „Migration" at the International Women's University, Hanover 2000, and co-coordinator and lecturer in the thematic field „Spaces, Cultures, Identities in Process". Her main research interests are Turkish internal and external migration, gender studies with an emphasis on the history of women's movements in Turkey and other Muslim countries, material culture, and intercultural communication. Among her publications is the reader on *Feminismus, Islam, Nation. Frauenbewegungen im Maghreb, in Zentralasien und in der Türkei"*, edited with Ayla Neusel and Mechtild Jansen (Frankfurt 1997)

Helen Schwenken is a graduate research and teaching assistant at Kassel University in the field of Globalization and Politics. She graduated from Bochum University with her M.A. in Social Sciences. She is member of the PhD programme „Gender Democracy and Organisational Change in a Global Context" of the Heinrich Böll Foundation and currently works on her dissertation „The self-organisation of migrants in the European Union". She was a visiting scholar at the International Women's University (*ifu*). Her research interests lie in the area of (international) feminist theory, migration studies and social movements. With a women's group she organises the annual Feminist Winter University in Bochum/Germany and is involved in political youth exchanges, especially to Latin America. Her publications include: Editor (with Ilse Lenz) of the special issue „Lokal, national, global? Frauenbewegungen, Geschlechterpolitik und Globalisierung", *Zeitschrift für Frauenforschung und Geschlechterstudien,* 1+2, 2001.